INTRODUCTION TO PROCUREMENT IN THE PUBLIC SECTOR

Public procurement is an exciting, challenging profession that is responsible for the procurement of goods, services, and construction at every level of government, estimated at nearly 13 trillion US dollars worldwide. Public procurement professionals often work behind the scenes to promote responsive and responsible government, improving the quality of life for the people in their communities. *Introduction to Procurement in the Public Sector, Fourth Edition* is designed to provide an overview of the field, introduce the reader to the public procurement profession, and explore the wide variety of responsibilities and practices that must be addressed throughout the public procurement cycle.

This book offers a thorough and complete overview of the function and profession of public procurement, explores legal frameworks, examines contract administration, and investigates a variety of solicitation methods and processes, with an emphasis on what happens post-award, including surplus and disposal. *Introduction to Procurement in the Public Sector, Fourth Edition* provides the reader with a comprehensive understanding of the public procurement profession, as well as insight into methods, strategies, and tools for successful and ethical procurement practice. The book is an ideal primer for those entering the field of public procurement and serves as a comprehensive textbook for courses in public administration, supply chain management, and related fields of study.

Theresa R.M. Bauccio-Teschlog, MBA, NIGP-CPP, CPPB, began her career in private sector supply chain management in 1997. In 2001, she shifted to public procurement. Since 2001, she has worked for both cities and transits and has extensive knowledge of federal grants. Theresa currently serves as the Procurement Manager for the City of Everett, Washington, and as both a Subject Matter Expert and an NIGP instructor.

Ronald L. King, MA, NIGP-CPP, CPPO, has more than 40 years of purchasing experience in both the private and public sectors. He retired in 2018 as Deputy Director, Sourcing & Contracting for the VA Department of General Services/Division of Purchases & Supply in Richmond, VA and again in 2023 from the position of Content Developer for NIGP: The Institute for Public Procurement. He currently is a Consultant with NIGP Code and Consulting and serves as a Subject Matter Expert and an Instructor for NIGP.

William J. (Joe) Tommie Jr., MEd, CPPO, has over 40 years of experience in public procurement. In 2020, he retired as the Director of Purchasing for the Cobb County Government in Georgia. Prior to joining Cobb County, he served as the Director of Construction Procurement for the School District of Pickens County, as the Coordinator of Purchasing for the School District Five of Lexington and Richland Counties, and as the Manager of Purchasing and Inventory Control, Greenwood School District 50, all in South Carolina. He continues to serve in a consulting role with an Atlanta metro city government and currently serves as an NIGP instructor.

Cornerstones of Public Procurement

NIGP—The Institute for Public Procurement, USA

Recently Published Books

The Legal Aspects of Public Procurement, Third Edition
Michael Flynn, Kirk W. Buffington and Richard Pennington

Developing and Managing Requests for Proposals in the Public Sector, Third Edition
Theresa Bauccio-Teschlog, Dennis Carney, Joyce D. Foster, Ronald King and Christine Weber

Managing Logistics and Transportation in the Public Sector, Second Edition
Darin Matthews and Linda L. Stanley

Strategic Sourcing in the Public Sector
Barbara A. Grilli and Theresa G. Webb

Contracting for Design and Construction Services in the Public Sector
John O. Adler

Introduction to Procurement in the Public Sector, Fourth Edition
Theresa R.M. Bauccio-Teschlog, Ronald L. King and William J. Tommie Jr.

INTRODUCTION TO PROCUREMENT IN THE PUBLIC SECTOR

Fourth Edition

THERESA R.M. BAUCCIO-TESCHLOG, RONALD L. KING AND WILLIAM J. TOMMIE JR.

Routledge
Taylor & Francis Group
NEW YORK AND LONDON

Designed cover image: © Getty Images

Fourth edition published 2025
by Routledge
605 Third Avenue, New York, NY 10158

and by Routledge
4 Park Square, Milton Park, Abingdon, Oxon OX14 4RN

Routledge is an imprint of the Taylor & Francis Group, an informa business

First edition published by NIGP: The Institute for Public Procurement 2004
Third edition published by NIGP: The Institute for Public Procurement 2009

ISBN: 978-1-032-93580-5 (hbk)
ISBN: 978-1-003-56656-4 (ebk)

DOI: 10.4324/9781003566564

Typeset in Adobe Garamond Pro
by codeMantra

Contents

List of Tables

Part I

Procurement as a Function and as a Profession in the Public Sector

Chapter 1

What is Procurement?

Procurement is a dynamic, ever-changing, strategic field of business that encompasses the process of acquiring goods and services for an entity to operate. Procurement professionals worldwide are the unsung heroes of an entity by keeping the flow of materials going, mitigating supply chain challenges, negotiating contracts, and ensuring that business requirements are met. Chapter One will introduce the field of procurement by first discussing the history of procurement and its impact on the profession and processes today, providing an overview of the differences between private and public procurement as well as the overall goals and influences of procurement, and introducing common terminology.

History of Procurement

The journey to understanding modern-day procurement practices and the role procurement plays in all organizations begins in 3000 BC when the Egyptians used scribes to manage the supply of materials when building the pyramids. According to historians, the scribes recorded the amount of materials and number of workers required to complete the task on papyrus

DOI: 10.4324/9781003566564-2

scrolls (Collins 2022). This historical task is like modern-day specification development. While the Egyptians began documenting their requirements, the Syrians are believed to have issued the first purchase order by using a red clay tablet somewhere between 2400 and 2800 BC. The order was for "fifty jars of fragrant smooth oil for 600 small weights in grain" (Coe 1989). While previous historical records are related to procurement functions, according to Professor Emeritus Harry Page of George Washington University, the first purchasing department can be traced back to the 13th century BC, while the historical records of the Phoenician traders refer to persons serving as purchasing agents (Page 1954). Professor Page also notes that ancient purchase orders were written on parchment scrolls in the days of Julius Caesar and called for the delivery of amphorae of wine, honey, and oil. Additionally, procurement has historical religious notoriety. "In the Holy Bible, the book of Deuteronomy provides instructions for buyers in the honest use of weights and measures and design specifications were introduced in Genesis with the Ark" (Davison and Wright 2004).

Contracting regulation in the United States dates as far back as the late 1700s. Enacted in 1795, the *Purveyor of Public Affairs Act* was the earliest law governing federal contracting opportunities and allowed the government to buy needed supplies and materials to perform government functions. Before that time, there were no laws or rules governing how to acquire goods, and, therefore, private individuals used to provide items from their own personal reserves. The next major law, the *Civil Sundry Appropriations Act*, was passed in 1861. This act began the principle of advertised procurements for supplies and materials. These two laws provided the structure for modern-day procurement practices in the United States and provided historical context for the laws and regulations that procurement professionals administer today. However, those two acts were just the beginning. Chapter Six will expand on additional laws and their impacts on public procurement.

Throughout history, a recurring theme has focused procurement activities on accountability, wise expenditures such as increasing value, and open, fair, and transparent competition. While laws and regulations have impacted procurement processes and procedures, the goals have remained constant: receiving quality goods and services on time for a reasonable price, while maximizing competition and ensuring the integrity of the process. Today, procurement professionals often refer to these principles as the five Rs, the right:

- Price
- Quantity
- Quality
- Place
- Time.

Each of these principles are interlinked and affect each other. Collectively, the achievement of all five provides a framework for effective purchasing and supply chain management that applies to all industries, sectors, and countries.

Procurement versus Purchasing

The terms procurement and purchasing are often used interchangeably. For example, depending on the entity, there may be either a purchasing or procurement department. Many people both in and outside of the supply chain field often wonder if there is a difference between the terms. NIGP: The Institute for Public Procurement's Dictionary of Procurement Terms recognizes that entities may refer to their supply chain function as either procurement or purchasing by acknowledging both in its definition of Purchasing (Procurement) department as "the staff of procurement professionals in an entity who act as the primary buyers of goods and services and oversee any delegated purchasing authority." While supply chain professionals can be called either purchasing or procurement, there is a difference between the two.

To fully understand, let's begin by reviewing the definitions. According to NIGP's Dictionary of Procurement Terms, purchasing is defined as obtaining, renting, or leasing needed goods or services without a long-term contract or ongoing relationship with a supplier, whereas procurement is defined as:

1. Purchasing, renting, leasing, or otherwise obtaining any supplies, services, or construction; includes all functions that pertain to the procurement, including description of requirements, selection, and solicitation of sources, preparation and award of contract, and all phases of contract administration.
2. The combined functions of purchasing, inventory control, traffic and transportation, receiving, inspection, storekeeping, salvage, and disposal operations.

If you work in the supply chain function for a municipality, then you work for a local public procurement unit which is any county, city, town, school district, special authority, or any other subdivision of the state, province, territory, or public entity of any such subdivision, or educational, health, or other institution spending public funds for the procurement of services, supplies, or construction.

If you were to ask a procurement professional the difference between procurement and purchasing, their answer is likely to be that procurement is a strategic function with an entity that is responsible for obtaining the best value for goods and services. Purchasing is a transactional function which is demonstrated in the earlier definition of obtaining items without a long-term contract or relationship. Others may contend that procurement is an organizational process. This is the point where the lines between procurement and purchasing can become blurry.

While many entities still refer to the procurement function as the purchasing group, the two terms are different. The *Merriam-Webster Dictionary* states that procurement is a noun while purchasing is a transitive verb. A transitive verb such as purchasing only makes sense if it exerts its action on an object. For example, the act of buying or purchasing an object such as a fire engine or design services. As a noun, procurement becomes the name of the group or function that performs the verb, or that completes the purchasing action. Similarly, the *Merriam-Webster Dictionary* defines procurement as the act or process of procuring (Merriam-Webster.com n.d.). Therefore, ultimately, purchasing falls under the umbrella of procurement.

Cooperative Procurement (Purchasing)

Examples of both procurement and purchasing can be found in NIGP's Dictionary of Procurement Terms. Within the dictionary, there are other instances where procurement and purchasing may also be used interchangeably, such as cooperative procurement (purchasing), most commonly referred to as cooperative purchasing or piggybacking, which is when two or more entities combine their requirements to obtain the advantages of volume purchases, including administrative savings and other benefits. Cooperative agreements can also be a variety of arrangements, where two or more public procurement entities purchase from the same supplier or multiple suppliers using a single Invitation for Bids (IFB) or Request for Proposals (RFP).

Internal versus External Procurement Units

The procurement function may reside internally within the entity or externally depending on the structure of the entity. Internal procurement functions reside and are overseen within the entity that they support. In contrast, external procurement functions reside outside of the entity. An external procurement authority is any buying organization not located in a state or jurisdiction that, if it were in the state or jurisdiction, would qualify as a public procurement unit. For example, an agency of the United States government is an external procurement unit as the United States government is decentralized, and the decentralized procurement unit often purchases for a department in another state (2023 New Mexico Statutes).

Joint Administrative Procurement

Another type of procurement arrangement is the joint administrative procurement department, which is defined in NIGP's Dictionary of Procurement Terms as "An arrangement under which part or all of the purchases of two or more entities are made by a procurement department that serves all of them." For example, there may be instances when multiple entities combine their separate public procurement departments into a single department, resulting in a joint administrative procurement department that performs the procurement and administrative functions for all partner entities. Such was the case when Yakima County, Washington contracted with the City of Yakima, Washington, a separate entity, to perform its procurement function on its behalf.

Public Procurement versus Private Procurement

Public and private procurement professionals must comply with their established policies and internal controls and share the same fundamental goal and objective of receiving the best value for the money spent. Oftentimes in the public sector, this is demonstrated by paying the lowest price. However, as the public sector progresses, more emphasis will be placed on life cycle costing as it is in the private sector. Additional similarities include analyzing spending data for opportunities to strategize purchases to save money. In both sectors, this is accomplished through strategic sourcing agreements such as bulk buying programs and bundling of like-kind items. Like-kind items are commodities such as tires, fuel, computers, uniforms, furniture, etc. that could be purchased in bulk or sporadically throughout the fiscal year. Additionally, both sectors recognize the importance of socially responsible contracting practices including the use of environmentally friendly and sustainable products.

While there are many key similarities between the sectors, the key difference is that private sector decisions are driven by profitability and increasing shareholder wealth, while public sector decisions are based on demonstrating responsive and responsible use of taxpayer funds with an emphasis on public need versus profit. As the City of Everett, Washington stated with its vision, "As a government agency, we are responsive, transparent, and accountable. We are good stewards of our resources, and we deliver essential services efficiently. We establish priorities and make decisions that honor our obligation to our community" (City of Everett n.d.). Since the public sector is spending taxpayer funds, there is significant scrutiny on how the funds are spent. In response, public procurement processes and procedures emphasize transparency and accountability, while the private sector is nontransparent about its business transactions and contracting agreements.

Another key difference is the cooperation between entities. Public entities commonly share procurement information and work cooperatively by sharing their contracts through cooperative purchasing agreements. Alternatively, two or more entities may work together through interagency purchasing agreements. This is vastly different from the private sector, where this practice would ruin a company's competitive advantage. Overall, public entities work cooperatively while private businesses work competitively. The table below describes additional key differences between public and private procurement.

Similarities and Differences of Public Procurement versus Private Sector Procurement

The following table compares public procurement and private sector procurement and identifies the differences between the two.

Table 1.1 Comparison of Private versus Public Procurement

Categories	*Private Sector*	*Public Sector*
Objectives	Maximizing profit	Transparency Fair and open competition Maximizing value for taxpayers
Accountability	Compliance with general standards of law, precedent, and ethical conventions	Taking ownership and being responsible to all stakeholders for our actions. This value is essential to preserve the public trust and protect the public interest.
Transparency	Do not need to provide equal opportunities. Often will withhold information that is not necessary to the bidding suppliers.	All communication and actions are subject to public disclosure.

(Continued)

Table 1.1 (Continued)

Categories	*Private Sector*	*Public Sector*
Funding	Revenue from sales, investments, and other business-related areas.	Tax revenue, fees, fines, grants. Tariffs, etc.
Budget Flexibility	Able to easily transfer money from one department to another if business conditions end up changing.	The budget is adopted by the governing authority. Budget changes require adoption.
Competition	Contracts are usually awarded through a negotiation process.	Contracts are awarded through a competitive bidding process.
Regulation	Largely unregulated, organizations are free to pursue their own procurement strategies.	Compliance with procurement laws at the local, state, and federal levels.
Legal Requirements	Fewer legal requirements, allowing organizations to pursue their own procurement strategies without having to worry about legal compliance.	Wide range of laws and regulations governing the procurement process.
Process Complexity	Relatively simple, governed by the organization's procurement strategy.	Detailed procedures dictated by laws and regulations to provide public oversight and transparency.
Commodities	Items to support production, manufacturing, and commercial resale such as supplies, raw materials, equipment, and other non-production purchases such as land.	Wide variety of goods and services to support government services including research, development, and major innovations.
Social Responsibility	Used to drive efficiency and reduce costs. Motivated by improving and increasing profit.	Used to advance social objectives. Motivated by public benefits and expectations.

Importance of Public Procurement

Public procurement exists at every level of society and within almost every government entity, from the local level to the federal level. According to NIGP, "Working in Public Procurement,"

> Public procurement refers to the purchase of any goods or services required to sustain communities. Public procurement professionals are public servants who work every day to make life better for people in their communities—whether it's a small township, a county, a major metro area, or an entire state or province.

Without public procurement professionals, roads would not become roads. Public parks, schools, libraries, and water treatment facilities would not be built or maintained. Water and electricity would not be provided to commercial buildings and private residences, and emergencies or catastrophes would not be responded to.

Goals of Public Procurement

If a procurement professional were to ask their clients what the goals of the procurement department are, the answers might vary widely. However, the common theme is likely to be for the Procurement Department (Procurement) to provide them with their requested items as soon as possible. At a basic level, that is the goal of public procurement, to provide our customers with goods and services that meet their needs while maximizing competition and optimizing market response. When competition is maximized, the entity is most likely to receive the best price. While maximizing competition and optimizing market response are important goals of public procurement, they are not the only goals. Earlier in the chapter, the primary goals of procurement were referred to as the five "Rs." The right:

- Price—paying a fair and reasonable price.
- Quantity and Quality—receiving exactly what is needed.
- Time and Place—arriving when it is needed at the location specified.

When procurement professionals provide goods and services that meet the five Rs, they have met the primary goals of public procurement. However, there are additional secondary objectives, such as minimizing business risk, achieving socioeconomic goals, and maintaining the transparency and integrity of the process while simultaneously maximizing competition, that are also important.

Price

As budgets tighten, stakeholders and end users are concerned about receiving the best price. If the entity receives federal funding, the federal grantor may require that the entity conduct a fair and reasonable analysis to determine that the price being paid is indeed fair and reasonable. Fair and reasonable analysis will be discussed later in the textbook in Chapter Nine. However, price is only one aspect of the overall cost of a good or service. Other cost considerations that could affect the total cost paid are shipping and delivery fees, surcharges, tariffs, maintenance plans, and extended warranties. Entities are strongly encouraged to consider life cycle costs. Life cycle cost is the total discounted dollar cost of owning, operating, maintaining, and disposing of an item over a period of time. Overall, while obtaining the best price is a primary goal of public procurement, the secondary objective is to pay the lowest overall cost, which requires consideration of all direct and indirect costs in addition to the purchase price. Direct costs are the costs that are directly related to providing the commodity, such as labor, supplies, equipment, or transportation. Indirect costs are expenditures other than the cost incurred to produce a good or deliver a service, such as insurance, rent, and utilities.

Quantity and Quality

Quantity is the amount of something. Quantity conformance is determined based on the supplier delivering the required or expected quantity of the commodity as contracted.

The NIGP Dictionary of Procurement Terms defines quality as:

> 1. [. . .] a function of excellence, intrinsic value, or grade, as determined over time by society in general or by designated bodies in specialized fields.
> 2. The composite of all attributes or characteristics, including performance, that satisfy a user's needs.
> 3. Conformance with the stated requirements.

While there are several additional definitions for quality, most procurement professionals understand quality as being how well the good or service conforms to the stated requirements as written in the specifications or scope of work. More simply, quality is how well the good or service meets the end users' requirements.

Time and Place

Suppliers must deliver goods and services to the end user by the time and at the place designated in the contract. For service contracts, this means that the supplier performs services at the time or per the schedule specified. For construction and information technology contracts, it means that the various project phases are completed as agreed to.

Managing Risks

Procurement should identify risk factors associated with each procurement, analyze the probability of the risk occurring, and consider the potential impacts. Various types of risks exist depending on the type of procurement. It is imperative that procurement professionals view risk as a continuum and understand that as risks shift in one direction or the other, costs will increase or decrease. For example, if the entity shifts risks to the supplier, the supplier will either increase the cost to compensate, or, if the risk is perceived to be too high, the supplier may be unwilling to contract with the entity. Risk management plans should be developed based on the decision to avoid, assume, or transfer the identified risks. Such plans are often developed in concert with the entity's risk management staff if the entity has a Risk Management Department.

Accomplishing Social and Economic Objectives

Laws have been enacted at all levels requiring suppliers to comply with various social and economic requirements, such as fair employment practices, safe working conditions, payment of fair or living wages, and refraining from polluting the air and water. Additional requirements encourage entities to use small and disadvantaged businesses, specify American-made products and components, or require the use of sustainable products. In general, most entities have adopted social responsibility goals. Social responsibility is an ethical theory that states businesses and people have a duty to act in the best interests of society as a whole. Depending on the funding source and the objectives of the local entity, each procurement may have unique social and economic objectives. In some instances, such as purchasing recycled paper, green cleaning products, or renewable diesel, the entity may determine that meeting a social responsibility objective justifies paying an initial higher price for the commodity. For example, recycled paper may cost more per ream but support the entity's environmental and climate initiatives. While renewable diesel may cost more initially, it lowers emissions and may improve vehicle performance such as fuel efficiency as well as reduce overall vehicle maintenance costs in the long run.

Maintaining Transparency

Transparency is one of NIGP's values and guiding principles and is essential to demonstrate the responsible use of public funds. Entities can demonstrate transparency with easily accessible and understandable policies and processes. Information must be clear, precise, accurate, understandable, and equally provided to all interested parties. Procurement professionals can ensure transparency by sharing information openly and equally, treating all potential suppliers fairly and equitably by providing transparency in each phase of public procurement. For example, publicly posting solicitation questions and answers during the open solicitation period and allowing free access to public procurement information, through an online portal, for all stakeholders, suppliers, and the public. Another example of transparency in public contracting is the disclosure of all public records including procurement file documents through public disclosure or *Freedom of Information Act* (also known as FOIA) requests.

Integrity

Integrity is crucial in public procurement. According to the Organisation for Economic Co-operation and Development,

> Public procurement is one of the government activities most vulnerable to corruption. In addition to the volume of transactions and the financial interests at stake, corruption risks are exacerbated by the complexity of the process, the close interaction between public officials and businesses, and the multitude of stakeholders. (OECD n.d.)

In its Dictionary of Procurement Terms, NIGP defines integrity as the quality of honesty and strict adherence to an ethical or moral code of conduct. Integrity is essential to preserve the public's trust. Procurement professionals can ensure integrity through general standards and procurement-specific safeguards, internal controls, developing training programs for procurement staff, and requiring high standards of integrity for all stakeholders in the procurement process. For example, requiring evaluators to complete conflict of interest statements documenting that the evaluators do not have any competing or conflicting interest in the commodity being evaluated. Entities can also develop compliance measures and anti-corruption programs for suppliers, including appropriate monitoring.

Maximizing Competition

In its Dictionary of Procurement Terms, NIGP defines Full and Open Competition as the process by which two or more suppliers attempt to secure the business of a third party by offering the most favorable price, quality, delivery terms, and service. The concept of competition presumes the existence of a marketplace in which there is more than one supplier that can provide similar goods or services. To maximize full and open competition, entities must promote a level playing field for suppliers so that all responsible sources are permitted to respond to solicitations. For example, specifying that procurement is the point of contact during the solicitation period ensures that all suppliers have an equal opportunity to ask questions, and that no supplier is given an unfair advantage.

Enabling Legislation

The overarching basis of public procurement is law. Imagine a three-tiered wedding cake. The laws and regulations adopted at the federal level provide the base layer. Then each state or province adds its additional laws and regulations, which for this analogy are additional, smaller tiers of cake. The top layer is the local jurisdiction's additional regulations. Court decisions are the filling between the layers. According to the US Department of the Interior, judicial decisions constitute one of the most important sources of legal authority, along with legislative and regulatory enactments, in our common law system (US Department of the Interior 2023). Even statutes must be read in conjunction with case law which construes the correct application of the legislation. Courts follow the doctrine of precedent or *stare decisis*, "let the decision stand," to create and build upon holdings of law to ensure that people in like circumstances of fact are treated alike.

While laws and regulations are the substantive cake that influences public procurement processes, there is often additional political influence from politicians. Political influence can be both indirect and direct, with politicians interfering in the process to secure their personal or party interests. For this analogy, political influence is the columns between the cake layers. Political influence can impact procurement in a variety of ways.

> Politicians' preferences for non-price criteria are strongly connected to ideological reasoning and to a limited extent to strategic reasoning. Regardless of their political ideology and financial situation of the municipality, politicians are willing to look beyond price, and consider environmental, innovative, and social criteria when awarding contracts. (Lerusse and Van de Walle 2021)

Terminology and Definitions

Understanding terminology is important to establish a base understanding for the rest of the textbook. The authors feel that the following terms will enhance the readers' experience and improve their understanding of the topics discussed throughout the textbook. The definitions are from NIGP's Dictionary of Procurement Terms, which can be found at www.nigp.org. NIGP frequently updates and improves its Dictionary of Procurement Terms. For additional definitions as well as the most up-to-date definitions, search "NIGP Dictionary-of-terms."

- **Client**—A client is an individual, department, or entity with whom procurement professionals consult and collaborate to procure a desired or required good or service. The client may also be the end user.
- **Commodity**—1. A marketable item produced to fulfill a need or want; may reference both goods and services. 2. A primary agricultural product or raw material that must meet specified minimum standards to be bought and sold in broad commerce.
- **End User**—The individual or department who uses a procured good or service. End users may also be clients. See also: Client.
- **Entity**—is the term used when referring to a public sector organization.
- **Exceptions**—is public sector procurement code (legislation) that waives competition requirements for the direct purchase of specific goods or services, e.g., authorized or mandated preferred source (prisoners, vision impaired, and disabled), emergency procurements, and other goods or services stipulated by local laws and regulations.
- **Procurement Department**—is the office, division, or unit with authority for contracting needed goods, services, or construction for the entity.
- **Stakeholder**—Any entity, group(s), or individual(s) that can place a claim on an entity's resources or services or are affected by what the entity does or the services it provides. Common stakeholders may be citizens.

- **Supplier**—An individual or business that provides goods or services, usually for other than low-cost, low-risk, and short-term engagements. May also be referred to as Vendor.

References

"2023 New Mexico Statutes :: Chapter 13 – Public Purchases and Property :: Article 1 – Procurement :: Section 13-1-56 – Definition; External Procurement Unit." 2023. Justia Law. https://law.justia.com/codes/new-mexico/chapter-13/article-1/section-13-1-56/

City of Everett. n.d. "City Priorities." City Priorities | Everett, WA—Official Website. https://www.everettwa.gov/2459/City-Priorities

Coe, Charles K. 1989. *Public Financial Management.* Englewood Cliffs, NJ: Prentice Hall.

Collins, Georgia. 2022. "Walk through the History of the Procurement Industry." May 11, 2022. https://procurementmag.com/digital-procurement/the-history-of-the-procurement-industry

Davison, William D., and Elizabeth Wright. 2004. *Contract Administration.* Herndon, VA: National Institute of Governmental Purchasing (NIGP).

Lerusse, Amandine, and Steven Van de Walle. 2021. "Local Politicians' Preferences in Public Procurement: Ideological or Strategic Reasoning?" *Local Government Studies* 48 (4): 680–703. doi:10.1080/03003930.2020.1864332.

Merriam-Webster.com. n.d. "Procurement." https://www.merriam-webster.com/dictionary/procurement

Merriam-Webster.com. n.d. "Purchase." https://www.merriam-webster.com/dictionary/purchase

NIGP. "Dictionary of Procurement Terms." https://www.nigp.org/dictionary-of-terms

NIGP. "Working in Public Procurement." https://www.nigp.org/our-profession/working-in-public-procurement#:~:text=Public%20procurement%20refers%20to%20the,an%20entire%20state%20or%20province

OECD. n.d. "Preventing Corruption in Public Procurement." https://www.oecd.org/gov/ethics/Corruption-Public-Procurement-Brochure.pdf

Page, Harry. 1954. "History of Procurement." Unpublished manuscript, George Washington University.

US Department of the Interior. 2023. "The Judiciary: Courts and Case Law." https://www.doi.gov/library/collections/law/caselaw

Chapter 2

Procurement as a Profession

Chapter Two describes the public procurement profession and what individuals considering procurement as a career could expect if they pursued a career in public procurement. The chapter includes a discussion of the values and guiding principles of public procurement while emphasizing the importance of ethics and professionalism. The chapter concludes with procurement career paths and opportunities, as well as common job titles and desired skills one should possess for each position.

Public Procurement as a Career

A career in public procurement is interesting, challenging, unpredictable, rewarding, and full of multitasking. For the procurement professional, every day feels like Christmas. The excitement, the surprises, and not knowing what to expect with each phone call, email, visitor, purchase requisition, or project that is assigned to them. If you are a planner, it is almost certain that your day will never go the way you think it will. So, if you enjoy doing consistent, repetitive tasks, this is not the profession for you! The procurement professional will rarely, if ever, feel bored.

DOI: 10.4324/9781003566564-3

To be an effective procurement professional, one must be able to set priorities and also be a good time manager. In addition, procurement professionals have a cache of skills at their disposal, for they must:

- Adhere to solid ethical standards.
- Communicate effectively with various people and groups.
- Demonstrate keen business acumen.
- Master research skills.
- Possess cognitive flexibility.
- Practice exceptional people skills.
- Provide excellent client service.
- Think critically and analytically.

Values and Guiding Principles of Public Procurement

NIGP has identified six values and guiding principles of public procurement to which all procurement professionals need to adhere (NIGP, "Values and Guiding Principles of Public Procurement"). They are:

- Accountability
- Ethics
- Impartiality
- Professionalism
- Service
- Transparency.

Accountability

Taking ownership and being responsible to all stakeholders for our actions. This value is essential to preserve the public trust and protect the public interest.

Principles:

- Apply sound business judgment.
- Be knowledgeable of and abide by all applicable laws and regulations.
- Be responsible stewards of public funds.
- Maximize competition to the greatest extent practicable.
- Practice due diligence.
- Promote effective, economic, and efficient acquisition.

- Support economic, social, and sustainable communities.
- Use procurement strategies to optimize value to stakeholders.

If procurement professionals are not accountable for their actions, then all credibility with the public and their other stakeholders will be justifiably lost. As Christopher Bovis states in his article "The Effects of the Principles of Transparency and Accountability on Public Procurement and Public-Private Partnerships Regulation" published in the *European Public Private Partnership Law Review*, "The regulation of public procurement, through the principles of transparency and accountability provides for a pedestal of the legal, economic and policy interface between public and private sectors" (Bovis 2009). Without credibility and trust, procurement professionals cannot perform their job effectively. No one, not management, end users, or suppliers, can work effectively with someone who shirks from their responsibilities. Procurement professionals must remember that there are consequences for any actions taken or not taken.

Ethics

Acting in a manner true to these values is essential to preserve the public's trust.

Principles:

- Act and conduct business with honesty and integrity, avoiding even the appearance of impropriety.
- Maintain consistency in all processes and actions.
- Meet the ethical standards of the profession.

Similar to accountability, if procurement professionals do not act ethically in all situations at all times, they cannot merit respect or inspire confidence, making it impossible for them to perform their jobs effectively. Every procurement professional should strive to uphold the NIGP Code of Ethics, or a similar code of ethics, in all of their business decisions and actions. It should be clear to all that a true procurement professional cannot be bought or persuaded to do anything dishonest.

Impartiality

Unbiased decision-making and action which is essential to ensure fairness for the public good.

Principles:

- Be open, fair, impartial, and non-discriminatory in all processes.
- Treat suppliers equitably, without discrimination, and without imposing unnecessary constraints on the competitive market.
- Use sound professional judgment within established legal frameworks to balance competing interests among stakeholders.

All concerns, problems, and challenges must be addressed objectively, without discrimination. If procurement professionals are not impartial, they will lose the respect of those who work below and above them. For direct reports, this can lead to low morale and high employee turnover. Lack of impartiality can also lead the entity to not be able to achieve its mission effectively or take appropriate actions.

Professionalism

Upholding high standards of job performance and ethical behavior which is essential to balance diverse public interests.

Principles:

- Be led by those with education, experience, and professional certification in public procurement.
- Continually contribute value to the entity.
- Continually develop as a profession through education, mentorship, innovation, and partnerships.
- Develop, support, and promote the highest professional standards to serve the public good.
- Seek continuous improvement through ongoing training, education, and skill enhancement.

Without exhibiting the qualities of professionalism, procurement professionals cannot obtain high job performance and success in their careers. Those qualities include, but are not limited to, the ability to learn, adaptability, conscientiousness, interpersonal skills, and reliability.

Service

Obligation to assist stakeholders, which is essential to support the public good.

Principles:

- Be a crucial resource and strategic partner within the entity and community.
- Develop and maintain relationships with stakeholders.
- Develop collaborative partnerships to meet public needs.
- Maintain a customer-service focus while meeting the needs and protecting the interests of the entity and the public.

Service for a public procurement professional means making a positive difference. Every day, across the world, an estimated 130,000 public procurement professionals serve their communities. Everyone is instrumental in championing for and protecting the taxpayer, improving procurement processes, and upholding public trust.

Transparency

Easily accessible and understandable policies and processes, which is essential to demonstrate responsible use of public funds.

Principles:

- Exercise discretion in the release of confidential information.
- Maintain current and complete policies, procedures, and records.
- Provide open access to competitive opportunities.
- Provide timely access to procurement policies, procedures, and records.

Transparency in government promotes accountability and provides all stakeholders with information about what the entity is doing. Without transparency, the procurement professional will lose the trust of those they serve, thereby creating mistrust and instability.

Ethics and Professionalism

As mentioned earlier, ethics should play an extremely important role in the life of all procurement professionals. Ethics needs to be at the core of every action and decision the procurement professional makes.

There are many different versions of codes of ethics for procurement professionals to adopt and follow. NIGP's Code of Ethics (Appendix A) has been adopted by many entities throughout the US and Canada. The principles included in that code, as well as many others, are:

- Accepting employment only in a position for which one is qualified.
- Acting in accordance with the highest ideals of honor and integrity in both public and personal relationships.
- Avoiding participation in any situation that involves a conflict of interest.
- Believing that accepting or seeking any type of profit or personal aggrandizement through the misuse of personal or public relationships is dishonest and is not to be tolerated.
- Dispensing or seeking no personal favors.
- Handling personnel matters on a merit basis without discrimination.
- Keeping one's entity informed, through appropriate channels, of any issues and progress of applicable operations by emphasizing the importance of the facts.
- Refusing to ever accept, directly or indirectly, gifts, gratuities, or anything else of value from suppliers that might influence or appear to influence the performance of one's personal duties.
- Serving in a manner that is in accordance with the dignity and worth of a trusted public employee.
- Supporting and subscribing to the objectives and aims of a professional, recognized organization within the field of public procurement.

Since these principles are the guide for all decisions made and actions taken by a good procurement professional, it is recommended to have a code of ethics prominently posted in the procurement department. This serves two purposes.

First, it is a constant reminder for all procurement personnel that their decisions and actions need to be above reproach. Procurement professionals are often held to a higher standard since we are spending large amounts of taxpayer dollars. As stated in one of the principles outlined above, procurement professionals must not only avoid improprieties, they must also avoid the appearance of improprieties. That is an extremely high bar! So, it is not just enough for us to know we are acting appropriately and in compliance with laws, policies, and procedures; we must also consider how our actions may appear to someone on the outside.

Second, it alerts anyone, especially suppliers, entering the procurement department that its personnel subscribe to and practice the principles outlined in the code. Ethics and policies followed by those involved in private procurement differ greatly from those involved in public procurement. So, suppliers may, from time to time, need to be reminded of those differences.

This is especially true when dealing with gifts and gratuities. Gifts, food, meals, trips, tickets to entertainment or sporting events, and other items or services of more than nominal value are often provided to buyers in the private sector. This is especially true during the holiday season. Depending on their employer's policy, this is an often accepted, and sometimes expected, custom. Public employees, particularly procurement professionals, are usually not allowed by law or policy to accept gifts or gratuities that are of more than nominal value, if at all. Some entities may set a dollar threshold for which their employees may accept gifts and gratuities. In legal terms, this is known as a *de minimis* benefit, defined as which, considering its value as well as frequency provided, is too small that the necessity to report or account for it is unreasonable or impractical. The key is to know your entity's policy regarding the acceptance of gifts and gratuities and be sure to follow it.

One of the most sensitive, and often controversial, issues revolve around food or meals. If your entity allows you to accept food or meals from a supplier, there are a few other issues for you to consider. Do you remember the above discussion regarding your obligation to avoid the appearance of improprieties? This needs to be considered when deciding whether or not to eat a meal in a public place with a supplier. Even if you are paying for your meal, how would it look to another supplier if they saw the two of you together? What would their likely assumption be regarding who is paying for both meals?

On occasion, we may need to work with a supplier during a meal period. A sensible solution in this case would be for your entity to have food delivered to you and the supplier to have a working lunch or dinner which your entity pays for.

What is the best way to handle food brought or delivered to you at your entity? Possible actions are declining the food if the supplier is delivering it in person, or accepting it then putting it out in the employee break room for all employees to enjoy. A third option would be to donate it to a homeless shelter or similar charity. The main issue is not to take it home for your personal use.

These issues and suggested approaches apply not only to the procurement professional but also to all entity employees, especially if they touch any part of a procurement with a contracted supplier or a potential supplier. This may cause some dissension in the ranks, but all public employees should strive to be above reproach.

Another ethical issue of which procurement professionals need to be aware is personal purchases. Is it okay for you to accept a discounted price offered to you by one of your suppliers on a laptop for your child to take to school or for your spouse to use in their startup business? The answer is no, because it violates the principle of not accepting or seeking any type of profit or personal aggrandizement through the misuse of personal or public relationships. If, however, the supplier is offering the discount to all entities or public employees, not just you specifically, then that would not be a violation of this principle.

Not only do procurement professionals and other public employees need to be mindful of ethical issues regarding gifts and gratuities, but the entity needs to be mindful of them too. How should an entity respond to a supplier who offers to give a backpack, with the company logo on it, filled with school supplies to all elementary students within the school district at the beginning of the academic year? On the face of things, this may seem a very generous gesture on the part of the supplier. Why wouldn't we allow them to do so? Well, there's that pesky issue of appearance and truth to the adage that nothing in this world is free. The supplier is getting something of value out of this transaction: free advertising. Just accepting the supplier's offer without giving other suppliers the same opportunity could be construed as favoritism or an unfair advantage.

Another ethical issue that both the procurement professional and the entity need to avoid is any conflict of interest. Conflicts of interest can arise when a public employee or the entity has a personal or direct interest in the result or outcome of a procurement decision. Personal preferences or personal gain, even for family members or friends, monetary or non-monetary, should not influence the decisions a procurement professional or any other public employee makes in the execution of their official duties. A conflict of interest occurs when public employees find themselves in a position to be, or appear to be, influenced by a personal interest that may lead to their gaining a personal advantage, monetary or otherwise, or to avoid a personal disadvantage. This can be actual, potential, or perceived, all of which can threaten to compromise our public duty as a procurement professional or as a responsible public employee.

As previously mentioned, there are a myriad of ethical issues that a procurement professional may face or must deal with. Along with that are all the specific circumstances surrounding the situation, which can create a lot of gray areas. Procurement professionals should rely on the code of ethics adopted by their entity and the newspaper test. The newspaper test asks, if the facts of the situation appeared in a local newspaper, would you be embarrassed? If you are interested in learning more, additional resources are NIGP's Global Best Practices entitled "Ethical Procurement" and "Transparency in Public Procurement." NIGP also offers a half-day Pathways course, "Ethics, Integrity, and Transparency."

Career Paths and Opportunities

As the NIGP website points out:

> Many people who go into public procurement do so because they want to serve the best interests of the public. Public procurement professionals are custodians of public trust. They always

> champion and protect the taxpayer. To be a successful public procurement professional, you must be dedicated to ethical practices and believe that the government can make a positive difference in the communities they govern through best practices.
>
> To excel in public procurement, you need to develop a broad base of skills and knowledge, and then work diligently to strengthen your abilities. In your roles as a government procurement agent, you will wear many hats. You will have the opportunity to be a strategic business person, establishing contractual relationships that leverage your buying power; a shrewd negotiator who understands how to achieve win-win solutions for both the agency and the supplier; a money manager who ensures that public funds are used in the best way possible; a visionary who creates meaningful change for the good of the community now and in the years to come; a champion of the public you serve, ensuring that tax dollars are spent responsibly and in the best interest of the community.
>
> Public procurement professionals are uniquely positioned to influence the way that government works to meet the goals of the community through the political process. While politicians may approve the building of roads, procurement professionals influence *how* the road is built. For example, they may identify that the road should be constructed using recycled materials and opt to install eco-friendly lighting or solar-powered traffic signals to best meet the needs of the communities they serve. (NIGP, "Why Choose a Career in Public Procurement?")

Once someone decides to pursue a career in public procurement, they have a wide range of jobs from which to choose.

First, several jobs fall within the category of Professionals. These include job titles such as:

- Bid Specialist
- Buyer
- Contract Administrator
- Contract Analyst
- Contract Coordinator
- Contract Specialist
- Procurement Administrator
- Procurement Analyst
- Procurement Coordinator
- Procurement Specialist

- Procurement Officer
- Purchaser
- Purchasing Administrative Clerk
- Purchasing Agent
- Purchasing Budget Analyst
- Regulatory or Legal Specialist
- Senior Buyer
- Senior Contracting Officer
- Senior Procurement Specialist
- Supplier Relationship Coordinator
- Vendor Performance Analyst.

An analysis of job postings for Professional positions by researchers for NIGP states:

> Most of the competence requirements for Professionals are in the Contract Administration and Sourcing and Solicitation areas. Policy, Legislation, and Program Oversight also becomes a relevant component. Interestingly, leadership skills still have a high importance; however, looking at the content, we can see that, compared to other positions, this high importance is due in large part because of the importance of communication skills and problem-solving abilities. Almost 40% of the job postings list professional certifications as required or desired. (Alkadry and Patrucco 2023)

The second category is Managers. Manager titles may include the following:

- Commodity Manager
- Contract Manager
- Proposal Manager
- Procurement or Purchasing Manager
- Strategic Sourcing Manager.

The above-referenced research for Manager positions observes that:

> The majority of competence requirements are in the [Pathways Focus Area of] Contract Administration area, followed by Policy, Legislation, and Program Oversight. Leadership skills are also significant, but less so than for Director positions. Over 50% of job postings list professional certifications as a requirement or preference. (Alkadry and Patrucco 2023)

The third, and final, category is Directors. Director job titles may include:

- Associate Director of Procurement or Purchasing
- Chief Procurement Officer
- Deputy Chief of Procurement
- Director of Procurement.

The NIGP researchers also state that:

> [m]ost of the competence requirements for Directors [. . .] are in the [Pathways Focus Area of] Leadership area, followed by Policy, Legislation and Program Oversight. A more detailed text analysis of the job posting content shows that it is also important to obtain professional certifications, as almost 70% of the job postings list this aspect as required or desired. (Alkadry and Patrucco 2023)

From this research, we see the skill sets needed for each of the three ranges of jobs open to those seeking a career in public procurement, with Policy, Legislation, and Program Oversight being the only areas of overlap. This, of course, makes sense because anyone in public procurement must be aware of and carefully follow all policies and legislation that relate to the profession. The research also shows that professional certifications are increasingly a requirement or a preference as one progresses up the career ladder.

Desired Skills

There are many desired skills that an effective procurement professional needs to possess and continually hone. Some of the top skills frequently identified are:

- Analytical skills
- Business acumen
- Client service mindset
- Communication skills
- Critical thinking ability
- Leadership skills
- Objectivity.

These are all learned, not innate, skills. They are acquired and honed through on-the-job training and in the classroom. This is only one of the many reasons that ongoing, life-long learning is so important for the true procurement professional.

Procurement professionals need to have strong analytical skills to interpret laws, regulations, policies, and procedures. Strong analytical skills are also needed to correctly assess situations regarding procurement issues to properly advise clients, management, and suppliers as well as to be able to make good business decisions.

Along with strong analytical skills, business acumen is also needed. This is the ability to combine knowledge and skill with experience to assess a situation, weigh options, make sound decisions, and then have the confidence to take the appropriate actions that will move the entity toward achieving its objectives while influencing others to agree with you. This trait is extremely important for procurement professionals because they are at times called upon to make quick decisions with incomplete or limited information. Business acumen is comprised of various skills which include, but are not limited to:

- Ability to discern cause and effect
- Ability to handle ambiguity
- Contextual knowledge
- Financial competence
- Organizational knowledge
- Self-awareness
- Stakeholder awareness.

Having a client service mindset, or philosophy, is essential for anyone in a service-oriented profession such as public procurement and includes much more than just answering emails and phone calls. It is not only essential that we provide our end users with the goods and services they need, when they need them, where they need them, and how they need them at the right price, but also that we make the procurement experience as pleasant, effective, and efficient as possible to foster long-term rapport, support, and loyalty. It is all about the end user wanting to use your services, even if they are required to do so because they recognize the value you can add to the process.

Of course, to provide client services, the procurement professional must be able to communicate effectively with the end user. Good communication skills are essential for anyone in the public procurement profession. In the workplace, we must be able to effectively, correctly, and consistently provide, extract, and exchange information on a variety of topics and issues to a multitude of different stakeholders at various levels from janitors to jailers, from supervisors to suppliers, and from the public to other procurement professionals. Depending upon who you are dealing with and the purpose, you need to adjust your language and communication style. When dealing with subordinates, you may use informal language. In communications with management or suppliers, however, it is normally better to use more formal language.

Strong written and verbal communication skills are critical for procurement professionals because we deal with so many challenges and types of people on issues that are critical to the operations and missions of our entities. Human Resource personnel often report communication skills as one of the most, if not the most, commonly requested skills in job postings. Improving and demonstrating effective communication skills can help procurement professionals advance in their careers and remain competitive in the job market.

Some top communication skills include, but are not limited to:

- Active listening
- Clarity
- Communication method
- Confidence
- Empathy
- Feedback
- Friendliness
- Honesty
- Presentation
- Respect
- Responsiveness.

To meet the main goal of communication, to convey a message that is not misinterpreted or misleading, one must develop, demonstrate, and hone a variety of skills. This will not happen overnight and must be a conscious and continuous effort of every procurement professional.

Along with good communication skills, the procurement professional must be able to think critically. Critical thinking has been defined as "the intellectually disciplined process of actively and skillfully conceptualizing, applying, analyzing, synthesizing, and evaluating information gathered from, or generated by, observation, experience, reflection, reasoning, or communication, as a guide to belief and action" (Google, 2024). Critical thinking enables us to evaluate information objectively, analyze situations effectively, and consider various perspectives while identifying biases, underlying assumptions, and the relevance and credibility of data, all of which are crucial abilities for a procurement professional.

Critical thinking is also one of the top skills often listed for leadership. Other abilities often noted for leadership include, but are not limited to:

- Adaptability
- Decision-making

- Innovation
- Integrity
- Motivation and team-building
- Negotiation.

Things move very fast, so a leader must be able to be quick and adaptable as well as anticipate change. A leader cannot be complacent. They must often make difficult decisions while maintaining the confidence of their team at the same time as navigating tough additional hurdles such as budget and time constraints. They must be open to innovative problem-solving while seeking to better inspire and achieve goals and move their teams to the next level. Demonstrating integrity in all they do is vital for leaders to gain and maintain the respect of their teammates, entity management, suppliers, and the public. Leaders must build and foster *esprit de corps*, also known as camaraderie, within their teams. This entails fairness, avoids inter-team resentments, and provides incentives that reward those who contribute toward the progress of a common goal. Finally, leaders need to be good negotiators to work with their teams to help set the vision for their department or entity, while making them feel heard and appreciated.

Lastly, a procurement professional must be objective. Objectivity is crucial in decision-making as it helps ensure fairness, accuracy, and inclusiveness while inspiring trust. This leads to a more positive, inclusive, and beneficial work culture for everyone.

Professional Development

Part of being a true procurement professional is subscribing to the ideal of life-long learning and continuous self-improvement. In her article "The Importance of Professional Development in Procurement," Amanda Moffo asserts that: "Professional development in the procurement industry is critical to evolving and staying relevant and well-rounded. The procurement landscape is constantly changing, so acknowledging that we need to continue to innovate and grow our skills is vital" (Moffo n.d.). Professional development has several components.

The first element is chapter and national membership in a public procurement organization dedicated to education and professional development for their members, such as NIGP. Other highly regarded organizations include:

- American Production and Inventory Control Society
- Chartered Institute of Procurement and Supply

- Institute for Supply Management
- National Contract Management Association
- Supply Chain Canada.

As noted on its website, NIGP's mission is "to develop, support, and promote the public procurement profession" (NIGP, "NIGP Mission Statement"), and its vision statement proclaims, "NIGP is a vibrant international association creating a world in which public procurement practitioners are highly regarded members of a respected professional order" (NIGP, "NIGP Vision Statement"). By being a member of NIGP and any of its chapters throughout the US and Canada, you are letting everyone know that you also subscribe to its mission and vision statement. Membership also provides you access to up-to-date, relevant information on various procurement issues through classes, webinars, learning labs, and conferences. NIGP membership provides access for you to network with some of the best and brightest minds in public procurement in North America through the previously mentioned learning opportunities and through participation in online communities where you can post questions and challenges you are facing for other community members to respond with their advice, suggestions, and points of view. What a great benefit to have such a brain trust at your disposal!

Additionally, NIGP offers you the opportunity to become certified as an NIGP-Certified Procurement Professional (NIGP-CPP), which is recognized throughout the US and Canada. As the NIGP-CPP Certification Handbook points out, the reasons for procurement professionals to seek certification are to:

- Develop and advance their knowledge, skills, and abilities
- Distinguish themselves in the job market
- Expand their career opportunities
- Network and connect with others holding the NIGP-CPP certification. (NIGP, "NIGP-Certified Procurement Professional [NIGP-CPP] Certification Handbook")

Going hand in hand with certification is continuous, or life-long, learning. True procurement professionals know that they do not know it all and that once they do learn something, it can often change. For this reason, procurement professionals must continuously seek opportunities to learn and stay abreast of new and evolving practices and developments within the field, thereby helping them to expand their skill sets and spawn new ideas as well as new perspectives. This will raise their job performance and promote confidence in their team members and entity management.

Procurement professionals should also seek to improve and give back to the profession. Many volunteer opportunities exist within NIGP. You can participate on boards, councils, or task forces. NIGP has a Governing Board and three councils: Finance, Member, and Talent. NIGP's website states:

> Committees are an essential link between NIGP's leadership and its members. There are two types of committees, Board & Council Committees and Operational Committees. A Board & Council Committee is an extension of one of the three Councils (Finance, Member, Talent) in the fulfillment of its responsibilities. An Operational Committee supports and advises staff in the development and implementation of programs and services produced by the institute. (NIGP, "Leadership Opportunities")

In addition to standing boards, councils, and committees, NIGP also relies on its members to help staff its annual forum, present workshops at the Forum and chapter and conferences, present webinars and learning labs, and help develop new training materials.

As one can see, there are several opportunities to volunteer your skills, abilities, and knowledge to give back to and help advance the Procurement profession. If we would all, or even if half of us, volunteer to help when and where we could, just think what a mighty force that would be!

References

Alkadry, Mohamad, and Andras Patrucco 2023. "2023 NIGP Workforce Competency Study." NIGP. https://s3.us-east-1.amazonaws.com/nigp-prod-media/assets/resources/research-papers/2023%20Workforce%20Competency%20Research%20Brief%20FINAL.pdf

Bovis, Christopher. 2009. "The Effects of the Principles of Transparency and Accountability on Public Procurement and Public-Private Partnerships Regulation." *European Public Private Partnership Law Review* 4 (1): 7–25. https://www.jstor.org/stable/26696197

Google. "Critical Thinking." September 13, 2024. https://shorturl.at/e6skB

Moffo, Amanda. n.d. "The Importance of Professional Development in Procurement." Sig.org. https://www.sig.org/blog_posts/the-importance-of-professional-development-in-procurement/

NIGP. "Leadership Opportunities." https://www.nigp.org/membership/leadership-opportunities#

NIGP. "NIGP-Certified Procurement Professional (NIGP-CPP) Certification Handbook." https://www.nigp.org/resource/certification/handbook/NIGP-CPP-Certification-Handbook.pdf?dl=true

NIGP. "NIGP Mission Statement." https://www.nigp.org/about-nigp/mission-and-vison#:~:text=NIGP%20MISSION%20STATEMENT,promote%20the%20public%20procurement%20profession

NIGP. "NIGP Vision Statement." https://www.nigp.org/about-nigp/mission-and-vison#:~:text=NIGP%20MISSION%20STATEMENT,promote%20the%20public%20procurement%20profession

NIGP. "Values and Guiding Principles of Public Procurement." 2020. https://www.nigp.org/resource/global-best-practices/2020%20Values%20and%20Guiding%20Principles.pdf?dl=true

NIGP. "Why Choose a Career in Public Procurement?" https://www.nigp.org/our-profession/working-in-public-procurement

Chapter 3

Procurement Influences

This chapter discusses the influences that impact procurement operations. It addresses internal and external challenges and opportunities that public procurement professionals must deal with and how procurement can impact the entity by adding value to the procurement process. It also addresses local, national, and international topics that impact the public procurement profession. Anyone new to the field of public procurement must have a clear understanding of these issues and their impact on how procurement professionals conduct their daily work.

Adding Value to the Entity

At the forefront of every procurement professional's mind should be how they can add value to their entity. According to Sievo, a leader in procurement analytics solutions, there are eight ways that Procurement can demonstrate value:

1. Cost savings and reduction by driving cost savings and improved financial performance through techniques such as spend consolidation, contract negotiation, and the pursuit of volume discounts.

DOI: 10.4324/9781003566564-4

2. Strategic sourcing through analyzing the entity's spending patterns, identifying opportunities for cost savings, and developing a sourcing strategy that leverages purchasing power.
3. Process improvement by identifying and eliminating inefficiencies in an entity's processes.
4. Risk management through evaluating business risks by severity and likelihood and taking preventive actions where the benefit supersedes the effort.
5. Compliance by ensuring compliance with laws, regulations, and policies.
6. Innovation and supplier development through building strong and collaborative partnerships with suppliers and integrating new and innovative techniques, technologies, and approaches to improve efficiency and effectiveness.
7. Sustainability by making environmentally responsible decisions.
8. Contribution to growth by sharing market knowledge (Sievo n.d.).

On the most basic level, adding value entails ensuring end users' and suppliers' needs are met when obtaining goods or services needed to keep the entity running, thereby helping to meet the entity's mission and goals while being a good steward of taxpayer dollars. To do this, we need to be able to plan strategically. Strategic purchasing leads to better procurement decisions and relationships with suppliers. Procurement professionals are essential in orchestrating resources that support the entity's goals, and they are orchestrators of effective and efficient supply chains. The procurement professional, therefore, must be a good strategic planner and act as a partner when the entity's strategic plan is being developed to ensure goals, objectives, and plans realistically and effectively align with reality, good business principles, and best practices. Since strategic planning is an entity's process of defining its direction or strategy and allocating resources to attain the goals set, one can easily appreciate its importance to the effective operation and success of an entity fulfilling its mission. More specifically, strategic planning is an organized management activity used to set priorities for the entity, improve operations, direct resources and energy, and ensure all are working toward common goals by establishing agreement for intended results or outcomes. All of this, however, must contain a means to assess and adjust the plan when changes occur or when unforeseen internal or external circumstances occur. In other words, the strategic plan articulates where an entity intends to go, the actions needed to make progress toward getting there, and a means by which to measure success.

Procurement and Continuity of Operations Plans

In addition to being involved in strategic planning, Procurement should also be involved in an entity's business Continuity of Operations Plan (COOP), which is used when the entity experiences an emergency. A COOP establishes operational procedures to keep essential entity activities up and running when normal operations are not possible or feasible with the aim of guiding the entity to the restoration of all of its full functions. COOPs normally provide for attaining operational capability within a few hours to two days and aim to sustain an entity's core business functions and activities for 30 days or more when a catastrophic event or a national security emergency affecting the entity occurs, while assuring compliance with legal and statutory requirements. Procurement, of course, plays a vital role in this process. It is especially vital during an emergency that the needed goods and services are sourced from suppliers that can provide them at the right time and place the most effectively and efficiently possible.

Contract Management

Another value that Procurement adds to an entity is in the form of contract management. Contract management aims to achieve the stated goals and objectives through contract performance during contract formation and contract administration. This is often done through the use of a contract administration plan, which may be carried out by a contract administration team that provides support to and oversight on the project. At the end of the contract, the team uses established close-out procedures not only to ensure the contract file is complete but also to determine if any changes that would be beneficial to similar future procurements should be made. The contract administration team is assembled before the contract; its purpose is to oversee the entire contract administration process. The team's goal is to ensure the contract is executed on budget and on time, as well as to handle any problems that may arise. The size of the contract administration team is dependent on the number of stakeholders. It will often consist of:

- Contracting officer
- Project manager
- Subject matter experts
- Stakeholders
- Procurement professional.

All team members should be able to contribute to the effort and be free from any real or perceived conflicts of interest. Many entities require them to complete a Conflict of Interest Form, which is retained in the contract file.

Cooperative Contracting versus Piggybacking and Joint Ventures

Other issues that are important for procurement professionals are cooperative procurement versus piggybacking and joint ventures. The NIGP Dictionary of Procurement Terms defines cooperative procurement as:

> 1. The action is taken when two or more entities combine their requirements to obtain the advantages of volume purchases, including administrative savings and other benefits. 2. A variety of arrangements, whereby two or more public procurement entities purchase from the same supplier or multiple suppliers using a single Invitation for Bids (IFB) or Request for Proposals (RFP). Cooperative procurement efforts may result in contracts that other entities may "piggyback." (NIGP, "Dictionary of Procurement Terms")

It defines piggybacking as a:

> Form of intergovernmental cooperative purchasing in which an entity will be given the pricing and terms of a contract entered into by a larger entity. Generally, the larger entity will competitively award a contract that will include language allowing for other entities to use the contract to their advantage in terms of pricing, thereby gaining economies of scale that they normally would not receive if they competed on their own. (NIGP, "Dictionary of Procurement Terms")

While a joint venture is defined as, "A business arrangement in which two or more parties pool their assets to accomplish a specific goal or task while maintaining their distinct identities" (NIGP, "Dictionary of Procurement Terms").

The procurement professional needs to distinguish between these terms as they are somewhat similar, though there are subtle but essential differences. In a cooperative procurement, all participating entities in the contract are identified in the solicitation, which includes all of their combined volume, or estimated volume. One of the main purposes of combining several entities' volumes to establish one contract is to get volume pricing, aka economies of scale, or a cheaper price per unit than each entity could obtain on its own. In a piggybacking situation, an entity that was not a party to the original contract is allowed to be added to the existing contract. In this situation, the added entity's volume was not included in determining the economies of scale pricing, but they can benefit from the pricing of the existing contract. In a joint venture, two or more entities pool their resources to accomplish a goal or task they both share, often to reduce administrative costs such as cooperative procurement, in which one entity may solicit and award a contract while the other entity provides contract administration services.

Electronic Signature

An electronic signature, or e-signature, is a commonly used, secure, and efficient way to sign electronic documents quickly. Electronic signatures can replace handwritten signatures in many cases. Most United States public entities and Canadian provinces accept e-signatures as a valid and legal method to ratify contracts and other documents. The new procurement professional, however, needs to check with management or legal counsel to verify whether or not their jurisdiction recognizes and accepts electronic signatures on documents. Some jurisdictions may accept electronic signatures on certain documents but require a handwritten signature on others.

Globalization

Globalization in simple terms is the increasing interdependence and interconnectedness of people all over the world, such as how they interact in terms of culture, politics, and economics. For the procurement professional, it is important in terms of how technology and trade have transformed the world into a more interdependent and connected place. As some have stated, "The world has shrunk." Procurement professionals now have access to goods, services, supplies, and suppliers that in the not-too-distant past were inaccessible or impractical. Globalization has fostered free trade among nations around the globe, thereby providing more options and diverse choices for buyers and increasing competition. Some downsides of globalization, however, include environmental challenges, such as a larger carbon footprint in the transportation of goods all over the world, and possible income equality because of greater competition. For example, some companies may pay their workers less to remain competitive in the marketplace. As a result, issues such as fair trade have come to the forefront for those in both public and private procurement. The choice to purchase only Fair-Trade Certified goods shows an entity's commitment to protecting the environment, empowering farmers and workers, and supporting responsible suppliers.

International Trade Considerations

The issue of governing law is one of the most basic and primary considerations for the procurement professional. Legal disputes and governing law and legal disputes for international procurements can be extremely complex. For this reason, a procurement professional may seek advice from a more experienced legal professional in this area. A procurement professional seeks legal counsel when:

- The parties are based in different countries.
- The laws of another country will govern a contract because it was formed in that country.
- Part or all of the contract will be performed in a country other than the one in which one or both parties are based.

If any of these three elements are present, the contract must clearly state which system of law will govern the contract, as well as which country's courts have authority if a dispute arises. It would be prudent for parties to seek advice regarding legal issues from lawyers in the specific jurisdiction where the contract will be performed. The procurement professional should choose a legal system that is known for certainty and fairness as well as one that is relevant and commonly used. The business community frequently uses English law for international contracts. Other systems that are widely used include French, Japanese, German, Swiss, Hong Kong, and Singapore. Additionally, procurement professionals would be wise to consider the applicability of rules such as the United Nations Convention on Contracts for the International Sale of Goods (the "CISG"), which applies only to commercial goods and products. The "conflict of laws" rules will be applied if a contract does not stipulate a governing law. Rules involving conflict of laws are complicated, and disputes are expensive for all parties involved. It is, therefore, extremely important and prudent for the procurement professional to expressly choose governing laws in a contract between two international parties.

An equally important concern for a procurement professional to consider when conducting an international procurement is the currency rate of exchange. Since the value of two currencies may change between the time the contract is signed and payment is made, there is a great potential risk for both parties, both the buyer and the seller, because of currency volatility. Two commonly used approaches that address this issue are a forward or futures contract and to negotiate favorable contract terms. In a forward contract, the parties agree to buy or sell the needed goods or services at a specific price on a future date. Favorable negotiated terms may be an agreement on a currency clause, a fixed exchange rate, or a payment schedule that protects the entity from any unfavorable movements in the currency market.

Because currencies differ considerably internationally, many trade agreements specify the International Monetary Fund's Special Drawing Rights (SDR) as the unit of account for determining thresholds. To determine the actual threshold value, establish the currency exchange rate relative to the SDR and calculate the value in your country's currency. A procurement professional could also contact the federal government department responsible for trade since this information is usually posted on their websites.

In addition to currency rate or exchange issues, procurement professionals must consider the issue of customs when buying goods from another country. For example, duty rates can range from $0 to 37.5%, with a typical rate of 5.63% in the United States. Besides adding to the cost of the goods being imported, there are several additional logistical issues added for the procurement professional to address. The importer is responsible for arranging for the examination and release of the goods. This is often an involved and complicated process. That being the case, many entities opt to hire a licensed customs broker to ensure federal requirements regarding imports are met since they are experts regarding valuation, entry procedures, valuation, admissibility requirements, and the rates of duty as well as applicable fees and taxes.

Another issue procurement professionals may have to consider is domestic preferences. For some procurements, laws mandate that designated goods and services must be purchased domestically. For example, in some cases, United States laws require that iron, steel, manufactured products, and construction materials used in infrastructure projects have been produced in the United States. For this reason, it is a good idea to search international trade agreements and determine how they impact your specific procurement.

Embargos can be a complicating factor and a potential political risk for procurement professionals. Embargoes are financial and commercial penalties applied by a country or countries against a specific self-governing state, group, or individual. Embargoes take on various forms of actions, including banning exports or imports, creating quotas for quantity, imposing special tolls and taxes, banning freight or transport vehicles, freezing or seizing freights, assets, and bank accounts, and limiting the transport of technologies or products. Examples include:

- US and EU on Burma (Myanmar)—Embargoes for human rights violations

- US and EU on China—Arms
- US and Cuba—Arms, consumer goods, money.

To avoid any potential political risk, the procurement professional needs to be aware of and stay up to date on any embargo issues as they emerge.

Ethical differences are yet another consideration for procurement professionals. We need to ensure that foreign suppliers have a level playing field to compete with domestic suppliers and understand how to handle situations caused by individuals involved in government procurement that are considered unethical. As a steward of public trust and resources, we must conduct all procurements ethically. Below is an example that illustrates how there can be differences between the international parties regarding acceptable business practices. What is considered ethical in one culture may not be considered ethical in another culture. Therefore, it is paramount that procurement professionals be aware of the business practices and ethics that are acceptable in the culture in which they are conducting business.

An example of this situation is when the Macmillan book publishing company in the United Kingdom was fined £11.3 million for "unlawful conduct" regarding a textbook deal it had made in Sudan. A subsidiary of Macmillan paid bribes to secure the contract. Because bribes are a common business practice in Sudan, they are rarely prosecuted. In the United Kingdom, however, bribes are illegal.

This is just one example of many potential challenges we can find ourselves in when dealing with differing ethical standards from one country to another. A best practice is to always take the high road and follow the highest ethical standards for any given situation. It is vital for the procurement professional, especially when conducting an international procurement, to set ethical expectations.

International copyrights, trademarks, and patents are also considerations for procurement professionals. No creative work is automatically protected worldwide. There are, however, international treaties that automatically provide instant protection for all creative works once they are fixed in a medium. There are two primary international copyright agreements: 1) The Universal Copyright Convention and 2) the Berne Convention for the Protection of Literary and Artistic Works. These two agreements, however, have lost some of their significance since members of the World Trade Organization now comply with the Agreement on Trade-Related Aspects of Intellectual Property Rights Agreement (TRIPS).

Along with international copyright, trademarks, and patents, there is the principle of Moral Rights. The *Cambridge Dictionary* defines moral rights as "a writer's or artist's legal rights to protect their work, for example, to prevent it from being changed: The author will always hold the moral rights over their work" (*Cambridge Dictionary* 2024). In other words, creators of copyrighted works can generally protect their work through civil law and potentially common law. However, it is important to note that some countries such as the United States have amended creators' protections through acts such as the Visual Artists Rights Act of 1990.

> [Moral rights] include the right of attribution which is intended to allow an artist to control whether and the manner in which his or her name is associated with his own work of art and the right of integrity is intended to allow an artist to prevent his or her work from being altered, distorted, or mutilated. (Copyright Alliance 2020)

Even though many may not have heard of Moral Rights, the procurement professional needs to understand they apply to any country where they conduct business. Moral Rights laws often vary among countries. For example, in Italy, Moral Rights are non-transferable, eternal, and inalienable. Even after the transfer of economic rights, the author of a work retains the right to claim authorship, as well as the right to oppose mutilation of that work or any act that is or would be considered to be prejudicial to their reputation or honor. The United Kingdom requires individuals who commercially sell, perform, broadcast, or exhibit musical, artistic, literary, dramatic, or musical works to identify the author. This requirement, however, does not extend to things such as encyclopedias, typefaces, or works subject to Crown copyright. Moral Rights in Canada are protected under the *Copyright Act of Canada*, which includes an author's right to integrity, attribution, and association of a work. Moral rights cannot be licensed or assigned, although they can be waived by contract.

As the examples above demonstrate, the rights, duration, and relief opportunities differ from country to country. It is important to note that while Canada adheres to the "Moral Rights" principle, the United States does not.

Treaties and International Dispute Resolution

As with any contract, one must consider and plan for possible disputes and their resolution when negotiating and drafting a contract with a supplier in another country. In addition to all of the usual issues surrounding dispute resolution and risk mitigation in this area, procurement professionals must determine if their country is also party to any treaties that the country in which the supplier that is being contracted is located has signed. All countries are obligated to fulfill each provision of the treaty once it is ratified.

Treaties, though, do not have absolute authority. Countries can reject or negotiate provisions. Because of this, the procurement professional must conduct extensive research in this area to gain a complete understanding of the treaty's terms and any of those terms that may have been modified. Negotiating or rejecting provisions of a treaty can be difficult, in part because of differing interpretations of national sovereignty. Rather than treaties fitting in with the hierarchy of a country's laws, they work alongside the country's hierarchy of laws. Laws, however, can be modified to oblige them.

International trade agreements are likely to apply when conducting high-value procurements. When they do apply, they take precedence over local procurement laws. So, it is incumbent upon the procurement professional to do their due diligence in researching and determining which international trade agreements pertain to their procurement. The most prevalent trade agreement for North America was the North American Free Trade Agreement (NAFTA), which was an agreement between the United States, Canada, and Mexico in 1992. Part 4 is of particular importance to procurement professionals because it provided the rules under which government procurement was to be conducted among the three countries. The United States-Mexico-Canada Agreement (USMCA) replaced NAFTA and went into effect on July 1, 2020. USMCA is also known in Canada as the Canada-United States-Mexico Agreement (CUSMA) and as the Tratado entre Mexico, Estados Unidos y Canadá (T-MEC) in Mexico. While the United States and Mexico still have procurement obligations under USMCA, Canada continues to have procurement commitments through the World Trade Organization Revised Agreement on Government Procurement (WTO-GPA or GPA), while the United States, Canada, and Mexico continue to have commitments through the Comprehensive and Progressive Agreement for Trans-Pacific Partnership (CPTPP).

Tariffs are another important consideration as they can greatly influence the cost of a procurement. NIGP defines the word Tariff as "1. A schedule containing the rate, rules, and regulations under which transportation carriers handle the shipment of goods. 2. A tax imposed on imported goods" (NIGP, "Dictionary of Procurement Terms").

Tariffs can be variable, by price, or fixed, per unit or percentage of price. The purpose of tariffs is to boost a country's economy by making imported goods more expensive, thereby discouraging citizens from buying foreign products while encouraging them to buy domestic goods. Tariffs reduce foreign competition and trade deficits, and they give an advantage to domestic suppliers in the marketplace.

Again, research on the part of the procurement professional is required to determine the exact monetary impact of any applicable tariffs for that procurement to protect the entity's economic interests to ensure the entity gets the best value for any funds expended.

Market Influences

Market conditions can play a dramatic role in a procurement professional's efforts to meet one of their most important functions: maximizing competition. There are three basic types of competition: pure or perfect competition, imperfect, and monopoly. The most favorable market conditions for competition exist in the realm of pure or perfect competition, while the least favorable market conditions exist where there is a monopoly situation. In the middle of these two extremes is imperfect competition, such as an oligopoly.

The NIGP Dictionary of Procurement Terms defines Perfect (Pure) Competition as, "A market in which no buyer or seller has market power. This market contains a large number of buyers and sellers of approximately equal importance" (NIGP, "Dictionary of Procurement Terms"). In this market, there are a large number of suppliers vying for an entity's business. There are no barriers or hindrances affecting competition. This is the procurement professional's dream because they only need to stay informed about what is happening in the marketplace to determine the best time to purchase any needed goods or supplies.

Imperfect competition is defined by NIGP as, "A condition that exists when the marketplace is dominated by only one or possibly a few sellers. This is referred to as an oligopoly" (NIGP, "Dictionary of Procurement Terms"). In this environment, many of the goods and services being sold may be similar but have distinguishable differences. Also, neither buyers nor sellers dominate the market, so they must work together to reach an agreement since neither one has an advantage over the other. It is, therefore, key for the procurement professional to be knowledgeable about current market conditions and influences to negotiate a good and fair contract with suppliers.

The third type of market condition, monopoly, is defined in NIGP's dictionary as, "A market characterized by a single supplier that sells a unique good or service" (NIGP, "Dictionary of Procurement Terms"). In a monopoly, since only one supplier can supply the needed goods or services, they can dictate price and other important terms such as quality and service. Since supply in this case is low, prices tend to be high. It is, therefore, incumbent upon procurement professionals to negotiate, or at least to attempt to negotiate, the most favorable prices and terms in this situation.

Partnering

Partnering can be described as, "Creating a mutually beneficial relationship with a supplier or contractor for the specific purpose of work in which the relationship is trusting and supportive rather than adversarial" (NIGP, "Dictionary of Procurement Terms"). It is an attempt by entities to improve the level of service for their stakeholders, often to also lower the overall cost for goods and services needed by an entity. Partnering involves developing a long-term relationship with suppliers that meets both the unique and mutually beneficial goals of both the supplier and the entity. For this effort to be successful, mutual trust and respect between the parties must exist. This philosophy and way of thinking is a radical departure from the "let's do business at arm's length," somewhat adversarial, philosophy held and practiced by procurement professionals in the not-too-distant past.

Public-Private Partnership (P3), a specific type of partnering, is defined by the NIGP Dictionary of Procurement Terms as,

> A broad term used to describe the public facility and infrastructure contracts that minimally include components of design and build e.g., construction, renovation, rehabilitation into one single contract. Components of financing, operations, maintenance, or management may be included within this single contract. A P3 contract allocates risks to the party, the government, or the contractor, best able to manage the risks and may assign a higher level of responsibility for means and methods to the partner. (NIGP, "Dictionary of Procurement Terms")

Some examples of P3s include the building of new highways, hospitals, and government buildings. Canada is one of the world's leaders in using P3s globally. Advantages of partnering include:

- Enhancing long-term competitiveness since both partners strive to improve the quality of goods and services.
- Bonding of the entity and the supplier as the result of a mutual dedication to success.
- Communicating more openly and effectively.

Disadvantages include:

- The perception is that longer-term relationships with suppliers reduces competition.
- The considerable administrative time to develop, analyze, procure, and administer.
- The resistance to obtaining buy-in from entity stakeholders.

Procurement professionals must consider and weigh the impact of partnering on the ethical, organizational, and personnel elements of the entity. Processes must be transparent and accountable to avoid corruption and favoritism. Procurement professionals must remain vigilant to protect the public interest by avoiding unintended consequences and unexpected costs. They must also ensure that any partnership created is the result of an open solicitation that indisputably offers all suppliers access to participate in competing for such a contract.

Political Influences

Procurement professionals are not only supervised by managers within their entity, but they also work under the perpetual oversight and sometimes, unfortunately, interference of elected officials. These politicians may put pressure on a procurement professional to award a contract to a supporter, or they may criticize valid procurement practices, policies, or procedures to curry favor and attract votes. Such actions, along with operating under the constant glare of a spotlight held by the media, can create an extremely challenging and stressful environment for those in the public procurement profession. It is up to the procurement professional to ensure that all procurement processes are handled with integrity and transparency, without undue influence from any outside or political influences. The potential ramifications of deviating from the profession's ethical standards and codes of conduct can range from losing one's job to being convicted and having to serve time in jail or pay penalties in addition to losing one's reputation. If political pressure is ever applied to a procurement professional, they should document the facts and then notify their supervisor.

Purchasing Cards

Purchasing Cards, also known as P-cards, are an essential tool for processing small purchases in most entities. They are used to obtain small-dollar goods and services in a manner that streamlines the normal purchase order process. They are used by entities to reduce internal department and Procurement staff burdens on small-dollar, non-repetitive purchases. They are like corporate card programs except that under a P-card program, the entire balance is always paid off each month. P-card programs provide accountability for each purchasing cardholder, and usage reports can easily be created. This streamlined process has many benefits which include:

- Reducing the cost of small purchases by increasing the productivity of entity personnel.
- Reducing entity administrative costs.

- Improving cash management.
- Allowing supplier flexibility.
- Improving procurement oversight, controls, and reporting.
- Increasing entity employees' empowerment and convenience.

Further, a P-card program can help an entity establish controls, including:

- Prohibited and blocked categories.
- Items are allowed only by the nature of the purchasing cardholder's position.
- Varying maximum limits.
- The ability to immediately dispute transactions.
- The ability to immediately increase or decrease limits and the ability to immediately close accounts.

Any P-card program must include policies that assign responsibility for card use, in addition to oversight and accountability for all purchases. It is important to adopt limits for each purchase and a list of approved goods and services to help avoid potential abuse, waste, and fraud. Diligent oversight will help to ensure that the entity will reap the benefits from a P-card program while helping to alleviate fears and criticisms of potential abuse.

Reverse Auctions

Reverse Auctions are the opposite of regular auctions, where a seller puts up an item for sale and buyers place bids, with the item going to the highest bidder. In the public sector, Reverse Auctions are conducted online with multiple suppliers competing for the business of an entity by submitting an initial bid price for the goods or services an entity is soliciting for and then submitting subsequent lower bid prices as they see the prices that other suppliers are submitting in real-time. At the end of the auction, a contract is awarded to the lowest responsive and responsible bidder.

Reverse Auctions have been found to work best for simple, easy-to-specify goods. Services are often too complex for this procurement method. Reverse Auctions have been used successfully to procure items such as tires, car batteries, and rolled tin for license plates.

Even though Reverse Auctions often garner lower prices, there are some drawbacks which include:

- Additional training is required for participating suppliers.
- Additional training is required for entity staff.

- The possibility that a supplier can hurt themselves by bidding too low.
- A greater possibility that something may go wrong with technology during the Reverse Auction event.

Not all entities, however, have the authority to use Reverse Auctions. The procurement professional must ensure that it is an approved method of procurement for their jurisdiction before using it to solicit needed goods or services.

Social Media

Social media has had a tremendous impact on society, including the public procurement profession. Because of the explosion of people, including entities and suppliers, using various platforms, standards, and common practices, formal guidelines have not been able to keep up with emerging and changing technology.

It is not unheard of for unscrupulous suppliers to exert undue influence on a selection process by contacting end users to ask for additional information about a project, or asking administrative personnel for information such as budgets, evaluator, or award information. Some may even try to discredit competitors by repeating rumors regarding their personnel and performance to entity employees. While suppliers certainly have the right to seek additional information, they need to do so by following the proper communication protocols, policies, and procedures that have been adopted by the procuring entity to help ensure equality and transparency for all suppliers. No offeror should try to unduly influence any entity employee regarding the selection of a contractor for the goods or services being solicited by the entity. Social media has added to the ease and speed with which entity personnel's names and contact information can be obtained. For this reason, many entities have implemented or expanded a Cone of Silence policy. The intent of such a policy is not to prevent suppliers from communicating with entity personnel but rather to channel all communication between potential offerors and the entity through the procurement professional. Following this process allows the procurement professional to know what is being asked by and told to suppliers so they can determine if that information needs to be shared with other potential offerors to maintain a fair and level playing field for all suppliers.

Many entities have a presence on websites and regularly post on social media sites such as LinkedIn, X, Facebook, and YouTube for marketing purposes. The entity, therefore, needs to monitor comments, opinions, and discussions related to procurement during the solicitation, evaluation, and selection process while shielding evaluation committee members and other procurement decision-makers from being exposed to these postings.

Another consideration for entities is the appearance of "friending" or "liking" suppliers on social media. Doing so, or even having other entity employees do so, may give the perception that the supplier or their employees are being given a preference or that some sort of relationship between the supplier and the entity exists. Remember, perception is reality! Procurement professionals, therefore, need to be fully aware of the pitfalls as well as the advantages of using social media.

Social Responsibility and Sustainability

Since entities are stewards of public resources, they have a responsibility to society, and procurement can be an essential, strategic partner in meeting that responsibility proactively. This can be done by:

- Optimizing, growing, and building Disadvantaged Business Enterprises programs.
- Supporting the local economy by including and utilizing local businesses.
- Incorporating environmental sustainability efforts into procurements.
- Supporting the local economy by including and utilizing local businesses.
- Mitigating challenges, particularly those that may occur through service contracts relating to labor issues.

Disadvantaged businesses, in many ways, are different from their majority counterparts. Many have fewer human and financial resources. This often means that disadvantaged business owners do not have a lot of time for networking, building client bases, education and training, and searching and responding to opportunities to do business with entities. So, procurement professionals need to be intentional in seeking and utilizing them when sourcing suppliers.

In addition to disadvantaged businesses, microbusinesses are a subset of the supplier community. According to Wolters Kluwer, a micro business "is a business operated by less than 10 people and generates less than $250,000 in revenue a year" (Nelson 2023). The difference between a small business and a microbusiness is that the micro business typically has fewer than 10 employees while small businesses may include up to 500 employees. Additionally, they have even less access to capital and human resources. As a result, microbusinesses often face even more challenges and adversity than small businesses. Microbusinesses comprise a large part of small businesses, which employ a majority of the United States workforce. For this reason, it is vital for the economy that their business thrives.

There are several easy and subtle strategies for a procurement professional to take to begin growing small business programs for their entity that require minimal effort. They include:

- Seeking Competition—Notifying Disadvantaged Business Enterprises (DBEs) of opportunities to participate in formal solicitation processes.
- Using Low-Hanging Fruit—Encouraging DBEs to participate in procurements that require little to no competition.
- Identifying Opportunities for Growth—Recommending modifications to policies or procedures, so that they support DBE goals.
- Monitoring Specifications & Qualifications—Drafting qualification requirements and scopes of work that are not unnecessarily or overly restrictive.
- Advocating for DBEs—Looking for opportunities to introduce specific DBEs that seem to be a good fit to end users and expanding entity-wide the general knowledge of DBE utilization.
- Seeking Help with Majority Suppliers—Since many large distributors have access to sophisticated reporting tools that identify DBEs in their supply chain, procurement professionals should discuss with these suppliers opportunities for them to use this data to support the efforts and provide the data that can increase their utilization of small businesses.

Procurement professionals should also be concerned about environmental sustainability. There are several environmental sustainability measures that an entity can take to address the stewardship of natural resources. These include, but are not limited to:

- Water Conservation
- Management of Wastes
- Carbon Emissions.

Procurement professionals can use their purchasing power to choose goods and services that have a reduced impact on the environment. By doing so, they can take a huge step toward attaining sustainability goals. Because of the plethora of resources regarding sustainability that are readily available, it should be an easy task for procurement professionals to research to learn ways of incorporating terms, conditions, and specifications that impact environmental sustainability into solicitations. One such resource is the Environmental Protection Agency's (EPA) "Significant Guidance Documents by Environmental Topic," which can be found on their website. Other useful websites include:

- Comprehensive Procurement Guidelines
- Sustainable Acquisition/"Green" Procurement Through General Services Administration (GSA) Schedules
- US Sustainability Policy & Laws
- Environmental Law: Government and Public Policy Toward the Environment
- Understanding the Environmental Protection Agency
- Electronic Product Environmental Assessment Tool
- Federal Strategic Sourcing Initiative
- EPA—Related Programs, Tools, and Resources
- Comprehensive Procurement Guidelines for Non-Paper Office Products.

Though it is not a simple process, opportunities abound for procurement professionals to include environmentally sustainable requirements or options in the scope of work. The procurement professionals who are successful in sustainability meeting goals will come to adopt a mindset for this pursuit, and they will continually seek ways to receive training related to green procurement.

Socioeconomic Policies

The use of public procurement systems by leaders in government to achieve goals such as advancing racial equality and favoring domestic or local suppliers is not new; in fact, it is becoming more commonplace. While the aim here is commendable, the effectiveness of leveraging the procurement system to achieve socioeconomic goals beyond the act of simply procuring goods or services has been met with mixed results that suggest this approach may not be the best method to meet societal goals. While socioeconomic goals have their justifiable values, a rigorous assessment of benefits and costs derived from the employment of socioeconomic policies to meet goals being embedded in the public procurement system should be made to ensure the value derived justifies any additional costs, if there are any.

Supplier Relationship Management (SRM)

Supplier Relationship Management (SRM) is a set of processes, principles, and tools that help entities maximize relationship value with suppliers, minimize risk, and manage overheads throughout the life cycle of the relationship with the supplier. SRM has two components:

- Clear commitment between the procurement professional and the supplier
- The objective is that both parties understand, agree, and, whenever possible, codify the interactions between them.

Successful SRM is driven largely by changes in processes, policies, supplier agreements, roles, and effective SRM systems. These systems introduce standardization and structure into the relationship between the entity and the supplier through the use of data management, tools, and templates, enabling relationship visibility. They form the foundation around which the entity manages its relationship with the supplier and, thereby, govern a majority of the aspects related to the supplier management process.

SRM enables entities to:

- Establish processes to effectively manage performance and develop supplier capabilities to continuously improve value to the entity.
- Establish the governance structure and process for internal and supplier interactions across the life cycle of the supplier relationship.
- Effectively identify strategic suppliers based on relative importance and define operational expectations and supplier stratification.
- Define formal processes for management involvement in the relationship and clarify internal roles and responsibilities.

There are many reasons why procurement professionals and their entities need to strive toward a formal SRM program. One of the primary principles of the public procurement profession is to grow a robust pool of ready, able, and willing suppliers who are capable of providing the goods and services required. In addition, values, transparency, equity, transparency, and the principle of maximizing competition mandate that we are inclusive in our opportunities for suppliers to do business with our entities. A more diverse and expansive supplier pool translates to better pricing, better value, and better quality for the entity.

Transparency in Public Procurement

Transparency in public procurement is essential because it promotes accountability, promotes fair competition, and provides public oversight. If suppliers know that procurement processes are fair and transparent and that they all have the same access to pertinent information, they are more likely to participate in the competitive process, thereby driving down prices for the entity by widening the supplier pool and increasing competition.

Transparency is important in this process because it allows oversight entities and the public to inspect procurement files to ensure that procurement professionals are adhering to the procurement laws, rules, policies, and procedures that are in place to protect the public's best interest. Ineffective accountability may lead to decreased efficiency, wasted public funds, and flawed decisions. It is, therefore, vital that accountability policies, procedures, and oversight through individual or team responsibility, informal or formal systems, explicit lines of authority, and measurement tools that hold procurement professionals and other public officials accountable are in place and are strictly adhered to.

Workforce Evolution

The workforce in public procurement has changed greatly in the last few decades and will continue to do so in the years to come. Gone are the days when the value and potential contributions of buyers were undervalued if valued much at all. Buyers were not seen as professionals, but merely clerks or paper pushers. Fortunately, that perception is no longer held by most entities. Buyers have demonstrated how they can add true value to the procurement process and strategically enable the entity to meet its mission and goals more effectively and efficiently. We are now properly considered professionals and have gained our seat at the management table along with other entity leaders.

As a result, the public procurement workforce has evolved and continues to evolve to meet this new role. Expectations of procurement professionals now include:

- Continued training
- Professional certification
- Stronger contract administration skills
- Stronger market analysis skills
- Demonstrated leadership skills which include:
  - Communications
  - Critical thinking

    - Driving change, innovation, and agility
    - Problem-solving
    - Relationship management
    - Succession planning
    - Talent recruitment and development
    - Technology acuity
- Mastery of business principles and operations which include:
    - Business management and continuity
    - Economics, budget, financial management, and accounting
    - Technology management.

A 2023 workforce competency research brief published by NIGP listed key takeaways for job listings for directors, managers, and professional positions in public procurement. Those takeaways are as follows:

> - Directors: Many competence requirements for Director positions are in the Leadership area, followed by Policy, Legislation, and Program Oversight. Professional certifications are highly valued, with almost 70% of job postings listing this as a requirement or preference.
> - Managers: For Manager positions, most competence requirements are in the Contract Administration area, followed by Policy, Legislation, and Program Oversight. Leadership skills are also significant, but less so than for Director positions. Over 50% of job postings list professional certifications as a requirement or preference.
> - Professionals: For Professional positions, many competence requirements are in the Contract Administration and Sourcing and Solicitation areas. Policy, Legislation, and Program Oversight is also a relevant component. Interestingly, while Leadership skills are still important, the emphasis is more on communication skills and problem-solving abilities rather than leadership skills per se. Almost 40% of job postings list professional certifications as a requirement or preference. (Alkadry and Patrucco 2023)

From this research, it is astounding how far our profession has come. There is, however, room for growth and further development in the areas of business management, leadership, and social responsibility. Entity management should provide targeted training in three areas and continue to encourage and support those in the field of public procurement to seek professional certification.

Surplus

Every entity needs to have in place clear policies regarding surplus that are easy for all employees to access and understand. These policies also must have a means for oversight and enforcement. This is usually accomplished by appointing someone as the entity's surplus property manager. The surplus property manager will be responsible for the safe and efficient movement of surplus property within and out of the entity as well as the maintenance of all records associated with this activity and the completion and submission of any required reports.

The surplus property manager is also the one to determine which method of disposal is most likely to bring the best value to the entity. Chapter Thirteen is dedicated to the discussion on surplus.

However, important terms that procurement professionals need to know regarding this topic include:

- Surplus—an overstock situation in which an amount of a good is left over after entity requirements have been met.
- Excess—an amount of a good that is more than necessary, desirable, or permitted by a department or area, but can be utilized by another department or area within the entity.
- Disposal—the action or process of getting rid of or throwing away a good.
- Close-out—the sale of goods at a reduced price to get rid of them.

References

Alkadry, Mohamad, and Andras Patrucco. 2023. "2023 NIGP Workforce Competency Study." NIGP. https://s3.us-east-1.amazonaws.com/nigp-prod-media/assets/resources/research-papers/2023%20Workforce%20Competency%20Research%20Brief%20FINAL.pdf

Cambridge Dictionary. 2024. "Moral Rights." @CambridgeWords. October 2, 2024. https://dictionary.cambridge.org/us/dictionary/english/moral-rights#google_vignette

Copyright Alliance. 2020. "Copyright Attribution and Integrity." November 4, 2020. https://copyrightalliance.org/education/copyright-law-explained/copyright-owners-rights/copyright-attribution-integrity/

Nelson, Nikki. 2023. "What is a Micro Business?" Wolters Kluwer. https://www.wolterskluwer.com/en/expert-insights/what-is-a-micro-business

NIGP. "Dictionary of Procurement Terms." https://www.nigp.org/dictionary-of-terms

Sievo. n.d. "Potential of Procurement: How to Get More Value for Your Business." https://sievo.com/blog/procurement-value

Part II

Procurement Organization and Framework

Chapter 4

Procurement Entities

Procurement is impacted by the global environment in which it operates. This chapter will discuss the differences between eight of the world's trading partners: the United States, Canada, Mexico, China, India, Japan, Sweden, and Australia. With the increasing global marketplace, procurement professionals need to understand not only how the form of government and legal system impacts their activities but also how to communicate effectively within as well as outside of their increasingly diverse workplaces and the risks associated with contracting with other countries. The chapter concludes with a comparison of the United States and Canada.

Global Procurement

Public procurement exists in countries across the globe. According to the World Bank, "public procurement represents on average 13% to 20% of gross domestic product (GDP). Global expenditure in procurement is estimated at nearly 9.5 trillion US dollars" (World Bank Group 2020). Meanwhile, the Open Contracting Partnership and Spend Network estimate that in 2018,

DOI: 10.4324/9781003566564-6

the global value of public procurement was $13 trillion US dollars (Hayman and Makgill 2020). With so much currency being spent, it is important to understand international public procurement as it gains importance to policymakers. Additionally, understanding public procurement's influence on the global economy is crucial for understanding the impact of policy decisions on the global socioeconomic landscape. According to Dr. Lucian Cernat of Utrecht University, "International public procurement involves a substantial amount of money and is an area gaining importance among policymakers. However, despite the size and importance of international public procurement, it is subject to hundreds of restrictive measures and discriminatory policies" (Cernat 2022).

Understanding the Differences Between Countries

As public procurement professionals, we must understand the global world that we work in. Note that no two countries operate in the same fashion. Each country is organized and operates differently. For this textbook, the authors are focusing on the main trading partners of the United States of America. The United States Central Intelligence Agency has a detailed website that details all the countries from which much of the information was gathered (Central Intelligence Agency, "Field Listing—Government Type"; Field Listing—Legal System"). The table below details some of the more significant differences.

Table 4.1 Significant Differences Between United States Trading Partners

Country	*Form of Government*	*Legal System*	*Communication Context*	*Risk Management—Risk Factors*
United States	Constitutional Federal Republic	Common Law	Relatively Low Context	Supply Chain, Contractual, Environmental, Social, and Governance (ESG)
Canada	Federal Parliamentary Democracy	Common Law & Civil Law	Low Context	Political, Legal, Environmental, Social, and Governance (ESG)
Mexico	Federal Presidential Republic	Civil Law	High Context	Environmental, Social, and Governance (ESG), Political, Supply Chain

(Continued)

Table 4.1 (Continued)

Country	*Form of Government*	*Legal System*	*Communication Context*	*Risk Management—Risk Factors*
China	Communist Party-led State	Socialist Legal System with uniquely Chinese characteristics	High Context	Supply Chain, Political, Environmental, Social, and Governance (ESG), Legal
India	Federal Parliamentary Republic	Common, Religious, and Civil Law	High Context	Legal, Financial, and Supply Chain
Japan	Parliamentary Constitutional Monarchy	Civil Law	High Context	Environmental, Social, and Governance (ESG), Political
Sweden	Parliamentary Constitutional Monarchy	Civil Law	Low Context	Financial and Political
Australia	Federal Parliamentary Democracy under a constitutional monarchy; a Commonwealth realm	Common Law	Low Context	Environmental, Social, and Governance (ESG), Political

Form of Government

The form of government can impact competition, determine policies, encourage or limit innovation, etc. Procurement professionals need to have at a minimum a high-level understanding of the government as well as those of its closest trading partners. There are many different forms of government. Each of the countries listed in the table varies in who has the authority and how decisions are made. For example, Japan and Sweden vary in rules of succession and distribution of power even though both countries are parliamentary constitutional monarchies.

According to the United States Central Intelligence Agency, the United States is a constitutional federal republic in which its government operates under an authoritative document, the Constitution, which "sets forth the system of fundamental laws and principles that determines the nature, functions, and limits of that government" (Central Intelligence Agency, "Field Listing—Government Type"). The United States is also considered a federal republic as the powers of the central government are restricted and in which the states retain a degree of self-government. Ultimate sovereign power rests with the voters who chose their governmental representatives.

In contrast, Canada is a federal parliamentary democracy. A parliamentary democracy has a political system in which the parliament selects the prime minister, premier, or chancellor along with the cabinet ministers.

Mexico is a federal presidential republic. In Mexico, the power is divided between three branches: the Presidency, the Congress, and the Courts.

China is a communist-led state in which the government controls the economy, and a single party holds power. Controls are imposed with the elimination of private ownership of property or capital while claiming to make progress toward a higher social order in which all goods are equally shared by the people.

India is a federal parliamentary republic with a parliamentary form of government. There is a Council of Ministers with the Prime Minister as its head to advise the President, who is the constitutional head of the country.

Japan is a parliamentary constitutional monarchy, with a parliamentary system of government. The emperor plays a diplomatic role and is the symbol of the state but does not hold political functions.

> The government is composed of the Executive, the Legislature, and the Judiciary, with separation of powers. Executive power is vested in the Cabinet, led by the Prime Minister as head of government. Legislative power is vested in the National Diet, a bicameral parliament. (Foreign & Commonwealth Office 2021)

Sweden is a parliamentary constitutional monarchy led by the Prime Minister, who is chosen by the Parliament. However, the formal Head of State is the oldest living monarch descendant, male or female as described in the Succession law to the throne.

Australia is a federal parliamentary democracy under a constitutional monarchy, a Commonwealth realm. The head of state is the monarch of the United Kingdom, while the head of government is the Prime Minister.

Legal Systems

Understanding the different legal systems is important if your entity conducts internal procurements and contracts with a supplier outside of your home country. Legal systems provide the framework for resolving disputes and contract enforcement. Challenges may arise because of differences in the laws of the countries involved or because of different interpretations of words or applications of laws. It is recommended to thoroughly research and understand a country before contracting with suppliers and establish which law will govern the resulting contract.

The United States has a type of common law legal system which is often referred to as case law and is based on past judicial decisions. Common law most often influences public procurement decisions. The basis of authority is derived from four sources: constitutional law, statutory law, administrative regulations, and case law.

Canada has a combination of English common law and civil law and affirms Aboriginal rights and treaty rights. Its federal, provincial, and territorial courts resolve disputes, and in doing so, they interpret and establish the law for all Canadians. However, the province of Quebec follows the civil law tradition through the introduction of the Charter of Rights and Freedoms to the Canadian Constitution.

Mexico follows a civil law system, and its constitution has supremacy over all other sources of domestic and international law. Mexico has both state and federal court systems. Federal courts have jurisdiction over cases involving federal statutes and constitutional questions.

According to the Foreign Law Guide, the Chinese government characterizes its legal system as The Socialist Legal System of Laws with Chinese Characteristics ("China, People's Republic of—Government"). Judiciaries Worldwide state that the sources of China's law include the Constitution of the People's Republic of China, national laws issued by the National People's Congress, administrative regulations disseminated by the State Council, decrees from local People's Congresses, administrative orders, and local rules (Judiciaries Worldwide n.d.).

According to the US Department of Justice, India's legal system is drawn from three primary sources: English common law, customary and religious laws, and civil law (Office of Justice Programs n.d.). The Indian Contract Act of 1872, often referred to as the Contract Act, codifies Indian contract law. Departures from English law have been in accordance with what India's legislators deem the unique conditions of India and considerations of equity. India differs from the other countries discussed in that it does not have a dual court system, although it does have a Federal Constitution.

Japan's legal system is structured as a "Civil Law" system, based upon codified statutes in the *roppō* ("Six Codes"), which include the Constitution of Japan, Civil Code, Code of Civil Procedure, Criminal Code, Code of Criminal Procedure, and Commercial Code.

According to the US Central Intelligence Agency, Sweden has a civil law system influenced by Roman-Germanic law and customary law, although it does not have a civil code (Central Intelligence Agency, "Field Listing—Legal System").

Australia has a common law legal system which was inherited from England. The two major sources of Australian law are cases from the decisions made by judges in the courts and legislation based on the legal rules made by parliament and by those to whom parliament has delegated authority.

Communication

Communication styles can vary greatly across cultures. Understanding the different communication styles and nuances is an important skill for all procurement professionals, and it is especially important if you are conducting an international procurement. Culture can impact business transactions or negotiations as miscommunication or misunderstandings can arise from interactions between people or groups who do not have a long-shared history. A long-shared history and homogeneous population tend to result in a high-context culture in which context is passed between generations (Meyer 2014). However, when individuals come from different cultural contexts, the likelihood of a misunderstanding increases (Meyer 2014). When two different cultures interact, the relative positioning of the two cultures in relation to one another determines how people view each other (Meyer 2014).

One of the most popular cultural communication continuum concepts was developed by Edward T. Hall, a popular anthropologist who is known for his development of high- and low-context cultural factors (Changing Minds n.d.). High- and low-context cultures refer to how important contextual cues are in interpreting a message. Typically, high-context cultures have a communication style based on body language, tone, and overall context including unwritten rules of the culture. In contrast, low-context cultures are more straightforward, direct, and clearer in communication. In a low-context culture, very little is taken for granted.

For example, if a procurement professional from the United States or Canada, both relatively low-context cultures, were negotiating with a supplier from China, a relatively high-context culture, there could be misunderstandings. The procurement professional may expect that the contract identifies all relevant issues, devoid of ambiguity, whereas the high-context supplier may agree to the arrangement with a handshake, leaving many of the contract details subject to interpretation. During discussions, it is common for high-context cultures to infer but not directly speak their thoughts. In many ways, the low-context party must read between the lines. For example, a high-context supplier may use a prolonged pause or an emphasis on a particular phrase to get their point across. These subtle cues may be overlooked or ignored by a low-context procurement professional. Another example is that in many Latin countries, including Mexico, businesspeople are not fond of overt disagreements, so rather than saying "no" they might say "maybe" or "I'll get back to you." If you are from a low-context country, be wary not to mistake this for interest.

Another example of the differences between high context and low context concerns the United States, where its citizens are taught to say what you mean and mean what you say (Meyer 2014). For example, in the United States and Canada, specifications are written as specifically as possible and avoid using ambiguous language that may cause confusion or misunderstandings. Procurement professionals spend hours learning how to identify vague and speculative language that can be misconstrued, such as the words usually, generally, often, normally, typically, flexible, proper, suitable, reasonable, appropriately, user-friendly, and approximately. Procurement professionals are encouraged to use clear and concise plain language in describing their requirements as misunderstandings can cause contract disputes and potential litigation. This communication approach differs significantly from China with its high-context culture. The Chinese are taught that the listener is responsible for understanding the speaker's intention (Meyer 2014). In a high-context culture, the real message is often implied; thus, the listener is encouraged to "listen to what is meant instead of what is said" (Meyer 2014).

To minimize misunderstandings, a best practice is to understand and learn about the cultures, practices, history, values, and expectations of the countries that your entity is doing business with before beginning negotiations. Generally, high-context cultures prefer a slower more relationship-oriented negotiation, while low-context cultures prefer a faster and more task-oriented negotiation. Remember to ask questions to clarify misunderstandings and confirm agreements. However, be careful not to ask questions that are too personal or intrusive. Other recommendations include:

- Openly discuss any cultural differences upfront.
- When two different cultures communicate, the best practice is to use low-context communication, such as putting agreements in writing to minimize potential misunderstandings (Meyer 2014).
- Recognize the etiquette of the culture that you are interacting with. Show deference to rank and position. Seat those of equal status next to each other and approach others based on their hierarchical order (Meyer 2014).
- Allow decisions to be made slowly. Avoid putting pressure on people to make decisions quickly, or it will likely lead to them shutting down and politely resisting you (LaMarco 2018).
- Develop a relationship with the person or people that you are working with. Take the time to get to know them and develop trust through a connection. The Chinese build loyalty with the individual, not the company (Meyer 2014). Take time to share a meal and have a few drinks. Worry less about efficiency, and instead focus on being transparent by being yourself.

- Conduct business before the actual meeting. Provide information in advance to allow for informal discussions to occur offline (Meyer 2014).
- Be willing and comfortable adapting to the style of the culture you are interacting with and doing business with (Meyer 2014). Specifically, remain flexible and go with the flow. Remember, flexible people do not get bent out of shape.
- If misunderstandings appear to arise, feel comfortable enough to stop and discuss the differences, preferably in private over a meal with a Chinese leadership-level equivalent.

Risk Management

Procurement professionals must understand the different risks of doing business with various countries. While the different types of risks will be covered in greater detail in Chapters Eight and Ten, this chapter will introduce its application to international procurements.

According to NIGP's Dictionary of Procurement Terms, risk management is defined as the process including the identification and analysis of risk; and the decision to either accept or mitigate the exposure to such risk when compared to the potential impact of the organization's objectives (NIGP, "Dictionary of Procurement Terms").

Before beginning an international procurement or sourcing from the countries listed, each identified risk should be analyzed, and a risk management and mitigation plan developed for any identified risks that will have the most severe impact and greatest possibility. An entity may elect to accept the risk by placing an order with a supplier in a country in which there is a high probability of a supply chain disruption because of an ongoing trade war. Another option is to monitor the risk by requiring a supplier to provide a mitigation plan for schedule delays along with frequent check-ins. A third option is to transfer the risk by requiring a performance bond.

Types of Risk

When discussing the different types of risks, it is important to understand what each risk includes. The list that follows describes in greater detail the risks presented in Table 4.1, but it is by no means a comprehensive list of business risks.

Contractual risks include risks associated with the failure of contractors to deliver services or products at the agreed cost and specifications, including delivery of substandard products such as out-of-date food products as well as the failure to meet specified outcomes.

Environmental risks include pollution, noise, or the energy efficiency of ongoing operations such as the reliance on unsustainable commodity sources.

Environmental, Social, and Governance (ESG) risks are risks associated with sustainability that extend beyond environmental risks. ESG risks include the risks associated with the entity's activities, including but not limited to corporate governance, company policies, operations, business practices, and ethics. Examples of ESG risks are energy efficiency, overall environmental impact, pollution and gas emissions, child labor, modern-day slavery, human rights violations, gender and diversity inclusion, data security, political contributions, lobbying, anti-bribery strategies, and corruption.

Financial risks are associated with the failure to secure the most economically advantageous outcome to an acquisition, such as not applying the correct costing or appraisal technique before contract award.

Legal risks are associated with breach of contract, failure to include contract terms, and violation of intellectual property rights including copyright and trademark infringement.

Legislative and regulatory risks are associated with current or potential changes in laws. Laws are written and enacted by the legislative branch of government, while regulations are written by governing entities to supplement laws that were passed by the legislature.

Political risks are associated with a failure to deliver goods or services because of political policies or constraints, including the failure to integrate sustainability requirements, changes in government, and the potential for political turmoil at home or abroad.

Supply chain risks include exposures, threats, and vulnerabilities associated with the goods and services throughout the supply chain.

Risk Factors by Country

While any type of risk could occur when contracting with the countries listed, Table 4.1 identifies the most common potential risks with each country. When contracting internationally, other universal risks that should be considered include schedule risk from customs delays, the legal risk from missing or failing to comply with statutory and regulatory requirements, breach of contract or infringement of intellectual property, differences between the governing law and jurisdictions and other parties' laws, as well as misunderstanding or lack of knowledge regarding the suppliers' laws. Additional generic risks include political risk from political unrest and violence, and contractual risk from a company going out of business or failing to deliver the contracted goods or services. Financial risks also exist from foreign exchange rates, non-payment, or late payments, and currency transfer and conversion risk. ESG risks, such as the impacts of doing business with a company that causes pollution or engages in questionable labor practices, such as human rights violations and corruption, can occur in any company in any country. Lastly, other factors to consider are the size and diversification of the economy, the risk of natural disasters, and any set-aside programs that can create barriers to conducting business across country borders. More specific examples of the country-specific risks are elaborated below.

When considering contracting with suppliers from the United States, considerations should include supply chain risk. It is not uncommon for one region of the United States to experience a weather event that disrupts the supply of a particular commodity. Additionally, weather events can create an expected demand for a commodity that disrupts the expected supply. Other examples of supply chain risk could be a transformer blowing at a manufacturing plant that disrupts the availability of the raw material which then impacts the downstream production of goods. Another general risk is ESG, from human rights violations, corruption, greenhouse gas emissions, water scarcity, air and water pollution, and impacts on the environment. For example, inadvertently contracting with a supplier that is transporting and disposing of waste in an unethical manner could result in the entity being on the front page of the newspapers.

When considering contracting with suppliers from Canada, Export Development Canada (2024) states in its White Paper on dealing with country risk that political risk is the most common consideration—specifically, changes in local laws and regulations making it harder to move your money out of the country. Restrictions on imports can make it difficult for Canadian procurement professionals to conduct business with other countries such as the United States. Provincial laws and taxes may also make it more challenging to conduct business with Canadian suppliers. Other political considerations include high tariffs for certain products, import licensing requirements, anti-dumping and countervailing duty measures, quarantine measures for agricultural products, and technical requirements and mandatory standards that are overly restrictive, discriminatory, or more burdensome than necessary.

When considering contracting with suppliers from Mexico, the largest consideration should be given to ESG risks. Specifically, violence and threats from organized crime can range from extortion to corruption as well as other security threats, which can jeopardize not only the safety of employees and facilities but also supply chain networks. Political risks include unpredictable changes in government policies, regulatory requirements, and labor laws including labor guidelines and tax regulations (Villarreal 2023).

When considering contracting with suppliers from China, considerations should include supply chain risk from current or potential trade wars, paying for products never received, orders getting damaged during shipment, as well as long lead times. Political risks arise from the conflict between the country's central government and the provincial and local governments over applicable law. Environmental social and governance risks concerns include the forced labor of Uyghurs and other mostly Muslim minorities, pollution, and toxic emissions. Legal risks include infringement of intellectual property rights.

When considering contracting with suppliers from India, considerations should include contract and legal risk. According to BTG Advaya (2021), India lacks central procurement regulations to exclusively govern public procurement, and regulations, rules, and policies can vary from state to state. Instead, public procurement regulation consists of a "framework of overlapping administrative rules and guidelines, sector-specific manuals and state-specific legislation," which can make contract enforcement challenging. Additionally, India's trade regulations and tariffs can increase financial risk and add complexity to any potential arrangement. India's poor (but improving) infrastructure can increase supply chain risk.

When considering contracting with suppliers from Japan, considerations should include ESG risks, specifically business practices such as the importance of personal relationships in business dealings and the cultural hesitancy to break or modify business relationships. Developing strong interpersonal relationships is a requirement for a successful business contract and subsequent relationship. An example of a strong political relationship is Japan's alliance with the United States, which is the cornerstone of its foreign and security policy (Foreign & Commonwealth Office 2021). The United States maintains a significant military presence in Japan and is committed through the alliance to guaranteeing Japan's security (Foreign & Commonwealth Office 2021). This presence can minimize political risk. However, Japan's geographic location near China, North Korea, and Russia, combined with ongoing political tensions, are political risks that must be considered.

Overall, Sweden is a low-risk country to contract with. Bribery is illegal, and Sweden ranks extremely positively on Transparency International's Corruption Perceptions Index (Transparency International 2020). Progressing and increasing respect for human rights is a Swedish foreign policy priority, and the European Convention on Human Rights has been incorporated into Swedish law since the country joined the EU in 1995 (Foreign & Commonwealth Office 2021). Additionally, Swedish businesses are leaders in promoting corporate social responsibility, specifically climate change, equality, human rights, and anti-corruption (Foreign & Commonwealth Office 2021). However, there is a potential financial risk from weak exchange rates between the Swedish krona and major currencies like the US dollar and the euro. Careful watch of Sweden's monetary policies and economic conditions is recommended. Additionally, political risk may increase depending on the results of future political elections and acceptance into NATO.

Australia is largely a low-risk country to conduct business with. Australia is a member of the World Trade Organization's Agreement on Trade-Related Aspects of Intellectual Property Rights and a signatory to multilateral treaties administered by the World Intellectual Property Organization (Foreign & Commonwealth Office 2021). However, risk considerations should include ESG risks from the prevalence of international organized criminal activity that takes place in parts of Australia, linked to drugs, people smuggling, and people trafficking (Foreign & Commonwealth Office 2021). Political risk should also be considered as Australia's largest trading partner is China, followed by the United States, Japan, the Republic of Korea, and the United Kingdom (Foreign & Commonwealth Office 2021).

North American Free Trade Agreements

While having a basic understanding of public procurement's influence on the global economy is important, it is equally important to understand the relevant trade agreements, history, and their impacts on a public procurement professional's ability to procure. Free trade policies reduce barriers such as government tariffs, quotas, subsidies, or prohibitions on imports and exports, which allows goods to flow more easily between the participating nations. Ultimately, free trade allows goods and services to be bought and sold across international borders more easily. For public entities, free trade policies can result in better prices, higher competition, and additional access to innovative products and services as well as intellectual property protection for suppliers.

North American Free Trade Agreement (NAFTA)

The original free trade agreement between Canada, the United States, and Mexico was the North American Free Trade Agreement (NAFTA), which established a free-trade zone in North America. NAFTA was signed in 1992 by Canada, Mexico, and the United States and took effect on January 1, 1994. NAFTA remained in effect until June 30, 2020. NAFTA immediately lifted tariffs on most goods produced by the participating nations. The primary objectives of NAFTA were to eliminate trade barriers; facilitate the cross-border movement of goods and services; promote conditions of fair competition in the free trade area; increase investment opportunities; and provide adequate and effective protection and enforcement of intellectual property rights (Global Affairs Canada—Affaires mondiales Canada 2016).

United States, Mexico, Canada Agreement (USMCA)

On July 1, 2020, the United States, Mexico, Canada Agreement (USMCA) replaced NAFTA. According to the International Trade Administration (n.d.), the USMCA is a more balanced, equal trade agreement that supports high-paying jobs for Americans and the growth of the North American economy. Some of the highlights include additional and increased intellectual property protections including agricultural chemicals, improved trade access for agricultural products, and improved efficiency of products traveling between the nations allowing certain shipments to enter with minimal formal entry procedures. Additional provisions provided improved market access and protections for financial service providers as well as textile manufacturers.

United States versus Canada

The two most economically developed nations in North America are the United States and Canada. While Canada is the largest nation in North America, the United States is number one when it comes to economy and population. In 2022, the aggregated GDP for the two countries combined came to about 27.6 trillion US dollars, with Canada representing about 2.14 trillion US dollars compared to about 25.46 trillion US dollars for the United States (Statista n.d.). In 2022, all levels of government in Canada excluding consumption of fixed capital, spent $962.7 billion (Government of Canada, Statistics Canada 2023). Comparatively, the United States federal government alone spent 4.1 trillion US dollars.

While there appears to be a vast quantity difference in government spending, there are many similarities between the two nations. Both countries function under legislation establishing a uniform approach to procurement. Additionally, both nations have developed comprehensive and detailed regulations, policies, and procedures to govern federal procurement. Lastly, both countries' federal contracting is subject to very similar oversight and scrutiny by central audit and policy agencies such as the Government Accountability Office. Table 4.2 provides additional high-level similarities and differences between the two nations and their federal procurement structures.

Table 4.1 shows that the United States of America and Canada both approach federal procurement in a similar way. While the regulations, policies, and oversight departments may have different names, both nations are concerned about promoting fair and open competition while maximizing

Table 4.2 Comparison of United States versus Canada Federal Procurement Structures

	United States	*Canada*
Centralized Federal Procurement	■ 1949 Federal Property and Administrative Services Act—Property Act established the General Services Administration (GSA) and was designed to increase the efficiency and economy of Federal government operations for the procurement, utilization, and disposal of property (General Services Administration, "Real Property Disposition").	■ 1969—The Department of Supply and Services was established as the purchasing and accounting function of the Canadian federal government (Department of Supply and Services n.d.). ■ 1993—the Department of Public Works and Government Services Act formed Public Works and Government Services Canada (PWGSC) in 1996 from the consolidation of Supply and Services and the Department of Public Works. The PWGSC is responsible for supporting all other government departments with the services and materials they require for operating.
Federal Procurement Policy	■ 1974 Office of Federal Procurement Policy was established by Congress to provide overall direction for government-wide procurement policies, regulations, and procedures and to promote economy, efficiency, and effectiveness in acquisition processes (The White House n.d.).	■ 2021—Directive on the Management of Procurement. The objective of the directive is that procurement of goods, services, and construction obtains the necessary assets and services that support the delivery of programs and services to Canadians while ensuring the best value to the Crown (Secretariat, Treasury Board of Canada 2021).

(*Continued*)

Table 4.2 (Continued)

	United States	*Canada*
Conflict Resolution	■ 2014 Office of the Procurement Ombudsman (OPO) was created to foster healthy and productive relationships between GSA and its industry partners. OPO provides an informal forum for suppliers and industry associations who do business with GSA to voice their concerns about acquisition programs, policies, and practices (General Services Administration, "Office of the Procurement Ombudsman").	■ 2006 Federal Accountability Act, which included the appointment of a Procurement Ombudsman. The Procurement Ombudsman is a neutral party to assist Canadian businesses and the federal government with any contract complaints and reviews the practices of departments for acquiring goods and services to assess their fairness, openness, and transparency and make recommendations to improve those practices (Government of Canada, Office of the Procurement Ombudsman 2013).
Public Procurement Goals	■ FAR Part 6 promotes full and open competition in the acquisition process.	■ Public Services and Procurement Canada—conducting procurement activities in an open, fair, and transparent manner.
Guiding Principles	■ FAR 1.102—Statement of guiding principles for the Federal Acquisition System. To deliver on a timely basis the best value product or service to the customer, while maintaining the public's trust and fulfilling public policy objectives.	■ The goal of the competitive process is to get the best value for Canadian taxpayers while enhancing access, competition, and fairness.
Ethical Conduct of Employees	■ Executive Branch—5CFR Part 2635.101 ■ FAR Part 3—Improper Business Practices and Personal Conflicts of Interest ■ 2 CFR 200.318 General Procurement Standards.	■ Modified 2011—Values and Ethics Code for the Public Sector. The Code outlines the values and expected behaviors that guide public servants in all activities related to their professional duties (Secretariat, Treasury Board of Canada 2011). ■ Directive on Conflict of Interest.

(Continued)

Table 4.2 (Continued)

	United States	*Canada*
Supplier Code of Conduct	■ 2021—FAR 52.203–13 Contractor Code of Business Ethics and Conduct provides a contract clause for contracts that exceed $6 million, and the performance period is 120 days or more. ■ Amended 2024, FAR Part 3, Subpart 3.10—Contractor Code of Business Ethics and Conduct, FAC 2024-03 (Acquisition.gov. n.d.). Prescribes policies and procedures for the establishment of contractor codes of business ethics and conduct.	■ Adopted in 2021 and amended in 2023, the code outlines expectations and obligations for suppliers and their subcontractors who respond to bid solicitations or provide goods and services to Canada (Government of Canada, Public Services and Procurement Canada 2021).
Whistleblower Protection	■ 5 U.S.C. § 2302(b)(8), the Whistleblower Protection Act. protects Federal employees or applicants for Federal employment from retaliation for making protected disclosures. The WPA also provides penalties for supervisors who retaliate against Whistleblowers (Federal Trade Commission 2020).	■ 2005 S.C. 2005, c. 46, Public Servants Disclosure Protection Act. Establishes a procedure for the disclosure of wrongdoings in the public sector, including the protection of persons who disclose the wrongdoings (Legislative Services Branch 2022).

value for the taxpayers. Both nations have strong codes of ethics requirements for employees and suppliers. Similarly, both countries have Federal Ombudsmen, who act as neutral parties for contract complaints and provide conflict resolution. Lastly, both countries provide whistleblower protection for those disclosing wrongdoing. Additional information on Canadian procurement systems and government spending can be found from Government of Canada Public Services and Procurement, Office of the Procurement Ombudsman, Global Affairs Canada, Secretariat, Treasury Board of Canada, and government statistics. Additional information on United States can be found from General Services Administration, Legislative Services Branch, and The Office of Federal Procurement Policy.

References

Acquisition.gov. n.d. "Subpart 3.10—Contractor Code of Business Ethics and Conduct." https://www.acquisition.gov/far/subpart-3.10

BTG Advaya. 2021. "Public Procurement in India Risks and Challenges Inherent in Supplying to the Government." Legal500. https://www.legal500.com/developments/thought-leadership/public-procurement-in-india-risks-and-challenges-inherent-in-supplying-to-the-government/

Central Intelligence Agency. n.d. "Field Listing—Government Type." https://www.cia.gov/the-world-factbook/field/government-type/

Central Intelligence Agency. n.d. "Field Listing—Legal System." https://www.cia.gov/the-world-factbook/field/legal-system/

Cernat, Lucian. 2022. "Dr. Lucian Cernat on the Role of International Public Procurement in the Context of Global Trade Negotiations Between the EU and Third Countries." Utrecht University. https://www.uu.nl/en/news/dr-lucian-cernat-on-the-role-of-international-public-procurement-in-the-context-of-global-trade

Changing Minds. n.d. "Hall's Cultural Factors." https://changingminds.org/explanations/culture/hall_culture.htm

"China, People's Republic of—Government." In *Foreign Law Guide*, edited by Marci Hoffman. http://dx.doi.org/10.1163/2213-2996_flg_COM_323948

Department of Supply and Services. n.d. https://www.thecanadianencyclopedia.ca/en/article/department-of-supply-and-services.

Export Development Canada. 2024. "Country Risk Quarterly—Winter 2024." https://www.edc.ca/en/guide/country-risk-quarterly.html

Federal Trade Commission. 2020. "Whistleblower Protection." December 29, 2020. https://www.ftc.gov/office-inspector-general/whistleblower-protection

Foreign & Commonwealth Office. 2021. "Overseas Business Risk—Japan." March 15, 2021. https://www.gov.uk/government/publications/overseas-business-risk-japan/overseas-business-risk-japan

General Services Administration. n.d. "Office of the Procurement Ombudsman." https://www.gsa.gov/about-us/organization/office-of-governmentwide-policy/office-of-the-procurement-ombudsman

General Services Administration. n.d. "Real Property Disposition." https://disposal.gsa.gov/s/act49

Global Affairs Canada—Affaires mondiales Canada. 2016. "North American Free Trade Agreement—Objectives." https://www.international.gc.ca/trade-commerce/trade-agreements-accords-commerciaux/agr-acc/nafta-alena/fta-ale/01.aspx?lang=eng

Government of Canada, Office of the Procurement Ombudsman. 2013. "The Office—Office of the Procurement Ombudsman." March 12, 2013. https://opo-boa.gc.ca/bureau-office-eng.html

Government of Canada, Public Services and Procurement Canada. 2021. "Code of Conduct for Procurement—Publications and Procurement Documents—Buying and Selling." August 12, 2021. https://www.tpsgc-pwgsc.gc.ca/app-acq/cndt-cndct/cca-ccp-eng.html

Government of Canada, Statistics Canada. 2023. "The Daily—Government Spending by Function, 2022." November 28, 2023. https://www150.statcan.gc.ca/n1/daily-quotidien/231128/dq231128a-eng.htm

Hayman, Gavin, and Ian Makgill. 2020. "How Governments Spend: Opening up the Value of Global Public Procurement." Open Contracting Partnership, Spend Network. https://www.open-contracting.org/wp-content/uploads/2020/08/OCP2020-Global-Public-Procurement-Spend.pdf

International Trade Administration. n.d. "USMCA vs NAFTA." https://www.trade.gov/usmca-vsnafta

Judiciaries Worldwide. n.d. "Country Profiles." https://judiciariesworldwide.fjc.gov/country-profiles

LaMarco, Nicole. 2018. "American vs. Chinese Business Culture." Chron. December 11, 2018. https://smallbusiness.chron.com/american-vs-chinese-business-culture-59039.html

Legislative Services Branch. 2022. "Consolidated Federal Laws of Canada, Public Servants Disclosure Protection Act." Justice Laws Website. July 26, 2022. https://laws-lois.justice.gc.ca/eng/acts/P-31.9/page-1.html

Meyer, E. 2014. *The Culture Map: Breaking Through the Invisible Boundaries of Global Business*. New York: Public Affairs.

NIGP. "Dictionary of Procurement Terms." https://www.nigp.org/dictionary-of-terms

Office of Justice Programs. n.d. "Indian Legal System." NCJRS Virtual Library. https://www.ojp.gov/ncjrs/virtual-library/abstracts/indian-legal-system#:~:text=India's%20legal%20system%20is%20drawn,India%20and%20considerations%20of%20equity

Secretariat, Treasury Board of Canada. 2011. "Values and Ethics Code for the Public Sector." December 15, 2011. https://www.tbs-sct.canada.ca/pol/doc-eng.aspx?id=25049

Secretariat, Treasury Board of Canada. 2021. "Directive on the Management of Procurement." June 17, 2021. https://www.tbs-sct.canada.ca/pol/doc-eng.aspx?id=32692

Statista. n.d. "North America: Gross Domestic Product 2018–2028." https://www.statista.com/statistics/527955/north-america-gross-domestic-product-forecast/#:~:text=In%202022%2C%20GDP%20of%20Canada

The White House. n.d. "The Office of Federal Procurement Policy." https://www.white-house.gov/omb/management/office-federal-procurement-policy/#:~:text=OFPP%20was%20established%20by%20Congress

Transparency International. "2020 Corruptions Perceptions Index." 2020. https://www.transparency.org/en/cpi/2020/

Villarreal, Alberto. 2023. "Council Post: A Guide to Mitigating Business Risks in Mexico." *Forbes*. July 18. https://www.forbes.com/sites/forbesbusinesscouncil/2023/07/18/a-guide-to-mitigating-business-risks-in-mexico/?sh=396582e13dfd.

World Bank Group. 2020. "Global Public Procurement Database: Share, Compare, Improve!" https://www.worldbank.org/en/news/feature/2020/03/23/global-public-procurement-database-share-compare-improve

Chapter 5

Organizational Structure and Framework

This chapter will highlight the different types of public entities in the United States and Canada, the role of the Chief Procurement Officer, and will conclude with different procurement organization structures.

Public Entities

The NIGP Dictionary of Procurement Terms broadly defines a public entity "as an entity subject to or created by a governmental jurisdiction." The United States of America and Canada, however, each define public entities slightly differently. For example, in the United States, a public entity is defined as (A) any State or local government; (B) any department, agency, special purpose district, or other instrumentality of a State or States or local government; and (C) the National Railroad Passenger Corporation, and any commuter authority, as defined in section 24102(4) of title 49 (Legal Information Institute n.d.). In comparison, a public entity in Canada includes local, provincial, or federal government, government service or agency, Crown Corporation, or a government-funded establishment such as a school, including universities or hospitals (Statistics Canada 2019).

 DOI: 10.4324/9781003566564-7

United States

In the United States, "governmental power is divided vertically across the federal, state and local levels and horizontally across branches of government and different general- and special-purpose government entities" (Federal Reserve Bank of St. Louis 2024). According to the 2022 US Census, in the United States, there are approximately 439 federal and 90,449 local governments, including counties, cities, townships, special districts, such as water districts, fire districts, library districts, mosquito abatement districts, etc., and school districts (United States Census Bureau 2023).

The US Census Bureau classifies an entity as a government if it possesses each of the following characteristics:

- It is organized.
- It has a governmental character.
- It is substantially autonomous in the sense that it determines its budget and is not directly controlled by a parent government such that it can distinguish itself as separate from the administrative structure of any other governmental unit within that state.

Essentially, entities that have the power to levy property taxes, issue interest-paying debt exempt from federal taxation, and perform a function commonly viewed as governmental are considered governments (United States Census Bureau 2006). Each public entity and quasi-public entity such as public utilities may have different enabling legislation, regulations, and varying degrees of flexibility.

Canada

The Canadian government defines a public sector entity as:

> A department or agency of the Government of Canada, a Crown corporation established by or under an Act of Parliament or any other entity to which the Governor in Council may appoint a person but does not include the Senate or the House of Commons. (Government of Canada 2024)

There are three levels of government in Canada: Federal, Provincial, and Municipal, each with its own sets of roles and responsibilities (Parliament of Canada n.d.).

Federal

The national government, also known as the federal government, makes laws for the entire country. It is responsible for areas of national interest such as immigration, defense, and trade with other countries. The federal government system has three branches: the legislative, the executive, and the judicial. Each one has separate powers and responsibilities that are defined in the Constitution: the legislative branch passes laws, the executive implements them, and the judicial interprets them. There are approximately 205 federal Canadian public entities.

Provincial and Municipal

According to Muniscope, Canada's national resource on municipal issues, there are more than 3,500 provincial and municipalities in Canada that have various powers and responsibilities suited to their classification (Secretariat of the Table of Provincial and Territorial Ministers Responsible for Local Government n.d.). Provincial governments are responsible for activities such as education, health care, social welfare, and highways, as they pass laws that affect only the people of their province. While municipal governments are responsible for areas such as parks, community water systems, local police, roadways, and parking, they receive authority for these areas from the provincial governments.

Procurement Organizations

There is no typical procurement organization. However, regardless of country or location, there are commonalities and similarities. For example, each organization has specific enabling legislation and a corresponding framework of bylaws, regulations, and policies. Every public entity is subject to political initiatives, public mandates, election cycles, and the impacts of strict financial rules. Every procurement professional serves the public trust and is directly or indirectly accountable to policymakers and the public; therefore, every procurement action must pass the tests for fairness, equity, and transparency.

Placement Within the Entity

The place of procurement refers to the horizontal separation from other departments which ensures organizational checks and balances as well as strengthening public trust.

Procurement's ability to impact, enact policies, and accomplish goals is influenced by its placement within the entity as well as the forces present in its environment. The American Bar Association's *Model Procurement Code* recommends that the policymaking function be separated from the operational procurement function, although few states have adopted this practice and have instead chosen to confer this power to the Chief or Central Procurement Officer (CPO) (American Bar Association 2000).

Ideally, Procurement's placement within the entity should be operationally distinct from other departments and divisions within the entity. In an ideal public entity, the CPO would hold an actual chief, Chief-level (C-level) executive management position and work alongside other chief positions such as Chief Executive Officer (CEO), Chief Operating Officer (COO), and Chief Information Officer (CIO). However, smaller public entities may not have C-level positions, and the head of procurement may hold the position title of director, manager, administrator, or other similar title. Regardless of the title, size, or structure of the entity, the head of Procurement should be a strategic partner by maximizing working relationships with departments and divisions including facilities, human resources, information technology, budget, etc. "Procurement's ideal inclusion as part of the entity's leadership team ensures that procurement strategies are aligned with the entity's organizational goals and enables the procurement team to proactively identify and capitalize on opportunities that improve operational and financial outcomes" (Demel et al. 2015). Ultimately, the expertise of the CPO is critical to the success of the entity and is best leveraged when Procurement is involved in the entity's strategic planning.

Chief Procurement Officer Structure and Role

Depending on the entity, the CPO may be called the Chief or Central Procurement Officer. For example, as defined by the National Association of State Procurement Officials (n.d.), the CPO is the state official who leads the state central procurement office and is responsible for the control of all procurement efforts across the state as established by law or statute. Many states have Central Procurement Officers that report to other officials in the Governor's cabinet, Secretary or Commissioner of the Department of Administration, or Treasurer. A Chief Procurement Officer is responsible for developing procurement policies for adoption by an executive or governing body as well as issuing procurement policies, guidance, and procedures. The CPO has overall responsibility and oversight for all procurement functions such as the procurement process, including approving supplier selection and award.

Authority of the Chief Procurement Officer

Depending on the governing legislation, the authority of the Chief Procurement Officer may vary from entity to entity. However, most often the CPO serves as an independent procurement professional, has been granted complete procurement authority, and is allowed to delegate responsibilities to procurement professionals within a centralized procurement division or department. This approach maintains the benefits of the best procurement practices conducted in a professional manner and preserves the transparency and accountability necessary for effective organizational management, thereby sustaining the public's trust (Lucas et al. 2014).

Factors Influencing Placement

While the best practice is for the procurement function to be aligned strategically within the entity, unfortunately, that alignment is not always possible. The placement of the procurement function within the public entity may depend on a variety of factors such as size, structure, and enabling legislation of the entity. For example, smaller entities such as towns may not have the resources to have a separate procurement function. In entities such as these, procurement is often considered a transactional function, and the responsibilities are often completed by an individual along with many other duties. Additionally, the structure of the entity may not support a separate procurement function. For example, the entity has adopted a decentralized procurement approach where many individuals across departments share the transactional procurement responsibilities along with other duties. Lastly, the entity may not have adopted enabling legislation to allow for a separate procurement function. For example, perhaps the entity has not elected to have a separate procurement function in its municipal code, governing charter, or other statutes.

Procurement's Role Within the Entity

Procurement is considered a strategic function of an entity. In most entities, only the amount that is spent on salaries and benefits exceeds the spending that Procurement is responsible for. For this reason, Procurement's visibility of entity spend allows for a unique cross-functional perspective of the entity. This high-level perspective provides value by contributing practical knowledge to the entity's strategic planning process. The Procurement team adds additional value through nurturing relationships with entity departments as well as suppliers, developing sourcing strategies, identifying opportunities to bundle purchases to achieve savings or unbundle, and right-sizing projects to encourage small business participation. Each of these responsibilities allows procurement professionals to play a variety of roles such as advisor, facilitator, moderator, collaborator, and champion. Often, procurement professionals will find themselves in multiple roles at the same time. For example, a procurement professional may be an advisor, facilitator, participant, moderator, collaborator, and champion during evaluations or negotiations.

- As an **advisor**, Procurement provides guidance and recommendations. In this role, procurement professionals act as consultants, offering options and making recommendations.
- As a **facilitator**, procurement professionals help guide and manage procurement processes such as proposal evaluations and guide discussions with stakeholders and end users. In this role, procurement professionals act as a neutral party, promoting open communication, fostering collaboration, and ensuring that all parties are heard and their contributions are valued.
- As a **participant**, procurement professionals may lead entity-wide initiatives or solicitation processes for commodities such as auction services, job order contracting construction services, or printing services. At these times, a procurement professional may become a participant or customer of the processes that it is responsible for.
- As a **moderator**, procurement professionals may lead activities such as independent evaluation scoring discussions, negotiations, discussions with auditors, or program implementations. In this role, procurement professionals lead activities such as negotiations and program implementations. During these activities and discussions, they will ensure that the atmosphere is friendly, everyone feels welcome, questions are asked, and discussion develops.
- As a **collaborator**, procurement professionals may support or assist in the development or execution of the entity's business or procurement strategy, or strategic planning process. In this role, procurement professionals add value by contributing their practical knowledge.
- As a **champion**, procurement professionals use their influence to communicate and assist in the achievement of the strategic plan. In this role, procurement professionals are powerful catalysts who use their integrity, passion, and charisma to guide the entity in the achievement of its strategic goals.

Procurement Authority

Procurement authority is the power to award, or to approve the award of, legally binding procurement agreements such as contracts and purchase orders on behalf of the public entity (Lucas et al. 2014). Procurement authority also includes management and oversight of the sourcing and contracting processes, including leading contract negotiations, and carries through to elements of contract administration and closeout. For example, after the contract award, the procurement authority includes the power to modify or amend existing contracts and agreements.

Procurement Authority Models

There are two different approaches to procurement authority models: structured and unstructured or ad hoc delegation. The structured authority model may range from broad to narrow.

Structured

A broad authority model delegates procurement authority horizontally across the entity to all individuals in a particular position such as directors, managers, supervisors, etc. at one or more levels in the entity. This authority model often lends itself to a structured decentralized organizational structure, where many individuals are responsible for the procurement process. With this model, everyone independently exercises divided procurement authority. Unfortunately, this approach increases the entity's financial, legal, and reputational risk and is less likely to achieve the strategic procurement objectives as it lacks central procurement oversight.

A narrow authority model delegates procurement authority to one person with the authority to delegate further. With this model, the delegation selection is based on the expertise, role, or duties of a single person such as the Chief Procurement Officer or Chief Financial Officer. This authority approach often results in a centralized procurement organizational model as discussed later in the chapter and allows the entity to take a strategic approach to procurement.

Unstructured or Ad Hoc

An unstructured or ad hoc authority model provides a case-by-case delegation of authority to one or more individuals by name or position, based solely on immediate needs, judgment, or discretion of the holder of the authority (Lucas et al. 2014). An ad hoc authority model is most often found in delegated authority to make purchases in response to an emergency, where a department director is empowered to engage a contractor to mitigate threats to human life or property. Ad hoc authority may also be granted to a project manager for a specific purpose, such as approving change orders up to a certain dollar threshold.

Organization Structure—Centralization versus Decentralization

Depending on the entity's organizational structure, the entity may centralize or decentralize its procurement functions. The NIGP Dictionary of Procurement Terms defines decentralized purchasing as:

> An organizational structure in which designated personnel and operating departments from within the organization have the delegated authority to select the sources of supply and contract directly with suppliers without consulting or receiving approval from the chief procurement officer. It should be noted that the scope and degree, if any, of decentralized procurement varies from entity to entity. (NIGP, "Dictionary of Procurement Terms")

NIGP further defines centralized purchasing as:

> An organizational structure in which the rights, powers, duties, and authority relating to procurement are vested in the chief or central procurement officer (CPO). While the CPO may delegate some of these powers to others, the final authority resides with them. (NIGP, "Dictionary of Procurement Terms")

Decentralization

In a decentralized procurement, entity departments are responsible for procuring goods and services in compliance with the entity's rules and regulations. In this example, there are individuals in each department who are responsible for managing purchasing requests and issuing purchase orders. Depending on the entity, oversight may fall upon the individual departments, the Finance Department, or another oversight function. The advantages of a decentralized procurement organization include:

- Faster decision-making and quicker purchases from not channeling requests through a centralized process.

- End users understand their needs better than a centralized procurement team.
- Shorter procurement process time resulting in quicker commodity delivery.
- Better response for local specific needs—for example, for less standardized goods such as infrastructure (Dimitri, Dini, and Piga 2006).

The disadvantages and risks of a decentralized procurement organization include:

- Costs can be higher as the entity loses the strategic viewpoint and consolidation of commodity purchases.
- End users spend their time and resources purchasing instead of focusing on their core competencies.
- Decreased likelihood of achieving the entities' strategic procurement objectives.
- Purchases may be non-compliant with entity policies and processes.
- Duplication of effort in supplier and contract management.
- Decreased risk mitigation and higher risk exposure to financial, legal, and reputational risks.
- Higher risk management challenges (Dimitri, Dini, and Piga 2006).

Centralization

In a centralized procurement organization, Procurement manages the purchases of commodities for the entire entity. In this example, Procurement is responsible for every purchase that the entity makes. Additionally, the professional procurement department holds procurement authority and guides and monitors the procurement processes that take place throughout the public entity (Lucas et al. 2014). In 1989, NIGP adopted Resolution 1002 regarding centralized purchasing (Appendix B), in which it strongly recommended "the adoption of centralized purchasing as the standard government organization" as openness, centralization, and professionalism serve a government well.

The advantages of a centralized procurement organization include:

- Provides a dedicated team of procurement professionals.
- Improved compliance, standardized processes, and risk mitigation.
- Increased savings from economies of scale, savings from volume purchases, and decreased processing costs.
- Better collection of entity spend data and visibility, leading to increased strategic sourcing and cost savings and better buying terms.

- Increased efficiency from making a single, large-scale solicitation for a commodity than carrying out multiple decentralized requests for quotes.
- Greater relationship management and one point of contact for key suppliers.
- Centralized application of strategic initiatives such as eProcurement solutions, small business, and environmental and sustainability programs.

The disadvantages and risks of a centralized procurement organization include:

- Strict interpretation of rules inadvertently creates inefficiencies or buying outside of contracts if Procurement is seen as a roadblock.
- Delays in the delivery of commodities to end-users or clients.

Influences on Centralization versus Decentralization

Many variables affect the structure of the entity's procurement function. The size of the entity is one factor. Smaller entities may not have the staff resources to have a centralized Chief Procurement Officer or centralized procurement professionals, while larger organizations such as states and federal governments are more likely to have a centralized procurement function. Other factors, such as the political environment and the perceived necessity or value of a centralized procurement function, may also affect the centralization decision. For example, an entity may remain decentralized until an audit finding occurs, demonstrating the need for additional compliance and oversight. Another example would be an internal department, such as the legal department, which may complain about its workload and request entity leadership to consider a centralized procurement professional. Additionally, laws, rules, and regulations may necessitate the degree to which the entity is centralized.

Centralization as a Spectrum

Centralization is typically a spectrum with centralization on one far side and decentralization on the opposite far side. Along the spectrum, many entities are not strictly one or the other, but rather a hybrid where internal departments can purchase goods and services up to a certain dollar threshold with minimal or no procurement assistance. After this, the purchase requests route through a central procurement office. Many hybrid entities consider themselves centralized as procurement is responsible for purchasing commodities above certain dollar thresholds. In this model, procurement is responsible for developing, writing, and administering procurement policies, processes, infrastructure, best practices, and sharing knowledge across the entity; therefore, procurement oversight is, in essence, centralized.

Either approach involves trade-offs, most often of efficiency versus price. For example, it may be faster for an end user to request a quote and direct contract with a supplier. However, the trade-off for that efficiency comes at a potential cost to the public entity because the end user may not have received the best price or considered potential risk factors. Centralization offers a way of aggregating entity demand and garnering the benefits of scale effects by reducing the per-unit fixed cost, thus enabling governments to purchase the same products at lower prices (Karjalainen 2011). Research suggests that a centralized approach is effective if the entity is receiving compliant solicitation responses. However, centralized procurement can become ineffective and more costly when it does not receive compliant offers. The research results suggest that the use of mandatory framework agreements absent of market bids is not economically advantageous for the public sector (Petersen, Jensen, and Bhatti 2022). Instead, public entities should consider adjusting their policies and procedures to allow for market situations, thereby allowing flexibility for end users to purchase commodities based on local knowledge and demand (Albano and Sparro 2010).

Regardless of which approach the entity takes, it is important to balance the pros and cons of both options to ensure that safeguards are in place with a flexible and efficient customer service focus on meeting the end users' needs. For example, the United States federal micro-purchase threshold as defined by FAR 2.101 is $10,000 for supplies and services, which allows end users to purchase goods and services up to $10,000 without competition (Acquisition.gov. n.d.). The micro-threshold allows US federal agencies the freedom to purchase goods and services without additional steps or requirements. With this centralized hybrid approach, the entity achieves the value from centralized procurement oversight and monitoring while also allowing for efficiency from end users to purchase smaller or less expensive items.

References

Acquisition.gov. n.d. "FAR 2.101. Definitions." https://www.acquisition.gov/far/2.101

Albano, Gian Luigi, and Marco Sparro. 2010. "Flexible Strategies for Centralized Public Procurement." *Review of Economics and Institutions* 1 (2). doi:10.5202/rei.v1i2.4.

American Bar Association. 2000. "The 2000 Model Procurement Code for State and Local Governments." Public Procurement International. https://publicprocurementinternational.com/wp-content/uploads/2019/04/2000-ABA-Model-Procurement-Code.pdf

Demel, Steven M., Theodore G. Lucas, Sandra E. Clifford, H. Arthur Roberson, and Jon M. Walton. 2015. "The Strategic Value of Procurement in Public Entities, A position paper from NIGP." NIGP.

Dimitri, Nicola, Federico Dini, and Gustavo Piga. 2006. "When Should Procurement Be Centralized?" In *Handbook of Procurement*, edited by Nicola Dimitri, Gustavo Piga, and Giancarlo Spagnolo, 47–81. Cambridge: Cambridge University Press.

Federal Reserve Bank of St. Louis. 2024. "Local Governments in the U.S.: A Breakdown by Number and Type." March 14, 2024. https://www.stlouisfed.org/publications/regional-economist/2024/march/local-governments-us-number-type#:~:text=In%20the%20most%20recent%20Census

Government of Canada. 2024. "Consolidated Federal Laws of Canada, Conflict of Interest Act, Conflict of Interest Act." Justice Laws Website. https://laws-lois.justice.gc.ca/eng/acts/C-36.65/section-2.html#:~:text=public%20sector%20entity%20means%20a,public%20servant

Karjalainen, Katri. 2011. "Estimating the Cost Effects of Purchasing Centralization: Empirical Evidence from Framework Agreements in the Public Sector." *Journal of Purchasing and Supply Management* 17 (2): 87–97.

Legal Information Institute. n.d. "42 U.S. Code § 12131—Definitions." Cornell Law School. https://www.law.cornell.edu/uscode/text/42/12131#1

Lucas, Theodore, Melissa Wilson, Scott N. Guzzy, Dan Stoltman, Joan Daniels, Jon M. Walton, Patricia. M. Innocenti, John O. Adler, Sandra E. Clifford, and Steven M. Demel. 2014. "Procurement Authority in Public Entities. NIGP. https://www.nigp.org/resource/position-papers/Procurement%20Authority%20in%20Public%20Entities%20Position%20Paper.pdf?dl=true

National Association of State Procurement Officials. n.d. "What Is Procurement?" https://cdn.naspo.org/RI/ProcurementToolboxIssue1_IntroductiontoProcurement.pdf

NIGP. "Dictionary of Procurement Terms." https://www.nigp.org/dictionary-of-terms

Parliament of Canada. n.d. "The Branches of Government." https://learn.parl.ca/understanding-comprendre/en/canada-system-of-government/the-branches-of-government/

Petersen, Ole H., Mads D. Jensen, and Yosef Bhatti. 2022. "The Effect of Procurement Centralization on Government Purchasing Prices: Evidence from a Field Experiment." *International Public Management Journal* 25 (1): 24–42. doi:10.1080/10967494.2020.1787278.

Secretariat of the Table of Provincial and Territorial Ministers Responsible for Local Government. n.d. "Provincial and Municipal Statistics." Muniscope. https://www.muniscope.ca/research/municipal_facts/Provincial_Municipal_Statistics

Statistics Canada. 2019. "Classification of Industry Sectors, Private or Public—1—Public Sector." September 24, 2019. https://www23.statcan.gc.ca/imdb/p3VD.pl?Function=getVD&TVD=1255295&CVD=1255295&CLV=0&MLV=1&D=1

United States Census Bureau. 2006. "Classification Manual." https://www2.census.gov/govs/pubs/classification/2006_classification_manual.pdf

United States Census Bureau. 2023. "About the Government Units Survey." https://www.census.gov/programs-surveys/gus/about.html#:~:text=The%20summaries%20are%20divided%20according

Chapter 6

Public Procurement Laws and Regulations

This chapter covers the legal framework and laws essential for the procurement professional in establishing legally binding contractual agreements. It discusses the sources of public procurement law and examines various legal considerations that impact public procurement, including the government's authority to contract formation and contract performance.

Legal Framework

Even though governmental representatives have been procuring goods and services for thousands of years, as evidenced by a clay tablet found in Syria which was estimated to have been created between 2400 and 2800 BCE, containing an order for oil and grain, it was, however, only in the nineteenth century that procurement began to be studied extensively and legal provisions enacted to govern the spending of taxpayer dollars. As early as 1823, court cases in the US codified the government's authority to contract with suppliers. In 1910, Oklahoma was the first state to create a board dedicated to centrally procuring goods and services for all state entities. In 1919, a book entitled *Principles of Government Purchasing* was published due to studies

DOI: 10.4324/9781003566564-8

conducted by the Rockefeller Foundation regarding government administration and public procurement problems.

Public procurement has existed in one form or another since early civilizations developed. However, it has only been in the last 200 years or so that there has been any conscious, substantive, concerted effort to regulate public procurement and harness its potential powers for the benefit of governments and taxpayers.

Sources of Public Procurement Law

Entities that receive federal funding must expend those funds in a manner consistent with the principles specified by the donor or granting entity. Principles generally included are:

- Adherence to acceptable review procedures
- Assurance of proper competition
- Use of appropriate procurement methods.

Sometimes, the entity's procurement rules may not align with those specified by the federal agency that supplies funds for the project. When this is the case, procurement professionals must adhere to the stricter requirements regardless of whether the more stringent requirements are from the federal agency or their entity.

Besides following federal laws and procedures when spending federal funds, procurement professionals must follow their state and local laws, which are usually the basis for the entity's procurement policies and procedures. The principles upon which these laws are based should include:

- Accountability
- Competition
- Consistency
- Effectiveness
- Fair-dealing
- Integrity
- Transparency
- Value.

Such policies and procedures are known as administrative law. Administrative law is defined in the NIGP Dictionary of Procurement Terms as "Rules, regulations, and executive orders promulgated by governmental administrative or regulatory entities. Generally enacted to make statutes and ordinances more specific. Has the force and effect of law" (NIGP, "Dictionary of Procurement Terms"). In other words, administrative law describes how an entity can operate.

Another type of law that is important for procurement professionals to know and be acquainted with is common law. Common law is not outlined in regulations, statutes, or ordinances. It is established by practices that have evolved over the years through the decisions of judges in courts, which have come to have the same legal effect as statutory law, namely, written law embodied in code. These uncodified judicial decisions are generally published, and courts must adhere to them just as they are charged to adhere to the principles contained in a statute. They are legally binding precedents.

Another type of law is civil law, which takes the form of legal codes and deals with behavior that injures an individual or a private party, such as breach of contract, defamation, negligence resulting in injury, and property damage. Civil law is non-criminal and normally not germane to procurement professionals, except in cases where a contract is breached.

History of Government Procurement Legislation

A far-reaching Supreme Court case that has had ripple effects throughout the US is the *City of Richmond v. J.A. Croson Co.* The verdict handed down in this case in 1989 was that the minority set-aside program that the City of Richmond, VA, had in place was unconstitutional under the Fourteenth Amendment's Equal Protection Clause. The set-aside program required companies awarded city construction contracts to subcontract 30% of the contract's value to minority businesses. In a 6-to-3 decision, the Supreme Court of the United States stated:

> We, therefore, hold that the city has failed to demonstrate a *compelling* interest in apportioning public contracting opportunities based on race. To accept Richmond's claim that past societal discrimination alone can serve as the basis for rigid racial preferences would be to open the door to competing claims for "remedial relief" for *every* disadvantaged group. The dream of a Nation of equal citizens in a society where race is irrelevant to personal opportunity and achievement would be lost in a mosaic of shifting preferences based on *inherently unmeasurable* claims of past wrongs. [. . .] Courts would be asked to evaluate the extent of

> the prejudice and consequent harm suffered by various minority groups. Those whose societal injury *is thought* to exceed some *arbitrary* level of tolerability then would be entitled to preferential classification. We believe such a result would contradict both the letter and the spirit of a constitutional provision whose central command is equality. (Wikipedia, "The City of Richmond")

Based on this outcome, many entities had to reevaluate their set-aside programs to ensure they were based on a proven, documented basis of discrimination in order to comply with the court's decision.

Procurement is also rich in anti-competitive practices laws. These are primarily federal statutes aimed at protecting competition. It is important for procurement professionals to be aware of them so that they can report any suspected violation to legal counsel.

The first antitrust act in the US was passed by Congress in 1890—the Sherman Antitrust Act. This act makes it unlawful for businesses to restrict or conspire to restrict or monopolize foreign or interstate trade. It also makes bid rigging, boycotts, price fixing, some types of tying arrangements, and territorial market allocation illegal.

In 1914, the US Congress passed the *Clayton Antitrust Act* to add further substance to the United States' efforts to prevent anti-competitive practices. This act prohibits certain mergers and acquisitions, interlocking directorates between competing companies, price discrimination, tying arrangements, and specific exclusive deals and refusals to deal where the aim is to monopolize or substantially lessen competition in interstate commerce.

The *Federal Trade Commission* Act was also enacted in 1914. It created the Federal Trade Commission to protect competition and consumers by empowering it to investigate and prevent unfair competition and deceptive or unfair acts and practices that affect commerce. The Commission can seek monetary compensation and other relief for conduct it finds injurious to consumers.

The *Robinson Patman Price Discrimination Act* of 1936 amended the *Clayton Antitrust Act.* Its purpose is to protect small businesses from being shut out of the marketplace by preventing price discrimination in interstate trade.

Legislative and administrative laws significantly impact public procurement. Public procurement, by design, is solely restricted to activities that are specified and authorized by law. This is in stark contrast to our counterparts in the private sector, who are allowed to do anything except what is prohibited by the law. Procurement professionals, therefore, are highly encouraged to influence positive changes that reflect the profession's best practices through enabling legislation and administrative laws. As pointed out in an earlier edition of a NIGP text on this topic, this can be done by continually seeking legislation that empowers procurement professionals by:

- Addressing environmental and social concerns
- Allowing for "total cost" evaluations and "best value" procurements
- Allowing for contract incentives and performance-based contracting
- Allowing for creative financing vehicles
- Providing clear ethical guidelines for anyone involved in the procurement process. (Pitzer and Thai 2009)

Since we must work within the strict confines of the law, it is our duty as procurement professionals to resist any changes to legislation that do not align with our core ethical values or our purpose of maximizing fair and open competition while promoting and supporting laws that do align.

American Bar Association *Model Procurement Code* for State and Local Governments

After five years of intense development, the *Model Procurement Code* for State and Local Governments (*MPC*) was issued in 1979 by the American Bar Association, the largest national organization of lawyers in the US. It was updated in 2000 to include such topics as electronic commerce and cooperative purchasing. The *MPC*'s purpose is to aid state and local jurisdictions that do not have suitable processes in place for public procurement. It is a model, rather than a uniform, code that can be adapted and tailored, if needed, by states and localities to meet their needs for the spending of public funds in a prescribed method that protects the taxpayers and ensures transparency, consistency, and fairness for suppliers. This was the first time that the fundamental principles of a sound public procurement system had been documented in one place. These basic principles are covered in 12 sections of the *MPC*. They are:

- Article 1—General Provisions
- Article 2—Procurement Organization
- Article 3—Source Selection and Contract Formation
- Article 4—Specifications
- Article 5—Procurement of Infrastructure Facilities and Services
- Article 6—Modification and Termination of Contracts for Supplies and Services
- Article 7—Cost Principles
- Article 8—Supply Management

- Article 9—Legal and Contractual Remedies
- Article 10—Intergovernmental Relations
- Article 11—Assistance to Small and Disadvantaged Businesses; Federal Assistance or Contract Procurement Requirements
- Article 12—Ethics in Public Contracting

This document has served as a rich resource not only for procurement professionals but also for jurisdictions seeking a model for statutory principles and policy guides for managing and controlling public procurement. It has been adopted in full by 16 states, in part by several others, and by thousands of jurisdictions within the United States (2000 ABA Model Procurement Code).

The *Uniform Commercial Code*

Another essential document for procurement professionals is the *Uniform Commercial Code* (*UCC*). It has been called one of the most critical developments in American law. It applies only to the interstate sale of goods; the *UCC* does not apply to the sale of services or real estate. One requirement of the UCC is that contracts for the sale of goods valued at $500 or more must be in writing and signed by an authorized representative of the entity or supplier the contract is being enforced against. The NIGP Dictionary of Procurement Terms describes the *UCC* as follows:

> Published in 1952 and revised and amended in 2003, the UCC was formulated by the National Conference of Commissioners on Uniform State Laws (NCCUSL) and the American Law Institute. The Code covers various commercial activities but does not apply to United States federal government contracts. The UCC determines rights and obligations based on fairness and reasonableness in the light of accepted business practices. All fifty states have adopted the UCC. Article 2, entitled "Sale of Goods," is the most essential part of the UCC for procurement professionals. Absent a specific state or federal statute or administrative regulation, Article 2 will govern a contract for the sale of goods. (NIGP, "Dictionary of Procurement Terms")

Below is a list of sections of the *UCC* which states have most widely adopted according to the Cornell Law School:

- U.C.C. - ARTICLE 1- GENERAL PROVISIONS (2001)
- U.C.C. - ARTICLE 2- SALES (2002)

- U.C.C. - ARTICLE 2A - LEASES (2002)
- U.C.C. - ARTICLE 3- NEGOTIABLE INSTRUMENTS (2002)
- U.C.C. - ARTICLE 4- BANK DEPOSITS AND COLLECTIONS (2002)
- U.C.C. - ARTICLE 4A - FUNDS TRANSFER (2012)
- U.C.C. - ARTICLE 5- LETTERS OF CREDIT (1995)
- REPEALER OF U.C.C. - ARTICLE 6- BULK TRANSFERS and [REVISED] U.C.C. - ARTICLE 6- BULK SALES (1989)
- U.C.C. - ARTICLE 7- DOCUMENTS OF TITLE (2003)
- U.C.C. - ARTICLE 8- INVESTMENT SECURITIES (1994)
- U.C.C. - ARTICLE 9- SECURED TRANSACTIONS (2010). (Cornell Law School n.d.)

While the *UCC* is not a federal law in the US, it is a uniformly adopted state law whose purpose is to coordinate and unify the law of sales and other commercial transactions throughout the United States, making business transactions consistent and efficient. Each state, however, may make its modifications; for example, Louisiana has not adopted Article 2, or they may reorganize various sections. One of the most critical aspects for the procurement professional is that the *UCC* can be used to fill any gaps that may exist in a contract for the interstate sale of goods. For example, if a contract does not address the issue of a warranty for goods sold, the UCC could be used to step in and fill that omission.

On the topic of warranties, there are two types that every procurement professional should be aware of. The first is an express warranty, which is defined as "A written description of the responsibilities of a seller if a product is found to be defective or otherwise unsatisfactory" (NIGP, "Dictionary of Procurement Terms").

An express warranty is a statement made in writing or verbally to a buyer by a seller regarding the quality of a good or service. Descriptive literature supplied by a bidder identifying specific qualities or performance levels a good may possess may be considered an express warranty.

An implied warranty, on the other hand, arises by law without the seller's need for expression. The UCC creates various implied warranties. The two most important ones for procurement professionals are the Implied Warranties of Merchantability and Fitness for a Particular Purpose.

Implied Warranty of Merchantability is defined as, "A promise, arising by operation of law, that something that is sold will be merchantable and fit for the purpose for which it is sold. Implied warranties come in two general types: merchantability and fitness" (NIGP, "Dictionary of Procurement Terms"). Under the *UCC*, if the seller of the goods is considered a merchant of those goods, an implied warranty that the goods meet industry standards is implied, meaning that the goods will "pass in the trade under the contract description" and that they are "fit for the ordinary purposes" for which those goods are to be used. So, if a procurement professional buys a step ladder from a hardware store, there is an implied warranty that the ladder will hold an average-sized person without breaking or folding when they climb it.

An Implied Warranty of Fitness for a Particular Purpose is defined as, "A warranty that applies to an instance in which the seller, at the time of contract, has reason to believe that the buyer wants the goods for a particular purpose, and the buyer is relying on the seller's skill or judgment to select or furnish suitable goods" (NIGP, "Dictionary of Procurement Terms"). This warranty exists under the UCC if the seller knows facts about the buyer's needs and understands they want to use the goods for a particular purpose, then suggests or recommends a specific good the buyer purchases based on the seller's recommendation. An example would be if a procurement professional tells the hardware clerk they need to buy oil for a specific make and model of chainsaw and then buys the recommended type and brand suggested by the clerk. If that oil is not the right type and causes the chainsaw to seize up or be damaged, the seller is liable for any damages caused by the oil.

Government's Authority to Contract

A constitution or charter usually grants the government the inherent power to contract, not government officials. Executive branch officials must authorize procurement professionals to enter into contracts. The most effective procurement ordinances and statutes establish a general framework for a procurement professional's contracting authority and grant the authority to develop policies, procedures, and regulations necessary to implement that authority.

Typically, statutes and ordinances do not specifically authorize procurement professionals to enter into contracts for their entities. The law typically grants contracting authority to an entity head or chief procurement officer. That person then delegates contracting authority for the entity to the procurement professional. This delegation may be oral, but ideally, it should be written and specifically detailed, detailing what decisions the procurement professional can make, the documents they can sign, and the dollar limits associated with the delegation.

This type of authority is known as express authority. Express authority is defined as, "Authority that is expressly given in direct language rather than inferred from conduct" (NIGP, "Dictionary of Procurement Terms"). It can be specific, for example, saying the procurement professional can enter into contracts for up to $100,000. Express authority may also be general, for instance, saying the procurement professional has the authority to enter into any contract for any goods or services the entity needs.

Implied authority is a rational extension of express authority. For example, the chief procurement officer who has express authority has implied authority to delegate that authority to another person or persons within the entity. Another example is the procurement professional who has the express authority of $100,000 to enter into contracts, signing a purchase order for a service costing the entity $25,000. Even though the written express authority specifically states the procurement professional can sign purchase orders, doing so is a logical extension of their duties.

Apparent authority is, "The reasonable impression that an agent is permitted to act on their principal's authority even though that authority has not been granted" (NIGP, "Dictionary of Procurement Terms"). This most often comes into play to protect a supplier. For example, an entity employee who has no delegated procurement authority goes to an office supply store to buy a case of copier paper, shows her entity ID badge to the clerk there, and tells him to charge the paper to the entity's account. The clerk has no way of knowing who has and has not been granted delegated procurement authority by the entity. The ID badge can lead one to assume that a person is authorized to purchase logically. For this reason, even though the entity may not be legally liable for unauthorized acts, an entity employee with actual authority may ratify the purchase in fairness to the supplier under the concept of apparent authority. It would then be up to the entity to deal with the employee who made the unauthorized purchase.

Elements of a Legally Binding Contract

There are six essential elements that all contracts in the US and Canada must contain to be legally binding and enforceable. It is the responsibility of a procurement professional to ensure that every contract issued by their entity includes all six. They are:

- **Offer and Acceptance**
  The formation of a contract requires an agreement between two parties, consenting to the same terms. The process by which persons reach

an agreement is the offer and acceptance process. An offer generally involves a promise or commitment to do or not to do a specified thing in the future. That promise demonstrates a person's intent to assure that the thing promised will or will not be done. In public procurement, a solicitation, such as an Invitation for Bids (IFB) or Request for Proposals (RFP), is not an offer. Instead, it is a request to suppliers to submit offers. The bids or proposals submitted in response are offers. Acceptance occurs when the entity agent who is authorized to award contracts signifies that the jurisdiction has selected the supplier as the winner.

- **Definiteness**
  Essential terms include subject matter, price, payment terms, quantity, quality, duration, and the work to be done. Suppose the parties purport to agree on a material term but do so in a vague manner, as contrasted with omitting the term altogether. In that case, there is no agreement because it is too indefinite. Because of the formal competitive process that most governments follow in purchasing items above a certain dollar limit, the indefiniteness of the offer is not a problem. Remember that the bid or proposal that a supplier submits is the offer. Under the law of public contracts, that bid or proposal must be responsive—it must show the supplier's commitment to comply with the solicitation's requirements, which includes supplying a set price. If a supplier submits an offer that says the price will be in effect at the time it supplies janitorial services, the offer is not only non-responsive, it is also indefinite.
- **Consideration**
  The person making the promise does or promises to do something they are not legally obligated to do. An excellent example of a consideration issue in the government contracts setting arises under what are called term or indefinite quantity contracts. Under this type of contract, a supplier agrees to supply particular goods or services at a set price for a specific period of time. Still, the quantity of the goods or services that the entity will need is unknown, only estimated. If a dispute arises because a supplier claims that the entity has ordered too great a quantity of the items under the contract, the estimated quantities in the contract and the size of past orders will define whether the disputed order is reasonable. If the contract does not require the entity to buy all those specific goods or services that it needs from that supplier but reserves the discretion to buy them elsewhere, the entity has not given any consideration; it has not obligated itself legally to the terms of the contract. That consideration problem is solved by mandating that the entity purchase all the specific goods or services it needs under the contract.

- **Mutuality of Obligation**
  Regarding consideration, both parties have promised to do something they are not legally obligated to do; otherwise, it is generally not a contractually enforceable promise.
  This element is a sub-element of consideration. It applies when the offer requires the person accepting it to make a promise in return rather than immediately performing. A simple statement of this element is "both parties must be bound, or neither one is bound." This means that both parties must give consideration to each other. For example, suppose a contracting party reserves a means by which it may altogether avoid performing. In that case, the contract may not be enforceable because both parties are not legally obligated to perform.
- **Competent Parties**
  It may refer to mental capacity or even age; it also refers to authority in public contracting contexts. A contract with an incompetent person is only voidable at the option of the incompetent person if the other party knew about the mental incompetence or ought to have known under the circumstances.
- **Legality of Purpose**
  Courts generally will not enforce an agreement, or part of an agreement, that violates statutory law or public policy. For instance, suppose a supplier does not have the appropriate license to enter into a contract to provide certain services to an entity but does so anyway. Another example is where a supplier submits a proposal to perform a study for an entity and receives a contract to do the work. It includes in its proposal a requirement for the government to make payments to it in advance of the work, but the law of that jurisdiction prohibits advance payments. In the first case, the entity must terminate the contract on discovering that the supplier does not have the proper license. If only part of a contract violates the law, as is the case in the second instance, the entity may ignore that portion of the contract because the law will not enforce it. A contract includes both traditional bilateral agreements, where signatures appear on the fully executed document, as well as purchase orders that are accepted through performance or in writing. As the NIGP Dictionary of Procurement Terms defines it, "[t]o be valid and enforceable, a contract must be consistent with the federal, state (province in Canada), or local law and cannot violate legal statutes of public policy" (NIGP, "Dictionary of Procurement Terms"). The legality of purpose is a general limitation on the "freedom of contracting."

Contract Performance

NIGP very simply defines breach of contract as, "Failure to live up to the terms of a contract without legal excuse" (NIGP, "Dictionary of Procurement Terms"). When either party materially breaches a contract, the non-breaching party has a legal basis to pursue a remedy, such as monetary damages and contract cancellation. A material breach is likely to occur early during the contract performance, is willful, and is significant. If the breach occurs after substantial contract performance has occurred, it is considered minor, and only limited remedies are available to the non-breaching party. Cancellation of the contract, however, is not an option.

Whenever a contract is breached, the breaching party is liable to the other party for the damages they caused by the breach and for any losses caused or any gains prevented. However, the non-breaching party may not unreasonably sit back to let damages accrue. It is their duty to take any actions that are reasonably necessary to prevent or reduce any damages caused by the breach. The common law remedy for breach is compensatory damages that equal the monetary value of any losses sustained and any reasonable potential gains lost. If the contract contains a liquidated damages clause that specifies a specific dollar amount to be imposed, this clause may be triggered by the breach. As a word of caution, the dollar amount specified in a liquidated damages clause must be a reasonable, defendable representation, often in the form of a dollar amount for each day of the breach, of the monetary value of the loss sustained by the non-breaching party. If this amount is determined to be excessive, courts will view it as a penalty and, therefore, not enforce it.

The *UCC* also specifies remedies for breach of contract:

- If the procurement professional unlawfully rejects the contracted goods, the seller may recover the difference in the value of the contract price and the market value or the price the seller obtained in reselling the goods.
- If the seller does not deliver the goods or if the delivered goods are defective, the procurement professional may recover from the seller the dollar value of the difference between the market price and the contract price for the goods or the difference in price between any substituted good and the unpaid contract price.
- If the seller breaches the warranty, the procurement professional may recover the difference in the value of the goods would have had if they had been as warranted in the contract and their actual value.

An important note for procurement professionals is that the entity must pay the contracted price of the goods to the seller once the entity has accepted the goods or if the goods are damaged or destroyed after the risk of loss has passed from the seller to the buyer.

Similar to the *UCC*'s Article 9 in the US is the *Personal Property Security Act* (*PPSA*) in Canada.

> The scope of the Act is extremely broad, as it is concerned with every transaction that, in substance, creates a security interest without regard to its form and without regard to the person who has title to the collateral. There are slight differences between the provinces regarding how far this extends, but the concept is basically the same. That said, however, there are some items that are specifically excluded:
>
> - liens
> - interests in annuities and insurance policies
> - interests in land (other than interests arising under a license), including leases
> - assignments for the general benefit of creditors
> - interests in any compensation for labor or personal services
>
> Personal property is classified into the following categories:
>
> - goods (further classified into consumer goods, equipment, and inventory)
> - instruments
> - documents of title
> - chattel paper (including leases and conditional sales contracts)
> - securities
> - money
> - intangibles (licenses and any other matter not included above). (Wikipedia, "Personal Property Security Act")

The PPSA is a real-time online registry for personal property that is or may be used as security. Its purpose is to offer better protection for creditors when their debtors become insolvent.

References

2000 ABA Model Procurement Code. https://publicprocurementinternational.com/wp-content/uploads/2019/04/2000-ABA-Model-Procurement-Code.pdf

Cornell Law School. n.d. "Uniform Commercial Code." https://www.law.cornell.edu/ucc

NIGP. "Dictionary of Procurement Terms." https://www.nigp.org/dictionary-of-terms

Pitzer, Jack, and Khi V. Thai. 2009. *Introduction to Public Procurement*. 3rd ed. Herndon, VA: National Institute of Governmental Purchasing.

Wikipedia. "Personal Property Security Act (Canada)." https://en.wikipedia.org/wiki/Personal_Property_Security_Act_(Canada)

Wikipedia. "The City of Richmond v. J.A. Croson Co." https://en.wikipedia.org/wiki/City_of_Richmond_v._J.A._Croson_Co

Part III

The Solicitation Process

Chapter 7

Pre-Procurement Planning

The role of public procurement has gradually evolved from a reactive support function that primarily focused on cost savings to a more proactive, strategic role that maximizes the value of public funds. Today's public procurement professional is responsible for a variety of initiatives and plays an active role in contributing to the entity's overall strategic planning process. The strategic value of public procurement provides opportunities for effective future planning, obtaining the best value, reducing risks, and ensuring that the organization delivers strategic value to the public entity.

To manage an effective public procurement program, the procurement professional needs in-depth knowledge of budgeting, strategic planning, pricing strategies, and analysis and forecasting methods. This chapter will explore the various strategies and methods that can be utilized by the procurement professional to ensure that goods and services will be purchased in a manner that results in the overall best value and establishes a reliable source of supply for their entity.

DOI: 10.4324/9781003566564-10

Budgeting

Budgeting is simply defined as the allocation of scarce resources among competing demands. The basic purpose of public budgeting is the efficient attainment of entity goals. Budget systems provide a means to evaluate competing demands for resources and a system to measure objectives to be obtained in meeting the goals of the entity.

Budget planning involves estimating anticipated expenditures and budget resources during the budget period. As an integral member of the entity organization's strategic planning team, the procurement professional will need to possess knowledge of the budgeting process and the various types of budgets. During the planning phase, the procurement professional will play a vital role in the budgeting process by providing cost and sourcing information for a wide range of goods and services.

Most public entities will follow a common four-phase budget cycle, which is described below.

Planning

The planning phase involves the identification of needs, budget objectives, estimated expenditures, and projected resources. During the planning phase, the Chief Financial Officer will estimate the revenues and expenditures for the budget period. Procurement professionals may occasionally be asked by departments to provide estimated costs or historical pricing for the various goods and services needed by the entity. At the end of the planning phase, a proposed budget document will be submitted to the entity's governing body.

Formalization

The formalization stage involves the legal adoption of the budget by the governing body of the entity. This can be a challenging and lengthy phase since it may involve various public hearings with citizen input where details of the budget are discussed. Occasionally, the governing body will need to pass interim budgets while budgets are being deliberated.

Implementation

The implementation phase is the execution of the budget during the budget period and involves collecting revenues and expending funds that support government services. Implementation involves allotting and allocating when expenditures can be made. The goal of budget implementation is to ensure that budgeted funds are being used legally and efficiently as directed by the governing body.

Evaluation

The evaluation phase involves monitoring the budget performance through periodic reports that show how much of the budget has been spent to date. An important goal of budget evaluation is to ensure that departments are meeting budget goals (Pitzer and Thai 2009).

Budget Types

1. **Line-Item Budget**
   Line-item budgets are the oldest and still the most common form of budgeting in the public sector. Line-item budgets are funded as fixed budgets with funds appropriated for a particular period, usually one year. They are easy to understand and designed to maximize control and ensure financial accountability.

   However, they can present some of the following weaknesses.
   - Focus on what is procured rather than on the achievement of goals.
   - Provide no criteria for evaluating funding to determine what is to be gained or lost by increasing or decreasing expenditures.
   - Make it difficult to determine efficient trade-offs among services and are prone to incremental increases in successive fiscal years.
   - Encourage a "spend it or lose it" attitude.
2. **Zero-Based Budgets**
   Zero-based budgeting is a method of budgeting in which all expenses must be justified for each new budget period. The process of zero-based budgeting starts from a "zero base," and every function within the entity is analyzed for its needs and cost. This budget type organizes budget presentations according to "decision packets" or cost centers for which alternative levels of service delivery can be specified. Decision packets are ranked by relative importance and allow for the elimination of entire packages.
3. **Program Budgets**
   Program budgets relate expenditures and revenues to public goals. Program budgets are meaningful to the entity and the public because

programs are directly relevant to how they experience public services. A program budget is organized into service areas rather than just by departments or budget line items. Program budgets are the most elaborate budget form and tend to be more long-range with multi-year plans prepared along with budget requests.

4. **Performance Budgets**
   Performance budgets relate expenditures and revenues to workloads. This budget type reflects both the input of resources and the output of services for each activity or performance unit. They provide a mechanism to improve the management of service delivery, with cost efficiency being the principal indicator of managerial effectiveness.
   Output or end-product measures are developed for each activity or performance unit.
5. **Results-oriented Budgeting**
   Results-oriented budgeting is an approach that attempts to link resource allocation decisions to performance criteria that include both output and outcome measures. Although there are some similarities to performance budgets, results-oriented budgeting considers performance measures that look at outcomes of activities rather than individual process steps (Georgia Municipal Association n.d.; King, Unesh, and Webb 2021).

Strategic Planning

What is a strategic plan and why is it important? Strategic planning is the process of determining the long-range goals of an entity and establishing how these goals will be met. It is a "road map" intended to help the organization respond to new challenges and develop future opportunities. Strategic planning is a disciplined effort to produce fundamental decisions and actions that shape and guide what an entity is, what it does, and why it does it.

Since the essential mission of the government is to preserve the health, safety, welfare, and well-being of its citizens, the procurement function should play a strategic role in accomplishing that mission. Effective procurement can impact an entity's ability to deliver needed goods and services to its citizens.

The strategic planning process for Procurement is divided into two phases. The first phase of developing the plan allows the Procurement Department to align goals, programs, activities, and resources with the mission of the entity. The second phase allows procurement to determine how it is going to accomplish the elements outlined in the strategic plan.

In the first phase, public procurement must understand its purpose in relation to the entity and constituency that it serves. The purpose should be clearly stated, in written format, through the development of a Mission, Vision, and Values Statement. Procurement should then develop a strategic plan that aligns goals and objectives in accordance with the Mission, Vision, and Values Statement while fulfilling the obligation to meet the needs of the entity.

Mission Statement

Strategic planning should begin with a Mission Statement. This statement should be specific to Procurement's purpose and role within the entity. The Mission Statement will state the reasons for the existence and purpose of procurement (Pitzer and Thai 2009; Sutler-Cohen 2019).

Vision Statement

The strategic plan should also include a Vision Statement. The Vision Statement should identify where Procurement wants to be in the future and develop possible improvement paths that may be linked to the goals.

An example of a public procurement Mission Statement is Dallas County, Texas:

> Our mission is to provide value-added professional procurement services to meet departmental goals while promoting an open and fair competitive process. The procurement team is committed to acting, in accordance with best practices, as a leader among service providers, recognized for innovative and high-quality, cost-effective approaches to meeting and exceeding our internal and external customers' expectations.

Dallas County's corresponding Vision Statement is, "To be recognized as an ethical, and transparent department" (Dallas County 2019).

Core Values

Following the Mission and Vision Statements, most public procurement departments will detail their core values. "Core values are the root beliefs that a person or organization operates from. They are the principal perspectives that guide a person or organization's behavior with others" (Sutler-Cohen 2019). Core Values, while listed after the Mission and Vision Statements, often guide the development of the Mission and Vision Statements. They demonstrate what is important to the entity. Dallas County (2019) explains, "Our core values will always be our central focus. Regardless of the activity or situation, we are committed to a steadfast embodiment of our core values." Dallas County's core values are as follows:

- Integrity
- Responsibility and Accountability
- Diligence in Pursuit of Excellence
- Respect
- Good Stewards of Taxpayer Dollars (Dallas County 2019).

Limitations and Challenges in Strategic Planning

As with any planning process, the strategic planning process can be challenging and there are considerations that the procurement professional must be aware of in initiating and establishing the strategic plan. Some of the main challenges are:

1. Entities commonly face rapidly changing environments in which influences from political, social, and economic issues can impact how the entity operates.
2. The potential for internal resistance to the plan. All entities face internal politics and power struggles. Without proper levels of participation and careful planning, entity members may reject proposed plans and objectives.
3. Lack of commitment by leadership or upper management.
4. Lack of time and resources. Effective planning requires large amounts of time and resources.
5. Lack of meaningful objectives that relate to the mission and goals of the entity.
6. Resistance to change.
7. Emergencies and crises can occur that divert attention from the strategic planning process (Pitzer and Thai 2009).

Strategic Procurement Planning (SP2)

Strategic Procurement Planning (SP2) is the transformation of an entity's mission, goals, and objectives into measurable activities to be used to plan, budget, and manage the procurement function within the entity. The ultimate goal is to effectuate positive change in entity culture, systems, and operational processes. A major goal of strategic procurement planning is to link resource allocation decisions in a priority-setting model. Some of the most common benefits of strategic procurement planning are:

- Focuses attention on the entity's mission and links procurement decisions to entity strategy.
- Assists in designing future procurement strategies.
- Assists in designing or redesigning the structure of the procurement functions and processes.
- Allows procurement professionals to verify the legitimacy of procurement strategy consistent with the entity's strategy.
- Creates a framework for communicating with suppliers and cross-functional team members.
- Allows procurement resources to be assigned according to opportunities and risks.
- Facilitates the identification of opportunities and threats for future procurement decisions (NIGP, "Public Procurement Practice, Strategic Procurement Planning").

Spend Analysis

Spend analysis is the formal process of collecting, cleansing, classifying, and analyzing expenditure data from all sources within the entity. Spend analysis analyzes current, past, and forecasted expenditures and can be beneficial in making future management and buying decisions. In addition, this process can be especially useful in determining the most cost-effective contracting method.

What is the value of conducting a spend analysis? Performing a detailed spend analysis can help entities find new areas of savings and answer the following questions:

1. What is the entity actually spending and how much did we pay for each item?
2. Who are we spending it with and how many suppliers were used?
3. Are we getting what's been promised for that spend?
4. Are we spending funds in the most cost-efficient and effective manner?

Performance Management

Public procurement departments should develop a performance management program that allows for a continuous cycle of improvement and added value. An effective performance management program aligns with and supports the goals and objectives of the strategic plan. After the development of the strategic plan and implementation of the program, progress should be monitored to ensure that goals and objectives are being achieved most efficiently and economically. The program should identify opportunities for improvement by evaluating reports to identify areas for performance improvement and correcting deviations from established goals and objectives.

A sound performance management program will assist Procurement in meeting both internal and external strategic plan goals and objectives and help the Procurement Department demonstrate its value to all stakeholders including upper management and elected officials (NIGP, "Global Best Practice—Performance Management").

Performance Measurement

Now that we have discussed the importance of strategic planning and an effective performance management program, Procurement measures and assesses progress toward the achievement of the strategic plan by having a performance measurement system. Performance measurement is the process by which Procurement establishes criteria, based on strategic planning goals, for determining the results and quality of its activities.

Good performance measures need to be meaningful for all participants including procurement professionals, end users, and suppliers. They should be fair, easy to collect, consistent, and objective. The process involves creating a simple, effective system of determining whether Procurement is meeting its objectives.

Methods used to measure performance should be designed to motivate staff at all levels to contribute to organizational improvement. The following are examples of methods that can be used to measure procurement performance.

- Performance reviews to share performance measures that identify accomplishments and areas of improvement.
- Regular staff meetings to share performance measures and progress.
- Performance indicators.
- Performance targets.
- Benchmarking measures processes, services, or products against the characteristics of the recognized leaders in the given area of review. The procurement department can also identify world-class entities to compare its practices, policies, and performance outcomes.
- Quality management tools such as checklists, progress charts, and graphs (Government Finance Officers Association, Best Practices, Performance Measures 2018; NIGP, "Public Procurement Practice, Performance Measurement").

Performance Metrics

Procurement professionals need to develop and track a standard set of metrics that are aligned with the strategic goals of the entity. These metrics represent a quantifiable way for Procurement to track and analyze results against the entity's goals. Tracking is an activity that must be measured against a metric to make sustainable improvements. Consideration should be given to collaboratively involving the individual(s) who will be responsible for decision-making and performance management when developing the metric. Metrics should be fair, relevant, and focused on customer needs and demands, and the data used be accurate, reliable, and simple enough to understand.

The following are types of metrics that are commonly used by Procurement for comparison of performance standards.

- **Input Metric**—Measures resources used. They include labor, materials, equipment, and supplies. Demand for services may also be considered an input metric.
- **Output Metric**—The recording of activity or effort that can be expressed quantitatively or qualitatively, such as the total number of new contracts, total number of employees who obtained professional certification, and total spend.
- **Outcome Metric**—Assessment of the results of an activity and shows whether the expected results were achieved such as customer service, improved delivery times, and employee retention. Outcomes must be benchmarked against other departments and outside organizations. Benchmarking is a point of reference that can be used as a standard to compare performance.
- **Efficiency Metric**—A ratio representing the ratio of inputs to outputs or outcomes such as turnaround time per purchase order processed, average administrative cost per contract, and number of small business contracts awarded as a percentage of total contracts awarded.
- **Effectiveness Metric**—The degree to which an activity is successful in producing a desired, positive result. Effectiveness measures quality and affects customer satisfaction (NIGP, "Global Best Practice—Performance Metrics").

Procurement and Requirements Determination

Requirements determination is an important function of public procurement and can result in significant savings to the entity and ensure a reliable source of supply. Implementing a successful requirements determination program requires teamwork, collaboration, and positive working relationships between Procurement and the end user.

Once a strategic plan and a budget have been established for the coming fiscal year, a buying plan should be developed. Several techniques and analysis methods can be used in developing an effective buying plan. An important consideration in developing a buying plan is being aware of the nature of volume and timing decisions. Determining the right time to purchase a commodity or service can result in significant savings to the entity and reduce delivery time.

Scenario

A public school district middle school budget includes $100,000 for the replacement of library furnishings. The district operates on a July 1–June 30 fiscal year. Sadie, a Senior Buyer, is assigned the responsibility of working with the school principal to develop specifications and a solicitation for the furnishings. The principal wants the solicitation developed quickly and the new furnishings delivered and installed by the opening of the new school year in August. What advice should Sadie provide to the principal regarding this purchase?

In considering the timing of the purchase, Sadie knows that the demand for school and library furnishings is greatest during the spring and summer months. Because of demand, she also understands that it will be difficult to have delivery by August and that the district will pay a much higher cost even if delivery can occur. After considering the timing and demand, Sadie advises the principal to solicit bids after the start of the new school year, preferably during the winter months when demand is lower with delivery at the end of the school year. This will maximize cost savings for the district and ensure that delivery and installation can be completed while students are not in school.

In developing the buying plan, the procurement professional must understand the stability of the market for the commodity or service for which they are purchasing. Market conditions can greatly affect the price and availability of goods and services.

Two Types of Markets

There are two types of markets: stable and unstable markets.

1. **Stable Markets**—Commodities that are produced in stable markets are usually standard off-the-shelf items. In a competitive economy, the forces of supply and demand determine the price, and these items usually exhibit little fluctuation in price.

2. **Unstable Markets**—Commodities in unstable markets can exhibit frequent, short-term fluctuations in price, and price and availability can be unpredictable. Prices for these commodities can be influenced by political situations, weather, growing conditions, and speculation. In unstable markets, timing becomes an important consideration. Careful timing by the procurement professional can, to some extent, control the price paid by the entity and maximize value (Pitzer and Thai 2009).

Demand, Market, and Supplier Analysis

Developing a solid and effective buying plan involves analyzing demand, market conditions, and supplier availability. In developing the buying plan, ensuring that purchases are conducted in a manner that maximizes competition will always be of utmost importance.

Demand analysis involves estimating annual requirements for the upcoming budget year based on the previous year's usage. The second analysis is very important and involves assessing market conditions of a product or service, and includes researching availability, market volatility, supply and demand, and price.

A market analysis can produce information regarding possible alternative goods or services and can provide information that will be useful in developing functional and technical specifications. Market analysis should be a continuous, ongoing process that will help procurement adjust buying schedules to achieve maximum availability and competitive prices.

Supplier analysis determines the availability of competition and ensures that there are an adequate number of capable suppliers able to meet the needs of the entity. Assessing the performance of current suppliers also is an important aspect of supplier analysis and will include an analysis of each supplier's past performance. Along with demand and market analysis, supplier analysis is critical to achieving maximum value and a reliable source of supply for the entity.

Make or Buy Analysis

A "Make or Buy" analysis involves comparing the cost and benefits of providing a good or service by using internal resources with the cost and benefits of contracting with a private provider. NIGP's Dictionary of Terms defines outsourcing as a version of "Make or Buy," and the terms are often used interchangeably. As a result of increased fiscal pressure and budget limitations, outsourcing or "contracting out" has become more prevalent in the public sector. Budget shortfalls have resulted in public entities considering outsourcing to avoid higher taxes or cuts in services. When comparing costs, three principles should be considered (Kenton 2024).

1. **Ensure that all costs are considered.** Excluding hidden costs can favor private providers. For example, the entity's cost to manage and ensure compliance with the contract is often overlooked in calculating the entity's cost to outsource.
2. **Evaluate only the costs that differ between providers.** If costs will be the same regardless of who provides the service, those costs are irrelevant and do not need to be included in the analysis.
3. **Ensure the costs evaluated are of the same level of quality and service.** For an accurate comparison of costs, make sure that there is no difference between the levels of quality of services being provided by the entity and the private provider. In outsourcing public school food services operations, some school districts have discovered during the contract period that the reduced quality of the food being served by the provider resulted in fewer students participating in the food service program.

The decision to outsource a service can be difficult and requires a careful and thorough comparison of costs and benefits, While the final decision to outsource usually is made by the governing body or upper management, the procurement professional is often called on to provide information on market conditions, costs, and competitive selection methods.

Lease or Buy Decisions

When considering the purchase of equipment items, the procurement professional will need to carefully evaluate the decision to lease or rent rather than buy the required equipment. A determination will need to be made as to which approach will be most advantageous to the entity. For entities considering leasing equipment, a common practice is to use full-service leasing firms, in which the leasing company owns the equipment, has its own source of financing, and assumes all the responsibilities of ownership for the lease.

Lease options include:

- **Operating Leases**
  Most operating leases are short term for a fixed time period that is considerably less than the life of the equipment being leased. These

leases are usually used to fill short-term requirements when budget constraints may prevent the purchase of the item or there is a danger of rapid obsolescence. Common equipment items currently being procured by public entities through operating leases include computers, copiers, vehicles, forklifts, and road maintenance equipment.

- **Financial Leases**
  Financial leases are usually long term with a fixed time period just short of the life of the equipment. Financial leases are used as a financing tool and may generate long-term benefits. Financial leases have been used by public entities to procure and finance large capital projects such as buildings, entertainment venues, and highways. There are two types of financial leases:
  - **Full Payout Lease**
    The lessee pays the full purchase price, plus interest charges, maintenance, insurance, and administration costs.
  - **Partial Payout Lease**
    The lessee is given credit for the residual value of the leased item after the lease period is complete. The lessee pays the difference between the original price and the resale value plus interest charges.

Advantages of Leasing

1. The risk of obsolescence can be minimized or reduced. A cancelable lease can be negotiated under which the lessor, the owner of the equipment, provides the latest and most up-to-date model available.
2. Equipment can be made available on a short-term basis for projects that do not justify a large and immediate outlay of capital funds. Procurement professionals should be cautious of leasing arrangements with exorbitant rental rates.
3. The burden of the lease is shifted to the lessor. The lessee's working capital can be utilized for other, more cost-effective, or profitable opportunities.

Disadvantages of Leasing

1. Lessors make their profit on the difference between the financial ownership costs and the assets and lease rate. Monthly fees paid over the useful life of the equipment can total approximately 120% to 135% of the purchase price.

2. Lessors retain control of equipment and may place restrictions on how the equipment can be operated and on the operating supplies that can be used. This control may include issues such as:

   - Modifications—Most leases do not permit the lessee to make modifications in any way without incurring a penalty.
   - Lessor Access—The lessor may require the lessee to access the equipment for periodic inspection and maintenance.
   - Location of Use—The lease may include language that restricts the location of equipment to the local area. For example, some automobile leases may prohibit vehicles from being driven outside of the United States.
   - Purpose—Some leases may prohibit the use of the equipment for commercial purposes.
   - Quantity of Use—Vehicle leases may limit mileage to a certain usage period or specified period, such as 12,000 miles per year. In these cases, the lease usually imposes an additional per-mile cost for all miles over 12,000 (King, Unesh, and Webb 2021).

Tools to Analyze Complex Procurements

Procurement should strive to ensure that they purchase goods and services that meet the needs and requirements of the end user at the lowest possible cost. In analyzing high-volume, more complex procurements, two of the most frequently used methods include value analysis and value engineering. How can these methods be used by Procurement to meet the needs of the client and maximize cost savings?

Value Analysis

Value analysis is an organized effort to analyze the functions of systems, products, specifications, standards, practices, and procedures to satisfy the required function at the lowest price without impacting the need of the user or suitability for the purpose.

We frequently utilize value analysis in our personal purchases and probably do not even realize it. For example, if we are purchasing a lawn mower for use at home and the yard is small, a small push or self-propelled, battery-powered mower will probably meet our needs and be most economical. For most of us, it would not be practical or economical to purchase a riding lawn mower. However, if someone is not physically able to use a push mower, a riding mower even for a smaller yard may represent the best value.

In conducting value analysis, the procurement professional should consider the following two approaches for reducing costs.

Cost Reduction

Cost reduction occurs when the current price paid is less than what was previously paid. There are several practical ways for procurement professionals to achieve cost reduction (NIGP, "Dictionary of Terms").

- Review specifications carefully to make sure that requirements are not restrictive and will allow for full and open competition.
- Select the appropriate procurement method to entice and motivate suppliers to participate in the solicitation process.
- Consider accepting an alternative bid or proposal that will still meet the functional requirements of the end user.
- Through supplier analysis, ensure that there are an adequate number of competitive suppliers qualified and available to submit a bid or proposal.

Cost Avoidance

Cost avoidance occurs when the procurement professional takes an action to avoid paying a type of cost. Actions that can result in cost avoidance include:

- Negotiating an extension to a current term contract when the entity becomes aware that a price increase is likely to occur.
- Using a state or cooperative contract to avoid the administrative cost and effort to develop and issue a competitive solicitation.
- Ensure that specifications represent the exact requirements and level of quality needed by the end user or client to avoid paying a higher cost for unnecessary product features and a higher quality level not needed.

Value Engineering

Value engineering is most often used by contractors in the construction industry and can either be voluntary or at the request of the entity. With this method, contractors will suggest a more economical method or approach that will satisfy the desired function. Value engineering promotes the substitution of materials and methods with less expensive alternatives, without sacrificing functionality. Value engineering may be applied to reduce either the initial or life cycle cost of the project.

Forecasting

Forecasting is a systematic process that includes anticipating the demand for goods and services for an entity or departments within an entity. Forecasting involves examining the amount of goods or services your entity is likely to need during a specified time period. It takes into consideration changes in the marketplace and general economic trends.

Proper forecasting allows procurement to anticipate and estimate needs, develop a buying plan that addresses product supply and timing, and plan accordingly more accurately. The selection of a forecasting method depends on the relevance and availability of historical data, the degree of accuracy desired, the time period of the forecast, and the time available for making the analysis.

Quantitative and Qualitative Forecasting

Forecasting techniques are generally classified as quantitative or qualitative. Quantitative forecasting is a group of statistical techniques for making future predictions that uses numerical facts and prior experience to predict upcoming events. Quantitative models work well when there are little or no significant changes taking place in the environment.

Qualitative forecasting refers to the process of producing estimates of future needs with the aid of non-statistical techniques. This forecasting method is often used when there is a lack of historical data or during new or unique market conditions and relies on opinion and subjective probability estimates. Expert opinion is often necessary because of a lack of available or appropriate information for using another method. Qualitative models work well when significant changes are anticipated in the environment.

Inventory Forecasting

A key function of inventory management is forecasting the anticipated need for the various commodities used by the entity. If an entity is maintaining an inventory of products, it is imperative that inventory forecasting methods be used effectively. Forecasting is usually done by analyzing historical data to determine if any changes in future requirements are anticipated. The most commonly used means of forecasting future usage is based on methods of averaging past usage. The methods are as follows:

Fixed Period Average

The fixed period average method is used to divide the total usage by a fixed period using the last fiscal year calendar by the number of months involved, generally, 12. The resulting average is the forecast for the entire comparable future period. This is a simple *mathematical calculation that does not take into consideration future trends.*

Moving Average

The moving average is a continuous average method used to gather the most current usage information about an item by taking into account current trends and always using the most recent data. When using this method for 12 months, as the year progresses, the forecast will be updated by dropping the oldest month's data and adding the most recent month's data. This is a much more accurate means of making projections than the fixed-period method.

Weighted Moving Average Method

The weighted moving average method improves accuracy by giving more significance to weighting specific information such as seasonal variations. For example, because more heating oil is used in the winter, a higher weight will be given to those months in which usage is higher (King, Unesh, and Webb 2021).

Economic Order Quantity (EOQ)

Ordering and stocking material in inventory is expensive, so it is important in inventory management to determine the optimal number of orders and the optimal amount in each order. EOQ is an inventory calculation method to determine stock-level reorder points. Calculations are based on the costs of acquisition, storage, administration, handling, and inventory investment to determine the most cost-effective time and quantity to reorder.

Two basic costs are associated with managing inventories: carrying costs and acquisition costs. Carrying costs represent the cost of maintaining the inventory including storage, insurance, the cost of invested funds, obsolescence and deterioration, and equipment and labor. Acquisition costs are those costs associated with making a purchase. These costs include the administrative costs associated with issuing competitive solicitations and issuing orders. Maintaining too much inventory can result in unnecessary costs and obsolete items. However, not stocking enough inventory can result in departments not having a reliable source of supply and service disruptions. Procurement professionals should strive to minimize these costs as much as possible by monitoring inventory usage and using inventory forecasting methods effectively.

Contract Pricing Strategies

The compensation arrangement or contract pricing strategy is an important consideration that procurement professionals must determine for each procurement. The pricing strategy will determine the relationship between the contractor or supplier and the entity and will influence contract administration efforts and responsibilities. Contract pricing strategy also determines the level of risk assumed by the contractor and entity, and choosing the most appropriate pricing strategy will help the entity regarding risk. There are two major types of pricing strategies: fixed price and cost reimbursement, with variations of each type (Christensen and Dawson 2021).

Fixed Price

Fixed pricing is appropriate when it is possible to accurately predict costs and when it is reasonable to ask the supplier to assume responsibility for all costs. The supplier accepts most, if not all, of the cost risk and is responsible for managing all costs, regardless of whether they exceed or fall below the contract price. The total amount of the predetermined payment cannot be exceeded and reflects the result of the contract effort.

Variations of Firm Fixed-Price Contracts

There are several types of fixed-price contracts, and the extent of administrative activity and effort may vary. The procurement professional will need to assess and evaluate each procurement to determine which type will serve the best interest of the entity and result in the overall best value.

Fixed Price with Escalation, also known as Fixed Price with Economic Price Adjustment

A fixed price with escalation contract provides for either upward or downward adjustment in price based on certain contingencies specified in the contract. This type of contract is used when there is uncertainty about the stability of the market and labor conditions during a period when production is to take place and when it is possible to identify contingencies. Prices are adjusted according to provisions in the contract that provide a basis for price escalation or decrease. With this type of contract, the supplier and entity share in the risks and potential benefits. The suppliers are protected against unexpected price increases, but the entity will save money if prices decrease. The supplier still assumes the primary performance risk, and the suppliers' profit will not change as a result of any cost increases or decreases. Fixed price with escalation contracts can be especially beneficial when the entity is establishing term contracts for goods and services when there is potential for market volatility and a risk of price increases.

Fixed Price Incentive

This type of contract provides for an adjustment of profit and the establishment of a final price through a formula that compares the total actual cost to initial target prices. It is used when achievable cost and performance goals exist beyond the target or minimum acceptable levels outlined in the contract, and goals may be achieved by giving the supplier a profit incentive. If final costs are above the target price or below the target for performance, the supplier's profit is reduced. If final costs fall below the target price, the supplier's profit is increased. This type of contract is often used for service contracts or in construction to reward high-quality performance or a reduction in cost. Often the contract will also have a reciprocating disincentive clause for contract delays.

Fixed Price with Redetermination

This type of contract is used when a firm, realistic price can be determined for initial periods but not for subsequent periods. Quantities of materials and labor may change and be unknown. The supplier assumes the cost risk for the initial price, and the public entity assumes the risk for the redetermination.

Scenario

Maxwell, a senior buyer for a city government, is assigned responsibility for establishing a multi-year contract for copy paper. The term of the contract will be one year with the option to extend the contract for three additional periods of one year each. The city administrator directs Maxwell to require bidders to submit a firm fixed price for the initial and option years. How should Maxwell respond to the city administrator's directive?

Maxwell has assessed the market and knows that the paper market can potentially be unstable, and there will likely be price increases or decreases during the term of the contract. Maxwell also knows that requiring a firm fixed price for a multi-year contract for paper will place unreasonable risk on the supplier and that the supplier will submit a higher initial fixed price to protect themselves against uncertainty in the market. Maxwell recommends that the city use a Fixed-Price with Economic Adjustment contract.

Cost Reimbursement Contracts

Cost reimbursement contracts are used when there is uncertainty in the market and a variety of unknown potential cost risks, and when it is unreasonable to ask a supplier to assume all these risks alone. With cost reimbursement contracts, the specification or statement of work may be less definitive, and the focus of contract administration is mainly concerned with establishing the precise methods and manner of performance as the work progresses. The supplier is reimbursed for all allowable costs, and although the total cost to be paid to the supplier is not fixed at the onset of the contract, it is highly recommended that a ceiling or not-to-exceed price be established. The initial contract cost can be increased by contract modification if warranted.

Payment for the supplier's effort is paid upon incremental receipt of that effort. With these types of contracts, the public entity assumes most, if not all risks. Therefore, the entity should be aware of the use of resources and how the work proceeds.

Cost reimbursement contracts are used when the parties are unable to assess the full cost of performing the work before the commencement of the work. These contracts are most commonly used for equipment repairs when there is a high degree of uncertainty regarding the extent of the repair needed and for building renovations where some demolition is required, and the contractor cannot determine the full extent of the work until after demolition. Note, if using federal funds, that cost reimbursement contracts are discouraged and may not be allowed as they do not encourage the contractor to control costs. For example, The Federal Acquisition Regulation prohibits the use of cost reimbursement contracts for the acquisition of commercial services, and The Office of Management and Budget has directed Federal agencies to steer away from cost reimbursement contracts in most situations and look first at firm fixed-price contracts.

Variations of Cost Reimbursement Contracts

There are a variety of cost reimbursement contracts which are described in greater detail below.

COST-SHARING

A cost-sharing contract can be used when it is impossible to estimate costs accurately, and there is a high probability that the supplier will receive a substantial or future commercial benefit. This contract type may be advantageous in research and development contracts.

COST-PLUS INCENTIVE FEE

Targeted minimum and maximum costs are established at the onset of the contract. The supplier receives reimbursement for all costs, but the fee is determined after the contract is completed according to a formula comparing actual to target costs as in fixed-price incentive contracts.

COST-PLUS FIXED FEE

Cost-plus fixed fee contracts are used when it is appropriate to reimburse the supplier for all reasonable costs. The supplier receives a fixed fee amount negotiated at the time of award or submitted in response to a competitive solicitation. The fixed fee represents the supplier's profit. Some public school districts have used this contracting method to establish contracts for a wide variety of food items for school breakfast and lunch programs. Since food prices can be unstable and vary greatly over short time periods, competitive solicitations are structured to allow the suppliers to submit their costs and a fixed fee or profit for each food line item (Pitzer and Thai 2009).

Time and Materials Contracts

This contract type provides for contractors to be paid based on direct labor, hourly rate that includes profit and overhead, and the cost of the materials and equipment used in the performance of the contract. This type of contract is used only when no other type of pricing is suitable. A contract ceiling price is negotiated at the onset of the contract and is generally used when it is not possible to estimate the extent or duration of the required work. Heavy equipment and vehicle repair contracts are examples of services where the use of a time and materials contract may be appropriate because it is often unknown what the extent of the damage is, what parts will be needed, and how much time will be required to complete the repairs.

Contract for Volume Purchases

Now that we have reviewed the various types of pricing strategies, let's explore the types of volume contractual agreements that can help decrease administrative costs, reduce processing time, and increase productivity. In addition, volume contractual agreements can ensure a continuous, reliable source of supply and may result in lower costs.

Types of Volume Contractual Agreements

1. **Blanket Order**—A blanket purchase order, also known as a standing purchase order, is an agreement to purchase a given quantity of specific goods over a specified time period. The contract is generally used for items or services on an as-needed basis. The contract establishes the prices, terms, conditions, and the period covered, although no quantities are specified. Shipments or deliveries are made when and as required by the purchaser, which, in certain cases, may be the end user. Blanket orders are typically used when the exact items for services cannot be identified and usually cover a specific time period and include a maximum expenditure for each purchase and a maximum, not-to-exceed amount for the contract period.
2. **Term Contracts**—A term contract is a type of contract in which a source of supply is established for a specified period of time for specified supplies or services. They are usually characterized by an estimated or definite minimum quantity, with the possibility of additional requirements beyond the minimum, all at a predetermined price. The structure of term contracts can vary and can include the following arrangements.

   - Definite quantity for a definite period
   - Definite quantity for an indefinite period
   - Indefinite quantity for a definite period
   - Indefinite quantity for an indefinite period.

The use of term contracts can save significant amounts of administrative time and effort and reduce costs through volume purchasing. The procurement professional will need to structure the contract in a manner that will result in the overall best value for the entity. Most states establish state term contracts for a large variety of goods and services, and local governments typically have the option to utilize these contracts.

Schedule Contracts

Schedule contracts consolidate entity requirements by pre-establishing a solicitation opening date and requiring departments to submit requirements by a specified time. With this contract type, procurement consolidates the internal clients', e.g. each department's, needs under a single solicitation, and establishes contracts to fulfill those needs. Prices are established for definite items and quantities with specified delivery requirements.

Systems Contracts

Systems contracts establish a source of supply for a specified period for a large group of related materials or items. This method is designed to improve the reordering of materials used repeatedly. These contracts can be used as an across-the-board catalog discount contract where a percentage discount is applied to all catalog items. System contracts can also be structured contracts where the most frequently used items i.e., top 100 items, are competed as a fixed-price contract. For example, an entity could identify its 100 most frequently used electrical supply items and establish a competitive fixed-price systems contract for those items, while all other items are priced by a percentage discount from the catalog list price. A number of public school districts have established systems contracts for percentage discounts on entire school supply catalogs covering hundreds of instructional supply items (King, Unesh, and Webb 2021).

Contracts for Fluctuating Market Conditions

Forecasting is an essential tool of strategic planning and requires up-to-date knowledge of the market and an understanding of the tools for market evaluations. Forecasting should be used to determine the most appropriate type of solicitation and strategy based on market conditions. The following contract types may be used to manage procurements in varying market conditions.

Spot Purchases

Spot purchases are typically used for one-time purchases. They may be used for occasional small requirements, requirements for emergency or unusual situations, or favorable market conditions. Spot purchases are used when requirements cannot be forecasted with accuracy.

Term Contracts

As previously mentioned in this chapter, a term contract is a type of contract established for a specified period of time for specified supplies or services. The specified period can vary based on the volatility of the market and the ability of the supplier to deliver for an extended period. Terms contracts can lock in prices on commodities that experience sudden, unexpected price increases. Term contracts can help ensure that entities get reasonable prices and have a reliable source of supply in the event of emergencies (King, Unesh, and Webb 2021).

Economic Evaluation Strategies

Another important step in the procurement planning process is economic evaluation. It is an important element that enables procurement professionals and users to determine value. The following are economic evaluation strategies that can be used to ensure that a price is fair and reasonable.

Price Analysis

Price analysis is the process of examining and evaluating price data without evaluating the individual elements of cost such as profit and overhead. Price analysis is only valid when there is adequate competition resulting in a fair and reasonable price. When the procurement professional compares and evaluates competitive prices offered and the lowest price to determine if the low bid is fair and reasonable, they conduct a price analysis. Comparing a bid price to the previous price paid is another way to conduct price analysis. However, this is not necessarily valid since market conditions affecting price may have changed.

Cost Analysis

Cost analysis is the review and evaluation of cost data for the purpose of arriving at costs actually incurred. It involves evaluating the individual elements or components of costs that comprise the total price (NIGP, "Dictionary of Terms"). Cost components include direct costs including materials, labor, profit and overhead, and general administrative expenses. A cost analysis can be especially useful in determining a fair and reasonable price when a single response to a solicitation is received and in evaluating construction change orders.

Life Cycle Costing

Life cycle costing is a technique to determine the total cost of ownership of an asset over the entire life of the item from purchase to disposal. It involves a much greater analysis than simply basing a purchase solely on the initial purchase price. Life cycle costing includes the initial purchase price and all associated costs over the life of the item. For example, when purchasing a vehicle, all related costs incurred during ownership would need to be evaluated to determine the total life cycle cost. These costs would include the purchase price, operating costs such as fuel, maintenance, insurance, taxes if applicable, and disposal costs, salvage, or possible trade-in. Life cycle cost analysis is very important when purchasing capital equipment items since an item with a higher initial purchase price may actually cost less over the life of the item because of greater productivity, lower operating costs, and the item having a higher trade-in or residual value.

References

Christensen, Zac, and Nathan Dawson. 2021. "Contract Management and Performance." NIGP.

Dallas County. 2019. "Purchasing Department | Mission Statement." https://www.dallascounty.org/departments/purchasing/mission.php

Georgia Municipal Association. n.d. "A Budget Guide for Georgia Municipalities, 2020–2024." https://www.gacities.com/Resources/GMA-Handbooks-Publications/A-Budget-Guide-for-Georgias-Municipalities/Budget-Types-(1).aspx

Government Finance Officers Association. 2018. "Best Practices, Performance Measures." March 31, 2018. https://www.gfoa.org/materials/performance-measures

Kenton, Will. 2024. "Make or Buy Decisions Explained: How to Make Outsourcing Decisions." Updated July 25, 2024. Investopedia. https://www.investopedia.com/terms/m/make-or-buy-decision.asp

King, Ronald, Kalina N. Unesh, and Christine Webb. 2021. "CPPO Certification Preparation." NIGP.

NIGP. "Dictionary of Procurement Terms." https://www.nigp.org/dictionary-of-terms

NIGP. "Global Best Practice—Performance Management." https://www.nigp.org/resource/global-best-practices/Performance%20Management%20Best%20Practice.pdf

NIGP. "Global Best Practice—Performance Metrics." https://www.nigp.org/resource/global-best-practices/Performance%20Metrics%20Best%20Practice.pdf

NIGP. "Public Procurement Practice, Performance Measurement." https://www.nigp.org/resource/global-best-practices/Performance%20Measurement%20Best%20Practice.pdf?dl=true

NIGP. "Public Procurement Practice, Strategic Procurement Planning." https://www.nigp.org/resource/global-best-practices/Strategic%20Procurement%20Planning%20Best%20Practice.pdf?dl=true

Pitzer, Jack, and Khi V. Thai. 2009. *Introduction to Public Procurement.* 3rd ed. Herndon, VA: National Institute of Governmental Purchasing.

Sutler-Cohen, Sara. 2019. "Core Values: What They Are, Why They Matter, and How to Define Yours." Medium. March 6, 2019. https://medium.com/@scoutcoaching/core-values-what-they-are-why-they-matter-and-how-to-define-yours-93164383eada

Chapter 8

Solicitation Selection and Development

This chapter is designed to cover the various solicitation and contracting methods that can be used to fulfill the needs of the entity in a fair, timely, and cost-effective manner as well as examining the key factors to consider in selecting the appropriate solicitation method and risks associated with the procurement process. In addition, the chapter assesses the importance of market research and examines the types of specifications.

Assessing Solicitation Risks

There are risks with every procurement. Project risks can and will affect the overall project costs. Understanding the potential risks will allow the entity to decide which risks it wants to own and which risks the entity wants to transfer to the supplier. As the entity shifts risk to the supplier, costs will go up. In exchange for accepting additional risk, the supplier will increase its prices to compensate for carrying the additional risk. Procurements that shift too much risk to the suppliers will reduce the attractiveness of the solicitation therefore reducing overall competition. As a best practice, procurement professionals must identify the risk factors and analyze the probability of the risk occurring.

DOI: 10.4324/9781003566564-11

Strategic Risks

Strategic risks are those that may hinder the entity's ability to achieve its objectives and strategic goals. Strategic risks must be considered during the solicitation planning phase. Strategic risks are most likely to impact the solicitation schedule. However, identified strategic risks may also impact the solicitation document, involvement level of stakeholders, or the entities' ability to contract. NIGP's Global Best Practice on Risk Management provides a list of the most common strategic risks (NIGP, "Public Performance Practice, Risk Management").

- **Political**: risks associated with a failure to deliver policy for the entity that is served, or to meet the local administration's policy commitments, e.g. a failure to integrate sustainability considerations into acquisition decisions, and the impact of social unrest, changes in government, and the potential for political turmoil at home or abroad.
- **Economic**: risks affecting the organization's ability to meet its financial commitments, e.g. failing to consider the consequences of proposed major investment decisions before an acquisition; effects of inflation, recession, and foreign exchange rates.
- **Social**: risks relating to the effects that changes in demographic, residential, or socioeconomic trends will have on the organization's ability to deliver appropriate services, e.g. failure to procure sufficient elderly care provision for an aging population.
- **Technological**: risks associated with the organization's capacity to deal with the pace or scale of technological change or its ability to use technology to address changing demands, e.g. a failure to procure the appropriate software to allow for the efficient financial management of the authority, failure to manage and protect the security of the data.
- **Legislative & Regulatory**: risks associated with current or potential changes in law, e.g. a failure to address a legal directive.
- **Competitive**: risks affecting the cost, quality, or competitiveness of a service, e.g. the failure to address a failing service through improvement, market testing, or outsourcing.
- **Client or citizen**: risks associated with the failure to meet the current or changing needs and expectations of clients and citizens, e.g. the demand to improve the availability of public transport.

Operational Risks

Operational risks are the risks that procurement professionals are likely to experience or encounter while working. Operational risks are more likely to affect the entity and are less likely to impact the solicitation process. NIGP's Global Best Practice on Risk Management provides a list of the most common strategic risks (NIGP, "Public Performance Practice, Risk Management").

- **Professional**: risks associated with the practice of procurement, e.g. the failure to develop and implement robust procurement processes.
- **Financial**: risks associated with a failure to secure the most economically advantageous outcome to an acquisition, e.g. the failure to apply lifetime costing techniques in a tender or solicitation evaluation or the failure to apply the appropriate financial appraisal techniques before contract award, leading to supplier failure.
- **Legal**: risks related to possible breach of legislation, e.g. failing to advertise a contract under required directives; failure to include specific contract terms leading to contract failure.
- **Physical**: risks related to fire, security accident prevention, and health and safety, e.g. failing to procure properly labeled cleaning materials.
- **Contractual**: risks associated with the failure of contractors to deliver services or products to the agreed cost and specification, e.g. delivery by contractors of substandard or out-of-date food products; failure to meet specified outcomes.
- **Technological**: risks relating to a reliance on operational equipment, e.g. exclusive reliance on an eProcurement system to deliver critical supply acquisition.
- **Environmental**: risks relating to pollution, noise, or the energy efficiency of ongoing operations, e.g. the reliance on unsustainable sources of commodities.

Market Research

Market research is an important step in the solicitation development phase. Market research is defined as collecting and analyzing information about capabilities within the market to satisfy entity needs. The results of market research are used to determine the best approach to procuring goods and services. Procurement professionals typically conduct market research before

- Developing new specifications.
- Issuing solicitations.
- Soliciting offers for small procurements when adequate information is not available.
- Making fair and reasonable determinations.

The extent of market research and analysis will vary depending on the urgency, importance, value, familiarity or unfamiliarity, complexity, and rate of innovation of the proposed procurement (Bauccio-Teschlog et al. 2020). Market research of goods may include lead time as well as the following:

- The availability of commodities that are suitable as is, or that can meet the entities' needs with minor modifications.
- Common practices of suppliers engaged such as shipping, warranties, buyer financing, maintenance, and packaging.
- Laws and regulations specific to that commodity, etc.

In addition to the elements provided earlier, market research for services may also include:

- trends and innovative services in the field;
- terminology to better describe the entity's needs;
- availability of suppliers, etc.

Assessment of Market Conditions

As procurement professionals gather information on market conditions, they are compiling market intelligence. Market intelligence includes industry trends and the factors impacting them. Innovations as well as changes in products, quality, materials, and suppliers would also be tracked as part of market intelligence.

Request for Information

A Request for Information (RFI) is a formal, public, non-binding market research method in which an entity publishes a request for information for potential suppliers that may be interested in participating in the upcoming solicitation. An RFI includes a general description of the entity's requirements and requests that suppliers respond to the RFI with advice, guidance, and information that the entity may consider when planning its procurement. Suppliers' responses are used to develop the solicitation and provide current market trends and data. The sharing of information benefits both parties and assists the entity in determining the best solicitation method. It is important to note that since the RFI is not a method of solicitation, no award can be made on the basis of responses received from the RFI.

Pre-Solicitation Conference

A pre-solicitation conference is a market research method in which a meeting is held with potential suppliers prior to developing a formal solicitation. The conference is often convened through an RFI and is useful when the procurement professional needs information to prepare a formal solicitation.

A pre-solicitation conference provides the procurement professional with a means to acquire a better understanding of the marketplace and can provide information on alternative solutions. Purposes and benefits of a pre-solicitation conference include:

- Allows suppliers to better understand the entity's needs and requirements.
- Allows the entity to obtain the industry's input on the most effective means of meeting the entity's requirements.
- Helps the entity to identify prospective suppliers.

Although Procurement may invite only those suppliers who are expected to make a substantial contribution, the best practice is to provide public notice of the conference and conduct an open meeting. It is important to note that a pre-solicitation conference is not used to award contracts and does not serve as any kind of agreement or contract with any party.

Request for Expression of Interest (EOI)

A Request for Expression of Interest is a document issued by a procurement professional during the early stages of the procurement planning process to provide potential suppliers with an avenue to register their interest in being involved in a particular project or job. An EOI is a non-binding document that can be used by Procurement to survey the market and gauge the level of market interest in a project before issuing a formal competitive solicitation.

For example, a public entity requiring temporary office space may issue an EOI to help identify potential firms or individuals interested and capable of meeting the entity's needs.

Developing a Supplier List

A list of potential suppliers can be gathered from a variety of sources. Many entities have an ongoing supplier registration database that suppliers can register on to be contacted for opportunities for a specific commodity. When a solicitation is posted, it is sent to all registered suppliers for that commodity. In addition to pre-registered suppliers, entities often reach out to other public entities to gather their supplier lists. Other places to gather suppliers for a list include internet searches, trade associations, published directories, industry sources, sales literature, word-of-mouth recommendations, and electronic solicitation notification boards.

Inclusion of Minority Women Disadvantaged Business Enterprises

It is in the entity's best interest to include small and disadvantaged businesses. When an entity contracts with small businesses, they can assist small businesses with growing their businesses, creating jobs, and providing opportunities to expand. For example, in Canada, 1.3 million small businesses employ over 11 million people (Canadian Chamber of Commerce 2024). In the United States, that number is even greater; the 33.3 million small businesses in the United States account for 99.9% of all US businesses and employ nearly half of all US employees (Main 2024).

Many states in the United States have offices for business inclusion that maintain lists of certified small and disadvantaged businesses. For example, Washington state has the Office of Minority and Women's Business Enterprises, Oregon has the Certification Office for Business Inclusion and Diversity, Illinois has the Commission on Equity and Inclusion, Massachusetts has the Supplier Diversity Office, etc. In Canada, the Women Business Enterprises Canada Council is a Canadian non-profit organization that is opening doors for Canadian women-owned businesses to supply chains across Canada, North America, and globally (WBE Canada 2024).

Procurement Thresholds

Each entity will adopt its own procurement thresholds by policy or resolution. To minimize confusion for internal departments when they are using federal grant money, many public entities adopt the United States federal procurement thresholds. The United States federal government has adopted a three-tier threshold which includes micro-purchases, small-dollar, and formal purchase limits.

Micro-Purchase

The micro-purchase threshold is defined by FAR 2.101. The aggregate amount does not exceed the micro-purchase threshold (MPT). Micro-purchases do not require competition, and commodities can be purchased directly from a supplier without competition. To the maximum extent practicable, non-federal entities should distribute micro-purchases equitably among qualified suppliers.

- **Supplies**: The MPT for supplies is currently $10,000. Examples of supplies are computers, office supplies, tools, parts, etc.
- **Professional Services**: The MPT for professional services is currently $10,000. Examples of professional services include lawyers, architect-engineering services, chemists, biologists, accountants, medical services, etc.
- **Nonprofessional Services**: the MPT for non-professional services is currently $2,500. Examples of nonprofessional services include janitorial, servicing equipment, laundry or linen supply, food service, snow, trash, or garbage removal, operation or maintenance of facilities, landscaping, etc.
- **Construction**: The MPT for construction is currently $2,000. Examples of construction are building a structure, repairing or patching asphalt, or replacing a leaking roof or window, etc.

Small-Dollar, Informal Solicitation, and Simplified Acquisition Threshold

Informal solicitations are solicitations that may be accepted in an informal way such as via email, fax, or in person to the procurement office. An informal solicitation may also be referred to as a quotation. Many entities identify a dollar threshold in which informal solicitations may be conducted. The United States federal government refers to this as the Simplified Acquisition Threshold, which is currently between $10,000 and $249,999. For United States federally funded procurement 2 CFR 200.320 requires that price or rate quotations be obtained from an adequate number of qualified sources as determined appropriate by the non-federal entity (The Federal Register n.d.). Many federal entities have determined that adequate refers to two or more responses. However, entities may have stricter requirements such as defining adequate to be three or more. A best practice is to clearly define how the entity determines adequate competition to be.

Formal Solicitation

The United States federal government requires formal solicitations to be conducted for purchases of $250,000 or more. However, many public entities have adopted a much lower formal purchasing threshold. Per 2 CFR 200.320, formal procurement methods require documented procedures and may also require public advertising (The Federal Register n.d.).

Considerations for Selecting the Appropriate Solicitation Method

Table 8.1 shows the different solicitation methods and considerations for choosing the appropriate solicitation method. Each solicitation method is described in greater detail following the table.

Request for Quotations

Request for Quotations (RFQ) is a solicitation method typically used for low dollar value purchases that are below the dollar threshold set by an entity's statutes, regulations, and policies requiring formal advertising and submission of sealed bids or proposals. This method is an informal competitive bidding method that can be utilized if the dollar value of a purchase is relatively small but exceeds an entity's minimum dollar threshold requiring competitive pricing. This method is an efficient means of obtaining some level of competitive pricing by phone or in writing. The lowest price serves as the method of award if requirements for responsiveness and responsibility are met.

Table 8.1 Considerations for Choosing the Appropriate Solicitation Method

Request for Quotation	*Invitation for Bid or Invitation for Tender*	*Request for Proposal*	*Request for Qualifications*
1. Informal solicitation method 2. Objective evaluation 3. Awarded to lowest responsive and responsible	1. Formal solicitation method 2. Objective evaluation 3. Awarded to lowest responsive and responsible	1. Formal or informal solicitation method 2. Subjective evaluation 3. Price is considered as part of the best value determination 4. Awarded to the highest scored, best-value response	1. Formal or informal solicitation method 2. Subjective evaluation 3. Price is not considered 4. Awarded to the most- or best-qualified responder

Invitation for Bids (IFB) and Invitation to Tender (ITT)

An Invitation for Bids is a formal procurement method that may be used when requirements are known and the award is based primarily on the lowest price, which can include the total cost of ownership. The ABA *Model Procurement Code* differentiated an IFB which is the solicitation document and the competitive sealed bid which is the supplier's response to the solicitation. To be eligible for an award, the bid response must be responsive, and the bidder must be determined to be responsible. An entity's procurement laws and policies generally set forth public advertising requirements and the dollar threshold for which sealed bids are required. In Canada, this method is typically referred to as an Invitation to Tender and is used when requirements for a purchase are estimated to exceed $25,000.

When deciding whether to use an IFB, the procurement professional should apply the following criteria:

- The requirements are known and can be clearly specified in a manner that is clear to both procurement and potential bidders.
- Price is the basis of the award.
- A competitive market is available and must have an adequate number of qualified sellers.
- The dollar value of the specific purchase must be large enough to justify the expense, time, and effort required for both procurement and potential bidders.
- Adequate time must be available to use this method. Procurement must ensure that enough time is available to develop and issue the solicitation document and that bidders have adequate time to prepare and submit a bid.

An IFB details the conditions, procedures, and requirements for the procurement of a specified commodity and should be easily understood by the bidders. The IFB should be a professional-looking document of consistent style and format, and detail in a clear, organized manner the entity's requirements and instruct potential bidders on how to prepare and submit a bid response. Procurement should develop a standard format that groups information into sections or parts. Recommended sections include:

- Instructions to Bidders
- Scope of Work and Specifications
- General Terms and Conditions
- Special Terms and Conditions
- Required forms
- Contract documents.

When developing an Invitation for Bid, the procurement professional needs to work closely with end users to ensure that the solicitation document clearly specifies the entity's needs and is developed in a manner that promotes fair and open competition.

Request for Proposal (RFP)

Request for Proposal is a formal solicitation method that is used when consideration of factors other than price is critical in making an award decision and the ability to negotiate is desired. This method is used when requirements are not known and is oriented toward obtaining the best value or quality. The solicitation for a competitive sealed proposal is called a Request for Proposal (RFP), and the competing suppliers are referred to as offerors, proposers, or respondents.

An RFP is typically used for most types of professional services and complex procurements. This method provides proposers with the ability to offer creative and innovative solutions and is referred to by some entities as a solution- or performance-based procurement method. In contrast to competitive sealed bids that are awarded solely on price, the RFP document serves to promote fair and open competition while allowing the entity flexibility in evaluation through weighted, pre-established evaluation criteria, with price usually being one of the criteria. The evaluation criteria and their weights must be stated in the RFP with sufficient detail to enable the proposer to know what information should be included in their proposal. The RFP must also state how proposals will be evaluated, including the conditions that must be met to advance proposals through the evaluation process. The procurement professional must exercise care when defining the evaluation criteria and associated weights, specifically when assigning a weight to price relative to non-price criteria. The assigned weights must reflect the relative importance of each factor to ensure that the entity's needs are satisfactorily met.

Procurement professionals must work closely with the end user(s) to ensure that they understand the user's needs before determining the appropriate evaluation criteria. The RFP process is complex and lengthy, and sufficient time must be allotted to use this method for the evaluation of proposals and the negotiation of all terms, including price, before contract award.

The Evaluation Committee or Team

Evaluation committees serve in an advisory capacity and are established to advise and assist the entity in evaluating proposals and recommending an award decision. Serving as an evaluation committee member requires a commitment to dedication and effort. The optimal composition and number of committee members should be determined by the nature and type of each procurement, balancing engagement, expertise, and available resources. The evaluation committee members should be vetted in advance by the procurement professional to ensure that each member is free of bias and conflict of interest. For procurements of a highly technical nature, it may be advantageous to include individuals outside the entity with special expertise as committee members. The procurement professional should ensure that the evaluation committee members adhere to the following guidelines. They should be:

- impartial, open-minded, and fair; score proposals independently and fairly
- professional and adhere to the entity's policies and practices
- familiar with the RFP including the Statement of Work and the terms and conditions
- able to demonstrate prior experience in evaluating proposals
- capable of applying good judgment in awarding points and consider only the evaluation criteria published in the RFP
- prepared to support the award decision and defend the award.

Once the evaluation committee is selected, the procurement professional shall provide them with a document describing the evaluation process and guiding principles. In addition, Procurement should provide training for the evaluators before the submission deadline to ensure that the evaluation process as detained in the RFP is understood by all. If possible, training should be scheduled for a time near the proposal's due date so that the information is clear to the evaluators when they receive the proposals.

Performance-Based Contracting

Performance-Based Contracting is a results-oriented contracting method that focuses on the contractor's quality or outcomes. The solicitation is structured around the purpose of the work to be performed with contract requirements outlined in clear, specific terms with measurable desired outcomes. This method describes the results required rather than specifying how the work is to be accomplished. At least a portion of the contractor's payment may be tied to the achievement of specific, measurable performance standards and requirements. Contracts may include both monetary and non-monetary incentives and disincentives. Performance-based contracting is a contracting method that can encourage competitors to develop innovative and cost-effective methods of performing the work (NIGP, "Public Procurement Practice, Sourcing").

The purpose of performance-based contracting is to obtain overall better value, better performance, lower cost, or both. It requires output or outcome-based specifications and requirements that require the contractor to propose the most innovative, efficient, and effective ways to perform the work. The procurement professional must ensure that a competent and qualified contractor is selected.

Qualification-Based Selection for Architectural and Engineering Services

NIGP's Public Procurement Practice on a qualification-based selection of architectural and engineering services (QBS) describes QBS as a "procurement process for the competitive selection of architectural and engineering services under which the most appropriate professional or firm is selected based on qualifications such as knowledge, skill, experience, and other project-specific factors, rather than on fees. Fair and reasonable fees are negotiated with the top-ranked firm for an agreed-upon scope of services" (NIGP, "Global Best Practice—Qualifications-Based Selection for Architectural and Engineering Services"). QBS is required for selecting architects and engineers when using United States federal funds. Additionally, most states have implemented some sort of QBS law, and numerous localities have also adopted laws modeled after the federal statute, known as "Mini-Brooks" Acts. The Mini-Brooks Acts require states and localities to use QBS procedures when procuring design services. Other states and localities have adopted regulations or executive orders that accomplish the same objectives as the statutes. Additional information about current United States QBS laws can be found on the National Society of Professional Engineers website ("Qualifications-Based Selection of Engineering Services").

An analysis of issues pertaining to qualifications-based selection on the use of QBS found:

- Ensures cost-effectiveness
- Lowers risk for complex projects
- Results in better projects and highly satisfied owners
- Does a better job taking into account emerging social issues
- Encourages innovation
- Does a better job protecting intellectual property
- Does a better job building the capacity of staff who work for the client-owner government.

In the study's conclusion, the authors note that "traditional measures including cost, schedule, and quality all indicate a positive response in projects that employ QBS as a procurement method" (Chinowsky and Kingsley 2009).

The Brooks Act

The *Brooks Act* was enacted into public law in 1972 and established the statutory requirement to utilize a qualification-based selection process when contracting for architectural and engineering services, which has since been known as the *Brooks Act*, as it was introduced by the US Representative Jack Brooks of Texas. The *Brooks Act* requires contracts for architectural and engineering services to be negotiated based on demonstrated competence and qualification for the type of professional services required and at fair and reasonable prices. Section 904 of Public Law 92–582, 40 USC 541 et seq.92–582 describes the process for selection and negotiation. The law states the entity must "conduct discussions with no less than three firms regarding anticipated concepts and the relative utility of alternative methods of approach for furnishing the required services and then shall select therefrom, in order of preference, based upon criteria established and published by him, no less than three of the firms deemed to be the most highly qualified to provide the services required" (1972. Congress).

United States Federal Funding

When an entity is using United States federal funding to pay for architectural and engineering services, the *Brooks Act* applies. While the United States federal government uses qualifications-based selection, as incorporated into *Federal Acquisition Regulation* (FAR) Subpart 36.6, this requirement also applies when an entity receives and spends federal funds for architectural and design services. 2 C.F.R. 200.320. (b.)2. (iv.) currently states,

> The non-Federal entity may use competitive proposal procedures for qualifications-based procurement of architectural and engineering (A/E) professional services whereby offeror's qualifications are evaluated, and the most qualified offeror is selected, subject to negotiation of fair and reasonable compensation. The method, where the price is not used as a selection factor, can only be used in the procurement of A/E professional services. It cannot be used to purchase other types of services though A/E firms that are a potential source to perform the proposed effort. (The Federal Register n.d.)

For non-federal entities, the 2 C.F.R. 200 restricts qualifications-based selection to only be used in the selection of design services.

Qualifications-Based Selection vs Request for Proposals

QBS differs from an RFP process in that with qualifications-based selection, price is not considered as an evaluation factor. Instead, the price is negotiated with the highest-ranked proposer. With a request for proposal process, price is used as an evaluation factor in scoring proposal responses but often does not exceed 30% of the overall scoring points.

Many states have specified in law or statute that certain professional services be procured through QBS selection, while the remaining professional services such as consulting services be procured through a request for proposal process. It is strongly recommended that Procurement professionals understand their local and state laws when using local funds to procure professional services.

Procurement of Architectural and Engineering Services—Canada vs United States

As previously discussed in this chapter, the *Brooks Act* requires federal agencies in the United States to utilize a qualification-based (QBS) selection process for procurement of architectural and engineering services. In addition, most states and many local entities have implemented "Mini-Brooks" laws requiring the use of QBS. Although Canada does not have a federal law such as the US *Brooks Act*, a qualification-based selection process is commonly used across Canada when contracting for architectural and engineering services, and this method is recommended by professional organizations such as the Royal Architectural Institute of Canada and the Ontario Association of Architects (Royal Architectural Institute of Canada n.d.).

Procurement professionals in Canada should refer to the Canadian Free Trade Agreement and the Canada-European Union Comprehensive and Economic Trade Agreement. These trade agreements establish the procurement dollar thresholds for the procurement of services as well as goods and construction for ministries and most provincial agencies as well as municipalities, school boards, and publicly funded academic, health, and social service entities.

When procuring architectural and engineering services, procurement professionals in the United States and Canada must have a thorough understanding of the laws and regulations that govern the procurement of these services since legal and policy requirements can vary from entity to entity.

Competitive Bidding Exceptions and Exclusions

There are circumstances in which non-competitive procurements may occur. These are usually identified by the entity's jurisdiction or governing law.

Procurement exceptions are goods or services that have been determined not to be practicable for competition or where competition may be waived. Procurement exceptions include sole source, single source, emergency, in some cases, and single response.

Sole Source

The sole source method of procurement is used when there is legitimately only one provider or source of a good or service. This may occur for a variety of reasons such as patented technology, replacement parts, or single distributor. Since the sole source method of procurement goes against one of the primary objectives of procurement professions by limiting, not maximizing, competition, it should be used judiciously and be well documented. For this reason, the process may require public posting and special approvals. Some jurisdictions even require that noncompetitive negotiations must be conducted with the supplier and documented before an award can be made.

An example of a sole source is for reagents for the state's health department laboratory. While testing for a disease that had broken out statewide, the lab needed to order additional reagents. The reagents needed to be exactly the same for all of the initial and subsequent tests for consistency and accuracy. Since the chemical makeup of each supplier's reagent is not the same, inconclusive or inaccurate results could occur if identical reagents were not used for each test. So, even though other suppliers could provide reagents, it was decided to purchase them using the sole source method of procurement because it was not practicable to risk the possibility of inaccurate test results that affected public health and safety. The purchase of reagents was sole sourced to the supplier of the reagents used in the initial testing of the disease.

Single Source

A single source procurement is a purchase that is directed to one specific supplier because of a warranty, legal requirements, standardization, or other factors. It differs from a sole source in that other competitive, practicably available sources for the needed goods or services exist. Like the sole source method of procurement, it also limits competition and should be used judiciously and may have special posting requirements and need additional approvals. A note of interest is that some jurisdictions do not recognize a single source as a method of procurement, or they do not separate it from the sole source method of procurement.

An example of a single source is the printing of the state's legal journals. The General Assembly had written into law that only one specific supplier was authorized to print them. For this reason, when a new set of legal journals needed to be printed, the procurement professional used the single source method of procurement for procurement.

Emergency

An emergency purchase is made as the result of an urgent and unexpected request that may affect public health or safety, or when public property or resources are at risk. In a true emergency, formal competitive solicitations procedures may be simplified, modified, or waived. Just because a procurement is an emergency, competition is not automatically waived, as some may believe. To be true to one of public procurement's primary principles, competition should be sought to the maximum feasible extent given the circumstances. If competition is not feasible, then and only then should competition be waived. Just as with sole source and single source procurement, public posting and additional approvals may be required.

Again, this method of procurement must be used judiciously. An end user may approach a procurement professional claiming a purchase that does not fit the criteria is an emergency. The procurement professional in the case is obligated to deny the request to procure the needed goods or services in an emergency. It is important to remember that poor planning is never a justifiable reason for an emergency purchase, just as an expiring grant or budget does not constitute an emergency.

Single Response

A single response is when only one offer is received by the entity in response to a competitive solicitation. A single response differs from a sole source. With a sole source, there is only a single source that can provide a particular commodity.

In a single response scenario, multiple suppliers can provide the commodity but only one company responds to the solicitation. For example, electric medical beds can be provided by multiple suppliers including electric bed manufacturers and ambulance companies that provide outfitted ambulances equipped with electric medical beds. However, when the entity conducts its solicitation for medical beds, only the manufacturer responds, providing a single response scenario.

In this scenario, competition is limited. For that reason, the procurement professional needs to take additional steps to investigate why other suppliers did not also respond. They need to contact the other potential suppliers to determine the reason(s) they did not submit an offer. If the reasons are such as they were too busy, the person in charge of responses was out of the office on leave, they put the solicitation aside and forgot it, or some other similar reason, then only documentation to the file is needed. If, however, they indicate that the response timeframe was too narrow, the specifications were too restrictive or drawn to favor one supplier over another, the terms and conditions were too onerous, or some other similar reason, then the procurement professional should consider addressing the issue(s) raised, canceling the procurement program, and reissuing the solicitation with the needed modifications.

In cases where the decision is made not to re-solicit and make an award to the single response supplier, many jurisdictions have policies and procedures in place that require the procurement professional to take additional steps before making an award. These steps may include public posting, determining that the price is fair and reasonable, or obtaining additional approvals. Additionally, depending on the funding source, there may be additional documentation requirements when an entity receives a single response. For example, the United States Federal Transit Administration (FTA) requires that the entity review the specification to determine if it was overly restrictive, i.e., if only one company could meet the requirements (Federal Transit Administration, "Single Bid"). If this is true, then it is a sole source and not a single response, and a sole source approval must be sought before the contract can be awarded. However, if it is determined that the specification is not restrictive and other companies could have met the IFB's specification but chose not to bid for other reasons, then you need to document the file with your determination that the competition was adequate. The FTA also requires that some form of cost or price analysis be done to determine that the price is reasonable. We would not think the state contract price could be used as a benchmark since that price was not arrived at competitively. You should look at the Best Practices Procurement Manual, section 4.6—Cost and Price Analysis, which has several suggestions for doing a price analysis (Federal Transit Administration, "Best Practices Procurement & Lessons Learned Manual").

Determining the Procurement Method

A procurement professional determines the solicitation method for needed goods or services after analyzing requirements and determining if the procurement should be a contract to fulfill repetitive, ongoing requirements or on a one-time basis. While the end user should be included in this process, it is ultimately up to the procurement professional to make the decision on which solicitation method to use to achieve compliance and cost-effective results.

Factors in Choosing the Best Procurement Method

There are numerous factors to consider when choosing the best procurement method. If the total cost of the needed goods or services is within the entity's single quotation limit, then the procurement professional may obtain just one quotation and award it to that supplier if the price is deemed to be reasonable.

If the total cost for the needed goods or services falls within the entity's small purchase procedures, the procurement professional may obtain the required number of quotations using approved methods and make an award to the lowest responsive and responsible bidder or the highest-ranking proposer.

If the total cost of the needed goods or services is above the entity's small purchase procedures dollar threshold, the procurement professional must use a formal, sealed solicitation. Generally, the solicitation will be an IFB or an RFP. An IFB is used when the entity's needs can be clearly defined in specific terms and price is the most important factor.

A procurement professional may choose to use the RFP method of procurement when the needed goods or services can only be described in general, not specific, terms or when factors other than price need to be considered or are more important. Those factors may include the supplier's reputation, the fastest delivery schedule, the approach to be taken to satisfy the entity's needs, etc.

Other factors a procurement professional may need to consider are if the needed good or service falls into the category of an exception for competition or if the needed service is defined as a professional service. Many entities are required by law to procure professional services using only the RFP method.

Laws and Legal Requirements

In the US, the ABA *Model Procurement Code* identifies six procurement methods that a procurement professional may use to acquire needed goods and services. They are:

- IFB
- RFP
- Small purchase procedures
- Sole source
- Emergency
- Special procurements.

In Canada approved procurement methods include:

- Invitation to Tender (known as an IFB in the US)
- RFP or negotiated RFP

- Informal quotes, which are done via email, phone, or any other means but should always have something in writing; used for simple, low-value goods and services that must be delivered quickly and can be easily described over the telephone or other means such as email.
- Request for Quotation, similar to small purchase procedures in the US.
- Request for Standing Offer is a unique procurement method that does not always result in a contract. It is given to a supplier for a specific good or service at a specified price for a designated time period. Only if and when the government purchases the good or service against this standing offer is a contract formed.
- Request for Supply Agreement, a second stage process from a previously created Standing Offer when end users solicit prices from a pool of prequalified suppliers.

Time

Time can be a factor in determining the best method of procurement. Lindsay Kroes, in her article "Your Guide to RFP Cycle Times in Public Procurement," states that "the average public sector RFP process took 57 days from posting to award. This does not include the additional time spent on pre-planning and requirements-gathering before the RFP is posted" (Kroes 2019). The state of Maryland's procurement manual states that the timeline for an RFP is generally 12 to 18 months and that for an IFB it is generally six to nine months (Maryland.gov n.d.). The University of Arkansas states that a typical timeline for an IFB is one to two months (University of Arkansas 2023).

The timeframe estimates can vary widely, and the timeframe for the RFP process is considerably greater than it is for an IFB. The procurement professional must consider the timeframe estimates when determining which procurement method to use for acquiring needed goods or services.

Adequate Number of Suppliers

Effective competition does not necessarily mean a large list of potential suppliers, but it does mean a list of dependable, competent suppliers. An adequate supplier base is essential for the well-being of any entity. The determination of the optimal number of suppliers is a critical and strategic issue. The argument in favor of one supplier is that better pricing will result from a higher dollar-volume contract and that the procurement professional will have more influence with that supplier. Additionally, lower administrative costs may result. However, an argument in favor of multiple sources of supply is the protection that will be afforded to the entity if a problem occurs with a single supplier. This provides an incentive for supplier performance.

It is important to note that a recent trend in the private sector is a reduction in the number of suppliers a company maintains. The private sector is subscribing to the philosophy that quality, not quantity, yields the greatest benefit. Many firms are now maintaining two suppliers, one as a primary supplier and the other as a backup. The process is that if the primary supplier does not perform, the firm can then order the needed goods or services from the backup supplier, thus saving time and preventing disruption in entity services.

In the public sector, however, our goal is to maximize competition. So, for now, at least, we will not follow the private sector's current trend of trying to reduce the number of suppliers we contract with.

Importance of Qualitative Factors Other than Cost

In some cases, the end user or the procurement professional may want to consider qualitative factors in addition to cost when awarding a contract. As stated earlier in this chapter, those factors may include the supplier's experience, reputation, capacity to provide the goods or services such as the fastest delivery schedule, sustainability, ability to achieve diversity or small business goals, the approach to be taken to satisfy the entity's need, etc. Other factors that the entity may want to consider are experience and proven capability when cost is not the most important factor.

Ability to Allow for Negotiations

If an entity wants to allow for the ability to negotiate an award, based on qualitative factors in addition to cost, and time is not an issue, the procurement professional may choose the request for proposal method of procurement for the needed goods or services. Even though the RFP process is time-consuming, it allows for achieving the best value for the entity, while competitive sealed bidding merely allows for good value. When using the RFP method of procurement, procurement professionals must be sure to comply with all relevant laws, regulations, and legal counsel.

Most jurisdictions do not allow for negotiations when the IFB process is used. Some, however, do allow for an exception in certain circumstances if a prescribed process is followed. Generally, in such a case, negotiations with the lowest, responsive bidder are allowed if the procurement professional has documented the file that the entity's market research indicates that all bid prices are likely to come in above the budgeted amount for the procurement. In this situation, the procurement professional must include in the IFB a term and condition stating that if all bids from responsive and responsible bidders are above the procurement's budgeted amount, negotiations may be held with the lowest responsive and responsible bidder to try to reduce the price to one that is within the set budget amount.

Construction Project Delivery Methods

When procuring construction services, choosing a project delivery method is one of the fundamental decisions that an entity must make in developing its procurement strategy. How the procurement will be structured is critical to a successful procurement and contract award. Laws, regulations, and policies governing construction procurement can vary greatly from entity to entity, and the procurement professional must ensure that the method chosen is permitted within the laws and regulations of the entity. There are various project delivery methods. Each method designates what the contractor is required to do and establishes the relationships among the parties to the contract. Commonly used project delivery methods are listed below:

Design-Bid-Build (DBB)

Design-Bid-Build (DBB) is the traditional sequentially phased method in which the owner has two separate contracts: Owner to designer and owner to contractor. Design plans, specifications, and drawings prepared by the designer serve as the basis of the contract. The award is typically made to the lowest cost, responsible, and responsive bidder, and usually results in a fixed-price contract.

Advantages of DBB are as follows:

- This method is well understood and clearly defines the roles of all parties involved in the contract.
- When adequate competition is available, the entity can be reasonably certain that the work is being contracted at the lowest cost.
- Both the designer and the contractor work directly for the owner, and the owner has a significant amount of responsibility for the success or failure of the project.

Disadvantages include:

- The process may be longer and design must be completed before solicitation of bids.
- There is no collaboration between the design and contractor during the design phase, and this may limit the effectiveness of the design.
- The owner may face exposure to contractor change orders and disputes since the owner accepts responsibility for project design.
- This method may lead to adversarial relationships rather than cooperation between the owner, contractor, and designer.

Construction Manager at Risk (CMR) or Construction Manager/General Contractor (CM/GC)

Construction Manager at Risk is an alternate method in which the owner has two separate contracts, owner to designer and owner to CM-constructor. However, with CMR, the contract with the CM is usually awarded early in the design phase, preferably at the 30% design stage. Selection of the CM is based on an evaluation of qualifications and price, and the CM offers a Guaranteed Maximum Price (GMP) instead of a fixed bid. The Construction Manager at Risk is responsible and accepts risks for the construction of the entire project for the GMP and is responsible for assembling and managing the team of suppliers and subcontractors.

Advantages of Construction Manager at Risk include:

- The owner gains the benefit of having collaboration between the contractor and the designer during a portion of the design phase. The contractor's perspective and input can be incorporated into planning and design decisions.
- More professional relationships between the owner and the Construction Manager.
- Earlier knowledge of costs.
- Earlier involvement of contractor expertise.

A main disadvantage of this method involves the lack of a direct contractual relationship between the contractor and designer, and the owner can sometimes be placed between those parties when resolving project issues. Disagreements regarding quality, completeness of design, and scheduling may occur.

Design-Build (DB)

Design-Build contracts involve two primary parties: the entity (owner) and the design-builder. One contract exists between the owner and the design-builder, and the design-builder is responsible to design and construct the project that meets the performance standards set forth by the entity. The entity's requirements are usually outlined in functional requirements instead of detailed design plans and specifications. This method is sometimes considered to be a "fast track" approach since the work may start before the design is completed. Advantages of Design-Build include:

- Since the designer and builder are working together through the entire design phase, the project can usually be delivered more quickly than DBB or CMR.
- Fewer change orders and claims which can result in less likelihood of litigation. Change orders are typically limited to changes initiated by the entity.
- Earlier knowledge of firm costs.
- The contractor guarantees the design.
- Enhance project coordination between the entity and the design-builder.

Disadvantages can include:

- The Design-Build team qualifications are essential for the success of the project and the entity should place significant emphasis on the qualifications portion during the evaluation process.
- The entity has less control over design and must be willing to allow the Design-Build team to handle design details.
- In some entities, fewer contractors have the experience and capability necessary to complete Design-Build contracts. This may apply especially to small and disadvantaged businesses.
- Since source selection is based on subjective evaluation criteria, there may be more opportunities for disputing the selection process and award decision.

Multi-Prime (MP)

Multi-Prime is similar to the DBB delivery method in that there are three sequential project phases and the entity contracts directly with the designer. However, with MP, the entity contracts directly with separate specialty contractors for separate specific trades or elements of the work rather than a single general or prime contractor. The entity performs a general contractor role and has multiple prime contractors. Some entities mandate the use of this method to enhance opportunities for small and disadvantaged businesses.

The main advantage of MP is that the entity has control over the entire process, and the designer and all contractors report to the entity. This method can be very challenging, and the contract requires a significant amount of coordination and administration on the part of the entity. The entity is responsible for the development of separate bid packages for each prime or specialty contractor, and there is a risk of problems arising resulting from a lack of coordination. With MP, the cost of the project is not known until all prime contracts are executed, and there is the potential for numerous claims among the various contractors.

Job Order Contracting (JOC)

Job Order Contracting (JOC) is an alternative construction project delivery method that is typically used for smaller construction projects. The contract is an indefinite delivery indefinite quantity agreement and usually provides for a maximum amount of work during a specified contract term. Construction services are ordered from the contract on an "as needed" basis.

A job order contract is a competitively bid, fixed-price contract based on established unit prices listed in a Unit Price Book (UPB). Well-developed unit price books provide competitive pricing on a wide variety of construction tasks, and some UPBs include fixed prices for over 250,000 construction tasks.

The contract price is established by applying an adjustment factor, called a coefficient, to the unit price costs for a project. An adjustment factor is a numerical factor that is not included in task prices in the UPB. The adjustment factor typically includes but is not limited to business costs such as overhead, including, but not limited to, office space, office equipment, office and management personnel, office supplies, and employee transportation and profit, insurance costs, bonding costs, Job Order development services, owner meetings, and other administrative services required by the Contract Documents, subcontractor's overhead and profit, cost of financing the work, business risks such as the risk of a lower than expected volume of work, smaller than anticipated Job Orders, poor subcontractor performance, and inflation or material cost fluctuations. Adjustment factors include all direct and indirect costs not included in the preset prices listed in the UPB.

In competitive solicitations for Job Order Contracting contracts, government entities typically require adjustment factor pricing for work performed during normal work hours, other than normal work hours, and for non-pre-priced tasks. The contractor calculates the total cost for a project by multiplying the adjustment factor(s) times the established unit prices listed in the UPB.

Job Order allows entities to complete multiple construction, renovation, and repair projects under a single contract and can result in faster project completion times, less administrative time and costs, and better-quality work (Tommie and Varda 2022).

Specifications and Standards

After an end user submits a purchase requisition to Procurement, the next step is to define and detail what must be purchased. Procurement regularly receives requisitions for a wide variety of commodities, and it can be challenging to ensure that the needs of the end user are being met while achieving maximum competition, fairness, and transparency. The NIGP Dictionary of Procurement Terms defines a commodity as a marketable item produced to fulfill a need or want and may reference both goods and services (NIGP, "Dictionary of Procurement Terms").

The key to a quality acquisition is the specification. A specification provides a precise description of the physical or functional characteristics of a product and details the requirements of the purchase. Developing detailed and concise specifications requires collaboration between procurement and the end user(s), and the procurement professional must ensure that the end user accurately and concisely describes the required product or service. Solicitations that are developed and issued with inadequate specifications can potentially cause several problems including disputes with end users, supplier protests, failure to meet the needs of the end user, increased cost, and, in some cases, litigation. Each solicitation must be developed with the most accurate and concise information possible and written in a language that can be easily understood by potential offerors.

Types of Specifications

When deciding which type of specification to use for the purchase of a specific good or service, the procurement professional should consider the intended use of the commodity, the degree of complexity, and the desired outcome. The three most common types of specifications are design, performance, and brand name. NIGP's "Public Procurement Practice, Specifications" is a great reference and identifies the following types of specifications.

Design Specifications

Design specifications define the precise requirements in terms of how a commodity should be manufactured or constructed and state in prescriptive terms what the potential offeror must provide. They detail physical characteristics and can include dimensions, weights, colors, product features, industry standards, inspection methods, and required materials. Design specifications can include engineering drawings, plans, and blueprints. Design specifications provide the end user with increased certainty about a commodity and allow for objective evaluation of offers. However, they also place high risk on the buying entity for design errors or omissions within the specification. A contract award is based on compliance with specifications with the award made to the lowest responsive and responsible offeror. Design specifications can be expensive and time-consuming to prepare and often require the assistance of an outside party such as an architect or engineer. For a design specification to be effective, the procurement professional should ensure that provisions for tolerances are made, and the specifications allow for the submission of alternates and establish minimally acceptable standards.

Performance Specifications

Performance specifications, which includes functional specifications, describes the desired outcome or intended use and how a product or service should perform to achieve a desired outcome or specific end result. Performance specifications also identify and describe the capabilities and expectations that a product or service must satisfy. Instead of describing an item in terms of specific detailed requirements, performance specifications describe what a commodity must do. Performance specifications allow offerors to use their expertise, creativity, and innovation in proposing a solution and are typically used when the means of achieving the desired outcome is unknown. Performance specifications place a higher degree of risk on the offeror and the offeror assumes the responsibility of achieving the desired outcome. In addition to offering a viable solution, they must be able to provide conclusive evidence that the product or service requirements are being met. When using performance specifications, it is important to consider the supplier's expertise and capability in meeting the stated requirements. Selection of the wrong supplier can result in a less-than-ideal outcome. Performance specifications are commonly used for the procurement of services, such as consultants for feasibility studies or assessments, and some construction services. They can also be used to purchase large equipment and vehicles such as police boats and fire apparatus.

Brand Name or Equivalent

The NIGP Dictionary of Procurement Terms defines a brand name specification as the use of one or more manufacturers' brand names, with identifying model numbers, used in a specification to invoke certain quality, performance, and other salient characteristics needed to meet solicitation requirements (NIGP, "Dictionary of Procurement Terms"). The use of brand name specifications in procuring goods can simplify the process for the procurement professional and make inspections and acceptance easier since the specified brand name represents the quality ordered. However, brand name specifications can greatly limit competition since offers can only be submitted by distributors that can provide the specified brand name product.

When using brand name specifications, the procurement professional should always use accompanying wording such as "approved equivalent" or "approved alternate" and include a statement such as:

> The brand name(s) being used are to describe and establish general performance and quality standards and such references are not intended to be restrictive. The brand name(s) specified are intended only to establish a desired level of quality. Bids are invited for these, and comparable brand names provided the quality meets or exceeds the quality of the specifications listed for any item.

Whenever possible, it is advisable to include three or more acceptable brand names that identify the characteristics and desired quality level of the item(s) being procured. There are some instances when the use of a name brand specification may be allowed and justified on an exception basis. For example, purchasing products for standardization programs or for maintaining compatibility with existing products or equipment. When considering acceptance of an alternate name brand product, the procurement professional, in collaboration with the end user, reserves the right to determine equivalency.

Common Solicitation Activities

After the development of the solicitation document is complete, the procurement professional will ensure that the solicitation of bids and proposals is conducted in an open, fair, and competitive environment. During the solicitation period, procurement will work closely with entity representatives to ensure that prospective bidders and proposers clearly understand the terms, conditions, and requirements of the solicitation. The procurement professional also has the responsibility of facilitating the solicitation process and ensuring that the solicitation is publicly advertised in accordance with applicable laws and policies, and adequate time is provided for bidders and proposers to ask questions and seek clarification. Effective management of processes during the solicitation period will be key to a successful contract award that results in overall best value to the entity.

While the actual solicitation process and activities may vary from entity to entity, several common critical solicitation activities must be considered and planned for regardless of solicitation type. The two most common activities are allowing for a question-and-answer period as well as deciding if the entity is going to offer a pre-bid or pre-proposal conference.

Questions and Answers

The question-and-answer period intends to allow potential offerors an opportunity to ask questions and seek clarifications about the solicitation. During the solicitation period, prospective offerors should be encouraged to freely ask questions and seek clarifications. It is important that a deadline date for submission of questions be clearly specified in the solicitation document and that adequate time be provided for offerors to submit questions. The solicitation must also provide notice of when the prospective offerors can expect to receive answers to their questions and how the questions and answers will be communicated. The procurement professional must ensure that all prospective offerors have access to all questions and answers.

Pre-Bid or Pre-Proposal Conferences

When planning a solicitation, the procurement professional will need to decide if offering a pre-bid or pre-proposal conference will be advantageous to the entity. A conference for an IFB is called a pre-bid conference, whereas a conference for an RFP is called a pre-proposal conference.

A pre-bid or pre-proposal conference is held after the procurement professional has issued the solicitation. The purpose of the conference is to provide an opportunity for suppliers to ask questions and seek clarification about the solicitation. Additionally, the conference allows entities to emphasize areas of importance in the solicitation and provides suppliers with an opportunity to see or visit the site. If conducting a site visit in conjunction with a pre-bid or pre-proposal conference, the best practice is to offer the site visit first to allow prospective offerors to view the site and develop questions that can be asked during the conference. The procurement professional should ensure that prospective offerors have sufficient time to review the solicitation and prepare an initial set of questions prior to the date of the conference. In addition to providing prospective bidders or proposers with vital project information and an opportunity to meet the project team, pre-bid and pre-proposal conferences can also be very beneficial in improving business and networking opportunities for small, disadvantaged, and women-owned businesses.

When conducting a pre-bid or pre-proposal conference, the procurement professional should state publicly that any verbal answers are tentative and that official answers will be provided in writing at some scheduled date and time following the conference. A sign-in sheet should be distributed at the beginning of the conference and becomes a public document that can be freely distributed. This practice is important since some contractors will attend conferences to connect with other contractors to seek partnering opportunities.

For especially complex projects or when a site may be restricted or secure, it may be advantageous for the entity to require a mandatory pre-bid or pre-proposal conference. However, the entity must be very clear that offerors that do not attend the mandatory conference will not be permitted to submit an offer. Mandatory attendance should only be required when necessary since it can exclude bidders or proposers and limit competition. If a mandatory pre-bid or pre-proposal conference is necessary, it is preferable to offer at least two conferences in the event an offeror has a conflict or an emergency and cannot attend the first offered conference. When deciding whether or not to make attendance at the pre-bid or pre-proposal conference mandatory, do so with caution.

Mistakes Prior to Opening or Closing

Many procurement professionals refer to bids as opening and requests for proposals as closing. The difference in terminology for the two different solicitation methods stems from bids having public openings where the submitted bidder and bid totals are read aloud. This practice differs from proposals which undergo a subjective evaluation process and are most often not opened publicly. In the instances where entities complete a public process, only the names of the submitting proposing companies are read because the submittal will undergo an evaluation process.

Before bids are opened publicly, a bidder may discover that they have made a mistake such as forgetting to include required information, or they may want to change their pricing. Following the entity's legal requirements and policies, a bidder may be allowed to withdraw their bid or correct mistakes before bid opening. After bid opening, but before an award is made and with the approval of the procurement professional, a supplier's mistake may only be corrected if it is minor, and the mistake is evident on the face of the bid. Mistakes that can be corrected after the award include obvious mathematical or clerical errors. Once an error is discovered, the procurement professional must require written documentation from the bidder verifying the mistake. Procurement professionals are strongly encouraged to confer with their legal counsel before taking any action any time a mistake is noticed or brought to their attention.

Once proposals are opened, most mistakes or discrepancies may be addressed and corrected through negotiations. Exceptions would be any issues that have been identified as mandatory in the RFP or the failure to sign any part of the proposal response. As with bids, procurement professionals are strongly encouraged to confer with their legal counsel before taking any action any time a mistake is noticed or brought to their attention.

Handling

It is essential that the procurement professional spell out for prospective offerors in the solicitation how and when offers are to be delivered to the entity. Instructions should be as clear and as detailed as possible to mitigate the risk of ambiguity or misunderstanding. Procurement professionals should be deliberate in their use of mandatory versus permissive verbs in the instructions. If the entity requires that all offers must be delivered to one specific place, office, or person before the due date and closing time, then it must be stated that no exceptions will be allowed. To verify that this requirement has been fulfilled, offers should be time and date stamped using a verifiable, reliable, and consistent method, either electronic or manual.

Some jurisdictions may have a more lenient approach regarding late offers. Some jurisdictions may allow for the acceptance of a late offer if the reason that the offer is late was not attributable to any actions or inactions of the offeror, but, rather, it was caused by a third party or an Act of God. For example, if the offer was in transit via a commercial carrier such as FedEx or UPS and the delivery was delayed because of a snowstorm, hurricane, technology failure, etc., then the entity's legal may allow the entity to accept the late offer as the offeror clearly received no advantage from the late delivery. Procurement professionals are strongly encouraged to consult with their legal counsel prior to accepting or rejecting a later offer.

Delivery of Solicitation Response to the Wrong Location

If an offer is delivered to the wrong location and does not make it to the location indicated in the solicitation by the due date and time, it will, in most cases, be deemed late and, therefore, not considered. Laws, policies, and procedures vary; therefore, it is recommended that the procurement professional confer with the entity attorney before a final decision is made.

References

1972. Congress.gov. October 27, 1972. Brooks Act. https://www.congress.gov/92/statute/STATUTE-86/STATUTE-86-Pg1278.pdf

2000 ABA Model Procurement Code. https://publicprocurementinternational.com/wp-content/uploads/2019/04/2000-ABA-Model-Procurement-Code.pdf

Bauccio-Teschlog, Theresa, Dennis Carney, Joyce Foster, Ronald King, and Christine Weber. 2020. *Developing and Managing Requests for Proposals in the Public Sector.* New York: Routledge.

Canadian Chamber of Commerce. 2024. "Unveiling the Portrait of Small Businesses in Canada: Insights and Challenges." January 29, 2024. https://chamber.ca/unveiling-the-portrait-of-small-businesses-in-canada-insights-and-challenges/

Chinowsky, Paul, and Gordon Kingsley. 2009. "An Analysis of Issues Pertaining to Qualifications-Based Selection Final Report." QBS. https://www.qbs-mi.org/files/2009_QBS_Study.pdf

Federal Transit Administration. "Best Practices Procurement & Lessons Learned Manual (Report 0105)." https://www.transit.dot.gov/funding/procurement/third-party-procurement/best-practices-procurement-manual

Federal Transit Administration. "Single Bid." https://www.transit.dot.gov/funding/procurement/third-party-procurement/single-bid

Kroes, Lindsay. 2019. "Your Guide to RFP Cycle Times in Public Procurement." Bonfire, October 17, 2019. https://gobonfire.com/blog/your-guide-rfp-cycle-times/

Main, Kelly. 2024. "Review of Small Business Statistics of 2024." *Forbes*, January 31, 2024. https://www.forbes.com/advisor/business/small-business-statistics/#:~:text=While%20large%20corporations%20often%20grab,employed%20by%20a%20small%20business

Maryland.gov. n.d. "Maryland Procurement Manual—3. Pre-Solicitation." eMaryland Market Place, October 13, 2023. https://procurement.maryland.gov/mpm-3-pre-solicitation/

National Society of Professional Engineers. 2013. "Qualifications-Based Selection of Engineering Services." https://www.nspe.org/resources/issues-and-advocacy/action-issues/qualifications-based-selection-engineering-services

NIGP. "Dictionary of Procurement Terms." https://www.nigp.org/dictionary-of-terms

NIGP. "Global Best Practice—Qualifications-Based Selection for Architectural and Engineering Services." https://www.nigp.org/resource/global-best-practices/Qualifications-Based%20Selection%20for%20Architectural%20and%20Engineering%20Services%20Best%20Practice.pdf?dl=true.

NIGP. "Public Procurement Practice, Risk Management." https://www.nigp.org/resource/global-best-practices/Risk%20Management%20Best%20Practice.pdf

NIGP. "Public Procurement Practice, Sourcing." https://www.nigp.org/our-profession/global-best-practices#sourcing

NIGP. "Public Procurement Practice, Specifications." https://www.nigp.org/resource/global-best-practices/Specifications%20Best%20Practices.pdf?dl=true

Royal Architectural Institute of Canada. n.d. "Qualifications-Based Selection." https://raic.org/qualifications-based-selection-qbs

The Federal Register, 200.320. n.d. "Methods of Procurement to Be Followed." https://www.ecfr.gov/current/title-2/subtitle-A/chapter-II/part-200/subpart-D/subject-group-ECFR45ddd4419ad436d/section-200.320

Tommie, William J., and Kristy Varda. 2022. "Job Order Contracting." NIGP, Inc.

University of Arkansas. 2023. "RFP/IFB Procurement Lead Time." https://procurement.uark.edu/_resources/documents/RFP_IFB_Procurement_LeadTime_Website.pdf

WBE Canada. 2024. "Meet WBE Canada." August 7, 2024. https://wbecanada.ca/about/

Chapter 9

Pre-Award Activities

This chapter covers all the considerations and the steps a procurement professional needs to take after receiving responses to a solicitation to fulfill legal, procedural, and best practices to protect the entity. This chapter focuses on considerations for determining responsiveness and responsibility, the evaluation process, the award, and post-award processes, and how to deal with protests.

Evaluation

After receiving offers in response to a solicitation, it is the procurement professional's responsibility to evaluate those responses. The exact steps and processes may differ from entity to entity based on laws, procedures, and standard practices as well as whether those offers are in response to an IFB, RFP, or some other type of procurement method. In all cases, however, evaluations must be made with reasonable promptness in a fair, impartial, and compliant manner. For example, a contract award is made to the lowest responsive and responsible bidder meeting all of the requirements and criteria

DOI: 10.4324/9781003566564-12

of the IFB, and the highest-ranking responsive and responsible proposer from an RFP process.

For an IFB, evaluation starts with a review of the bid from the lowest bidder. If the bid is responsive, in other words, it meets all of the criteria and specifications, then the procurement professional needs to determine if the bidder is responsible. If the bid is not responsive or if the bidder is not responsible, this process is repeated for the next lowest bid and continues until a responsive bid from a responsible bidder is found. An award is then made to that bidder.

For an RFP, all proposals received must be evaluated using only the evaluation criteria specified in the RFP. Normally, negotiations are then conducted with those found to be in the competitive range, and an award is made to the highest-ranking proposer that is found to be responsible.

The issue of determining responsiveness and responsibility before making an award is critical. These determinations can greatly affect the success or failure of a contract.

Responsiveness

The determination by the procurement professional as to whether or not an offer is responsive is made after the solicitation's opening or closing. A responsive bid, proposal, or offer is one that "fully conforms in all material respects to the solicitation and all of its requirements, including all form and substance" (NIGP, "Dictionary of Procurement Terms"). All suppliers responding to a solicitation must provide their offers based on the same effort to assure fairness and objectivity of the procurement process. An offeror must not be awarded a contract based on less effort, cost, or quality than other offerors could have also provided if they had known the entity would have accepted such. To be eligible for an award, the offer must respond and conform to the requirements of the solicitation. The matter of determining the responsiveness of an offer includes several issues that the procurement professional needs to evaluate and address as appropriate. Those issues include:

- Exceptions to terms and conditions
- Mistakes after opening or closing
- Minor informalities.

To be responsive, an offeror may not take exception to any mandatory term or condition. The procurement professional may reach out to the offeror to explain to them that if they do not agree to withdraw such an exception, their offer cannot be considered. If, however, the exception is for other than a mandatory term or condition, the procurement professional may accept or negotiate the issue.

The withdrawal or correction of an offer, before or after an award has been made, in cases where an inadvertent error was made, is permitted in accordance with a jurisdiction's regulations. Unless regulations state otherwise, any decision to allow for the correction or withdrawal of an offer, or to cancel an award or a contract resulting from a mistake, must be documented in writing and approved by the Chief or Central Procurement Officer or the entity head.

If a proposer discovers they have made a mistake in their proposal before the closing date, they may withdraw their proposal and submit a corrected proposal, if time allows. Mistakes found in competitive proposals after the closing date can normally be handled fairly easily through negotiations. That, however, is not the case with competitive sealed bidding. Bidders are usually not allowed to modify or withdraw a sealed bid after the bid opening date and time. Failure to sign a bid may make the offer non-responsive since it could be considered as not being a valid offer. Conversely, failure by a bidder to acknowledge a bid amendment that does not materially affect the procurement may be determined to be an informality. In this case, the procurement professional may allow the bidder to correct the situation by supplying the signed amendment within a given, reasonable time frame.

If the bidder makes a mistake in their bid price, they may withdraw the bid and submit a corrected bid if the mistake is discovered before the bid's opening date. After the closing date, the only option usually available to the bidder is for them to withdraw their bid. If, upon opening the bid, a procurement professional suspects a mistake in the price offered, they may request verification of the price. Normally, the procurement professional will notify the bidder of the suspected price error and request them to verify the correctness and accuracy of the price submitted. In the case of suspected clerical price errors, the procurement professional may permit correction by verifying the intended bid price if there is clear and convincing evidence of the mistake and the intention of the bidder unless such a correction would displace one or more other bids. It would be prudent for the procurement professional to consult with legal counsel before doing so. If it is not a clerical error, but a valid mistake that can be confirmed and substantiated with written evidence, the bidder may withdraw their bid. Acceptable written evidence may include the bidder's original worksheets, supporting data used to prepare the bid, and suppliers' quotes along with the intended bid price.

If the mistake causes the bid price to be significantly lower than a reasonable estimate or other bid prices, other considerations come into play. If the procurement professional has actual knowledge that a mistake in the bid price has occurred, or if they should have known, they cannot in good faith obligate the bidder to the erroneous price by awarding them a contract.

A minor informality or irregularity is simply a matter of form, not of substance, or pertains to an inconsequential or immaterial variation or defect of an offer from the exact requirement of the solicitation which, if waived, would not be prejudicial to any of the other offerors. A minor informality can be defined as something that does not affect price, quality, quantity, or delivery. The procurement professional may allow the offeror to cure the deficiency in this case or simply waive the minor informality, depending on which one is to the best advantage of the entity.

Responsibility

Another concern for a procurement professional before awarding a contract that goes hand in hand with responsiveness is responsibility. NIGP defines a responsible bidder, proposer, or offeror as, "A supplier with the integrity and reliability as well as the financial and technical capacity to perform the requirements of the solicitation and subsequent contract" (NIGP, "Dictionary of Procurement Terms"). Three major components of determining responsibility are:

- Capacity to perform
- Financial ability
- References.

Checking and documenting references is an integral part of determining responsibility. When doing so, the procurement professional needs to ask open-ended questions that allow the reference's contact person to describe their experience with the supplier. If yes or no questions are asked, they should be followed up with why. The procurement professional should be aware that some people are reluctant to give, or may even be prohibited from giving, a bad reference. So, they need to be listening not only to what the reference says but also to what they do not say.

Financial information from the offeror also needs to be reviewed, checked, and verified. In some cases, further digging may be warranted. Financial information can be confusing, so the procurement professional may seek help from someone more knowledgeable in reading, deciphering, and interpreting it.

Verifying the offeror's capacity to perform the requirements of the contract can also be challenging. It is the responsibility of procurement professionals to completely satisfy themselves that the offeror has the full capacity, capability, and resources to fully perform. So if the offeror does not have the

Table 9.1 Comparison of Responsiveness and Responsibility

Responsiveness	*Responsibility*
Focuses on the offer, response.	Focuses on the offeror, supplier.
The response conforms to the mandatory submittal requirements.	The offeror has capacity to perform the requirements of the solicitation and subsequent contract.
A determination that the offer conforms in all material respects to the solicitation and all of its requirements, including all form and substance.	A determination that the offeror possesses the experience, facilities, reputation, financial resources and is fully capable of performing the contract.
Determination is made upon reviewing responses.	Determination is made during the evaluation process.
Determines whether the response can proceed to be evaluated for responsibility.	Determines if the offeror can be considered for award of the contract.
Sample definition, Virginia, 2.2–4301. Definitions.	Sample definition, Virginia, 2.2–4301. Definitions.
"Responsive bidder" means a person who has submitted a bid that conforms in all material respects to the Invitation to Bids.	"Responsible bidder" or "offeror" means a person who has the capability, in all respects, to perform fully the contract requirements and the moral and business integrity and reliability that will assure good-faith performance and who has been prequalified, if required.

manpower, equipment, etc. at the time, they cannot be deemed responsible. In other words, a contract cannot be awarded to an offeror who promises to hire the required personnel or obtain the needed equipment or other resources needed to perform the contract's requirements. An offeror must be fully capable of performing at the time of the award. While many states have developed their own definitions for responsiveness and responsibility, the following table was developed from researching FAR 14.301, Virginia statute "§ 2.2–4301 and MRSC's article by Josh Klika (2024).

Intent to Award

Once it has been determined which offer will be recommended for an award, the procurement professional may choose to post a notice of intent to award before an award is made. This is normally done in cases where the likelihood of a protest is anticipated. The reason for this is that it is administratively easier and less complicated not to proceed with a contract if a protest is received and upheld than it is to cancel a contract that has been awarded and where work has already begun. The intent to award document is posted per the jurisdiction's requirements or the entity's policy for the number of days specified. If no protest is received, the procurement may proceed with the award process.

The requirement to post or provide an intent to award to offerors varies significantly. For example, in Virginia:

> A Notice of Award must be posted for a ten (10) day period immediately following the actual time of award. If a protest is anticipated, the Notice of Intent to Award must be posted ten days prior to the actual time of award (see also 4.12d). Emergency notices must state that the contract is being issued on an emergency basis while sole source notices must state that only one source was determined to be practicably available and both must also state that which is being procured, the contractor selected, and the date on which the contract was or will be awarded. Routine notices of award may be a copy of the bid tabulation sheet revealing bidders' prices and indicating the bidder receiving the award. IFB and RFP solicitations must contain the General Term and Condition on Announcement of Award. The Notice of Award shall be posted on the eVA and in any additional locations as prescribed in the solicitation for a ten (10) day period immediately following the actual time of award. (Code of Virginia, § 2.2–4360)

In contrast, in Washington, entities commonly provide the intent to award to begin the protest clock. For example, City of Everett Municipal Code, 3.46.050.C, bases its protest procedures off of notice of intent to award.

> 1. If the city provides at least three business days' notice to bidders or proposers of its **intent to award** or reject all bids or proposals, any protest must be filed with the city clerk no later than the business day prior to the date of proposed award or rejection of all bids or proposals. For the purposes of this subsection, the city may notify bidders or proposers by providing them with a copy of the tabulation of the bids or proposals.

2. If the city has not provided at least three business days' notice to bidders or proposers of its **intent to award** or reject all bids or proposals, any protest must be filed with the city clerk no later than three business days after award or decision to reject all bids or proposals.

Recommendation for Award and Approvals

In some cases, the procurement professional may then proceed directly with making an award. Some policies require approval from others before an award can be made. Often, depending on the dollar value, the procurement professional may have to seek approval for a recommendation for the award from management or a board with oversight responsibilities such as a Board of Supervisors or entity council.

Debriefs

Debriefing is, "A practice primarily used during the Request for Proposals process, whereby the contracting authority will meet individually, generally upon request, with each proposer whose proposal was not deemed appropriate for an award, to discuss the strong and weak points of that supplier's proposal" (NIGP, "Dictionary of Procurement Terms"). The purpose of debriefs is to provide value to both the offeror and the entity. The quality and value derived from a debrief is dependent upon the clarity of the solicitation, the evaluation process, documentation, and how skilled and well prepared the procurement professional conducting the debrief is. A debrief meeting can provide the proposer with constructive feedback they may use when preparing future proposals for other RFPs. Procurement professionals can benefit from information gleaned from the debrief that they can also use when preparing future RFPs. When conducted properly and with a positive attitude, viewing the meeting as a learning opportunity for all, debriefs may lead to a better relationship with the supplier through the development of added trust fostered by transparency.

NIGP's Global Best Practice on Debriefs states:

> The procurement professional's conduct and level of disclosure during a debrief is directed by policies and procedures, based upon laws, regulations, and other applicable legal guidance to which

the entity is subject or adopts, along with generally accepted ethical principles. Complying with the policies and procedures ensures the appropriate level of disclosure, type of information, and method of disclosure during the debrief. To ensure compliance, the entity should apply the strictest requirement as a standard.

[...]

Debriefs for large, complex, or high-profile procurements may warrant additional preparation. Be prepared for potentially difficult conversations. Conduct the debrief with no less transparency than the entity's legal requirements.

Discuss the strengths and weaknesses of the proposer's submission in relation to the evaluation criteria.

- Provide a general overview for each evaluation criterion, not a point-by-point comparison.
- Do not compare information between proposals.
- The debrief may include information on the proposer's ranking relative to other proposals.

Considerations and best practices for a valuable debrief while mitigating risk to the entity include the following activities by the procurement professional in preparing to conduct a debrief.

- Know the law and expectations for the debrief.
- Review the procurement file.
  - Assemble documents i.e., evaluation committee notes, proposal, etc.
- Gain familiarity with evaluation notes to communicate constructive feedback related to strengths and weaknesses.
- Prepare, and practice.
  - Anticipate potential questions or areas of concern from the proposer and prepare measured responses.
- Send a summary sheet to the proposer who requests a debrief before the debrief.
  - The sheet would include strengths and weaknesses from the evaluation and often negates the need for the debrief.
- Conduct the debrief
- Lead with strengths before discussing weaknesses.
- Be prepared to offer suggestions for improvements for future proposals Note: Do not provide an example of a suggested response.

- Be as transparent as the entity's legal requirements allow without disclosing any proprietary information.
  - Discuss strengths and weaknesses of only the proposer's proposal in relation to the evaluation criteria and requested scope of work, a general overview, not a point-by-point comparison.
- The debrief may include information on the proposer's ranking relative to other proposals.
- Designate a colleague to take notes during the debrief, documenting questions asked, comments made, and any other relevant information or observations.
- Act professionally.
  - Employ active listening skills, be focused no distractions.
  - Dialogue should be courteous and respectful.
  - Stay calm and professional.
  - Prepare statements to diffuse difficult situations or questions. (NIGP, "Global Best Practice, Debriefs")

It is, generally, not a good idea to have legal counsel attend the debrief meeting, unless the supplier's legal representative is attending. Having only the entity's legal representative in attendance can add tension and an elevated sense of tension for the supplier. The procurement professional's best tools are transparency, acting professionally, respect, and a good attitude. Most important of all, however, is good documentation. Good documentation can go a long way in avoiding a protest.

Protests

Protests are something that many procurement professionals dread and fear. Some view them as a bad thing as a sign of some sort of failure. This is not true. A protest may be lodged for a variety of reasons, some of which are valid and some of which are not. It is a check and balance mechanism in public procurement that allows for transparency and fairness for our suppliers. Protests are an important instrument for suppliers to have at their disposal to ensure public procurement is and remains fair and competitive. It provides transparency for not only suppliers but also for the public at large.

Procurement professionals must know their processes regarding protests, such as how long the entity has to respond to the protest. In any case, the response must be timely. After verifying the entity's protest policy and that both the entity and the protestor have followed the proper processes, the procurement professional should review the procurement file to ensure that it contains complete and accurate documentation that is relevant to the procurement concentrating on information relevant to the protest. Once this has been done, the decision of the need to involve legal counsel must be made. This decision should be guided by the complexity and gravity of the protest.

The procurement professional must determine through investigation of the facts of the cases, what has or has not happened versus what has simply been alleged. This is done by retracing steps with the person conducting the procurement, internal staff, and anyone alleged to not have followed the proper process, to get their side of the story. If it is determined that no violation occurred, document why there was no violation found and the process that was followed to make that determination. This information is included in a written response to the protestor, written in a legally accurate and defensible manner.

If, however, violations are found, determine specifically what violations occurred and why. The procurement professional may meet with entity management, including legal counsel if appropriate, to explain what happened and why, and to determine what appropriate corrective action should be taken. The protestor is then notified in writing of this information. Based on the protestor's response, the entity should act accordingly.

The protestor may then accept the decision, appeal the decision, or file a lawsuit. If a lawsuit is filed, involve legal counsel immediately and notify or escalate to any other appropriate parties.

Do not respond directly to the protestor or anyone associated with them going forward. All communication from this point forward should come from the entity's legal counsel.

Lastly, but very importantly, the procurement professional should conduct a lessons-learned exercise and document the file in writing of the results. Any processes that need to be added, deleted, or adjusted should be modified and implemented promptly.

References

Acquisition.gov. n.d. "14.301 Responsiveness of Bids." https://www.acquisition.gov/far/14.301

Everett Municipal Code. 2014. "Ch. 3.46 Bid Protest Procedures." https://everett.municipal.codes/EMC/3.46

Klika, Josh. 2024. "MRSC—Saying Yes to Responsive & Responsible Bids." https://mrsc.org/stay-informed/mrsc-insight/july-2022/saying-yes-to-responsive-responsible-bids

NIGP. "Dictionary of Procurement Terms." https://www.nigp.org/dictionary-of-terms

NIGP. "NIGP Global Best Practice, Debriefs." 2021. https://www.nigp.org/resource/global-best-practices/global-best-practice-debriefs.pdf?dl=true

Virginia.gov. 2024. "§ 2.2–4301. Definitions." https://law.lis.virginia.gov/vacode/title2.2/chapter43/section2.2-4301/

Chapter 10

Contract Formation

Contract formation is a series of pre-award procurement steps and activities that result in a legally binding contract between an entity and a supplier. The procurement department provides value during the contract formation process by providing a set of procurement tools that can be utilized to assess different types of risks for each type of procurement. Specific contractual goals can then be established to manage risk.

During the planning phase of the procurement process, much of the groundwork for contract administration is established. The primary goal of contract formation is the prevention of disagreements and disputes during the execution of the contract. In essence, the contract formation activities serve as a preamble to the administrative activities that will follow once the contract is executed.

This chapter will explore the specific pre-award activities that will occur during the contract formation process and will address assessing contract risks, identifying the elements of a binding contract, the six types of contractual risks, contract development, and signature authority.

DOI: 10.4324/9781003566564-13

What is a Contract?

A contract is an agreement between parties which is enforceable by law (NIGP, "Dictionary of Procurement Terms"). The term "contract" is generally used to mean a written agreement signifying an agreement between two parties. But in the eyes of the law, the term means the process in which the agreement is formed. A contract may be characterized as an obligation, a legally binding promise, or an agreement between parties with a binding legal and moral force. For this chapter, the term "contract" refers to promises or agreements for which the law establishes enforceable duties and remedies (*Ironclad Journal* 2024).

Contracts can be formed in different ways. Express contracts, which may be written or oral, are created when the essential elements for establishing a contract exist. Another type of contract is an "implied-in-fact" contract. With this type of contract, some of the formal elements occur through conduct rather than expressed words. An example of this contract type is when you hire someone to mow your lawn. Although no formal contract exists, it is implied that after your lawn is mowed, the person performing the work will be paid.

To form a contract, all of the following six correct elements must be present for a contract to be binding and legally enforceable. The six correct elements were discussed in great detail in Chapter Six. As a reminder, they are as follows:

- Offer and Acceptance
- Definiteness of Purpose
- Legal Consideration
- Mutuality of Obligation
- Capacity of Parties or Competent Parties
- Legality of Purpose (King, Unesh, and Webb 2021).

Scenarios

1. Joy, the Food Services Manager for a public school district, has responsibility for purchasing supplies and materials for food service operations. Joy calls a local custodial products supplier and inquires as to pricing for a specific cleaning product. The supplier offers a price, and Joy informs the representative that she will consider the offer and get back in touch later. However, the next day, 20 gallons of the product totaling $500.00 arrived at the school district's location. Does the supplier have a legally enforceable contract?

No, a binding contract was not created since the Manager never accepted the supplier's offer. For a contract to be legally binding, there must be a clear offer and acceptance.

2. Chad, the Procurement Manager for a small city government, awards a contract for the construction of a warehouse storage facility. State law requires all contractors to have a current General Contractors license. After awarding the contract, Chad discovers that the contractor's license has expired and they do not possess a current, valid contractor's license. The contractor states that he can have his license renewed before construction starts. Does a contract exist between the city and the contractor?

   No, the law will only enforce contracts with a lawful purpose. Since the contractor had not complied with the state's contractor licensing requirements, a legal contract did not exist. Furthermore, the contractor was required to meet the legal requirements of the solicitation at the time the bid was submitted.

Contractual Risks

A key responsibility of the procurement professional is identifying contract risks and establishing specific goals to manage risks. Managing risks involves identifying and analyzing risk factors and working closely with end users and contracting personnel to manage risk exposure to the entity. Managing and communicating potential risks to the entity is a key element in ensuring that risks do not stand in the way of achieving the entity's objectives.

Every procurement involves some degree of risk and should be evaluated for the following six types of risks:

1. **Proposal Risk**—This type of risk addresses the legal document, solicitation, that defines and specifies the item or service being procured, mutual areas of agreement, and how the risks will be allocated. Does the solicitation clearly and accurately define the needs of the entity? Do prospective offerors have a clear and thorough understanding of the needs of the entity?
2. **Surety and Liability Risk**—Does the solicitation include language and clauses necessary to protect the financial and legal interests of the entity? This can include insurance, bonding, and licensing requirements that are necessary to protect the entity in the event of performance issues, contract termination, or statutory requirements.
3. **Schedule Risk**—Does the solicitation include clear and specific language describing delivery deadlines, delivery terms, and any penalties for late delivery? Do the contract terms assure timely delivery?

4. **Contractual Risk**—Does the solicitation include language and clauses that will address unexpected or unforeseen conditions or events? Mitigating this type of risk can include establishing change order procedures, dispute resolution processes, termination procedures, who has the authority to authorize changes, and what changes can be unilateral.
5. **Performance Risk**—This type of risk involves defining acceptance. Does the solicitation adequately describe the desired level of quality, the conditions under which acceptance will occur, and what type of inspection will be required?
6. **Price Risk**—Does the solicitation adequately define the payment terms and how and when the contractor will be paid? Does the price submitted by the contractor accurately reflect the cost required to meet the terms and conditions of the contract? (Pitzer and Thai 2009).

Assessing Contract Risks

Effective contract formation begins with the organization of the solicitation. Well-written and well-developed solicitations are key to forming contracts and will make the contract administration process more efficient. To do this, the procurement professional needs to start the process with the end in mind. The solicitation forms the foundation of the contract and is often included as part of the contract along with the supplier's bid or proposal response.

Procurement, through collaboration with the end user, should identify the risk factors associated with each procurement, analyze the probability of the risk occurring, and consider the potential impacts. Risk management plans should then be developed based on the decision to avoid, assume, or transfer the identified risks. Procurement professionals must have a strong understanding of the relationship between risk transfer and overall project cost. For example, risk transferred to the supplier will increase costs as the supplier will likely charge higher prices to mitigate its exposed risk.

Various types of risks will need to be considered when developing the solicitation. It is important to identify where the risks are located. Risks can be external and internal, as well as strategic and operational. The types of risks to consider include:

Strategic Risks

Strategic risks are risks that need to be considered in relation to medium- and long-term goals and objectives of the entity. Strategic risks can include:

- **Political Risks**—associated with the failure to deliver policy for the entity that it serves or failure to meet the local administration's policy commitments and requirements.

- **Economic Risks**—affecting the entity's ability to meet its financial commitments such as the effects of inflation, recession, or changes in market conditions.
- **Social Risks**—relates to the effects that changes in demographics, residential, or socioeconomic trends will have on the entity's ability to deliver appropriate services.
- **Technology Risks**—risks associated with the entity's ability to deal with the pace or scale of technological change or the ability to use technology to address changing demands.
- **Legislative/Regulatory Risks**—risks associated with current or potential changes in law.
- **Competitive Risks**—risks affecting the cost, quality, or competitiveness of a service such as failure to address a failing service through improvement or consideration of outsourcing.
- **Customer/Citizen Risks**—risks associated with failure to meet the current or changing needs and expectations of customers.

Operational Risks

Operational risks are risks that managers and employees may encounter while performing their work.

- **Professional Risks**—risks associated with the practice of public procurement such as failure to develop and update procurement policies and processes.
- **Financial Risks**—risks associated with the failure to procure in a manner that represents the most economical outcome for the entity such as failure to consider life cycle cost for an equipment item.
- **Legal**—risks related to following and complying with legislative and policy requirements such as failure to publicly advertise a procurement per local or state laws.
- **Physical**—risks related to fire, security, accident prevention, and health and safety such as failure to procure properly labeled or tested cleaning products.
- **Contractual**—risks associated with failure of contractors to deliver goods or services in compliance with specifications and contract terms.
- **Technological**—risks associated with reliance on operational equipment and systems such as an eProcurement system to deliver critical supply and materials acquisitions.
- **Environmental**—risks related to pollution, noise, or ongoing operations (NIGP, "Public Procurement Practice, Risk Management").

Types of Risk Factors

The decision regarding which risk factors to focus on will vary according to the entity's goals, the type and complexity of the goods and services being procured, and how critical a good or service is to the entity's operational needs. Risk factors that should be considered when planning for a procurement include:

- Escalating costs and availability of fuel, energy, and materials
- Possible financial instability of suppliers
- Lack of internal risk management capability on the part of the supplier
- Conflicts and disruption in the supply chain
- Exchange rate fluctuations
- Sole source arrangements and products with no available alternatives
- Focus on cost-cutting over quality performance
- Supplier failure to deliver on contractual obligations
- Changes in legislation or environmental requirements may affect the supplier base
- Changes that can result in obsolete technology or products (NIGP, "Public Procurement Practice, Risk Management").

Contract Development to Ensure Contractor Performance

The process of planning a contract works best in reverse, beginning with the end goal that needs to be achieved by the contract and ending with the inclusion of the correct contract language. Planning for the completion of a project allows for all key stakeholders to participate in and optimize a plan for completing the contract. Since the purpose of the contract is to achieve a result via a purchase, it is important to define the characteristics and requirements needed for successful delivery. Specifications are precise requirements that the awarded contractor must meet. The specifications are a precise description of the physical characteristics, quality, or desired outcomes of a commodity to be procured, which a supplier must be able to produce or deliver to be considered for award of a contract.

Delivery of goods and services to any entity can be uncertain, and, as mentioned earlier, some degree or type of risk will exist for every procurement. However, there are several actions Procurement can take to mitigate risks and protect the entity.

1. When developing a solicitation, if allowed by local laws, require information that will inform procurement of each supplier's qualifications

and capabilities. This can include mandatory minimum requirements such as a minimum number of years in business or qualitative information such as company background, relevant experience, and references of past work of a similar nature.

2. Be diligent in preparation when developing the solicitation. For a project to be completed in a manner that meets the quality needs of the entity, completed on time, and within budget, Procurement will need to research the goods and services being procured and work closely with the end user or department early in the process.
3. Include requirements in the solicitation that will ensure that the financial and surety interests of the entity are protected. Procurement can help protect their entity by ensuring that contractors have adequate insurance coverage. It is a common mistake to rely upon written promises of a contract where the contractor promises to hold harmless and indemnify the entity from unexpected or catastrophic events. While it is important to include these clauses in the contract document, they are not enough in themselves to protect the entity. Many smaller contractors will not have enough resources and capital to possibly indemnify the entity, and if serious injury or property damage occurs during performance under the contract, the contractor could go bankrupt and place the entity under considerable financial risk.

Procurement professionals must ensure that the awarded contractor provides documentation in the form of a certificate of insurance verifying the required types and levels of coverage. It is also very important that someone in the entity, such as procurement or risk management, monitors the policies to ensure that they stay in force during the entire term of the contract. Policies that lapse during the performance of the contractor can result in serious financial problems and risks to the entity. Each contract has its own particular risks, and the required insurance must be appropriate for the particular type of contracted work. It is important to note that the actual price of the contract has little bearing on the degree of project risks.

Some small projects, especially those that have to be performed when staff or students are present, can present a higher degree of risk and financial liability to the entity than a high-dollar, lower-risk project. For example, a small weight room or gym remodel with offices on the other side of the wall can impact staff and cause disruptions, especially if the areas share electrical or ventilation. While the purchase of a fire ladder truck is much more expensive but has lower risk to the entity.

Insurance policies and clauses can be very complex and often will require the assistance and expertise of professional risk managers. It is incumbent on the procurement professional to work closely with the end user or contracting officer to identify and analyze all potential risks. The best protection that procurement can provide to the entity in mitigating and managing risks is to ensure that all solicitations are well developed, detailed, and address the possible risks to the entity and that the awarded contractor is qualified and meets all the requirements of the solicitation.

Relationships with End Users and Contracting Officers

One aspect of public procurement that can be both challenging and rewarding is the fact that the procurement professional must work closely with several stakeholders during the solicitation development process. Stakeholders can include end users, department managers, contracting and project managers, architects, engineers, and sometimes elected officials, and they can vary from project to project. Stakeholders are anyone who can place a claim on an entity's resources or services or is affected by what the entity does or the services it provides. Developing positive working relationships and rapport with internal and external stakeholders can make the solicitation development and risks analysis processes much smoother and ultimately help to mitigate risks to the entity. It should also be noted that educating internal stakeholders is very important in establishing positive relationships between internal stakeholders and Procurement. Ensuring that stakeholders are knowledgeable about the value of procurement as well as procurement policies and procedures will help to reduce the risks associated with the procurement of goods and services (Robinson 2019).

Organization of a Basic Contract

Contract documents typically have a common flow that includes the following basic sections. Contracts do not need to be of a specific length to be valid and basic, and handwritten contracts are legally enforceable.

1. **Document Title**—states the purpose of the document and is placed at the top of the document.
2. **Description of the Document**—identifies the type of agreement indicated in the title such as "Contract for Custodial Services."
3. **Caption**—identifies the parties to the contract and the legal action that they are taking.

4. **Transitional Language**—language indicating that the parties have agreed to the terms of the contract.
5. **Recitals**—provide background information for the purpose of clarifying the parties' intentions. Recitals are sometimes known as the "whereas clauses," and they should be short and consist of a concise statement of the key facts.
6. **Definitions**—includes explanations of key terms of the contract.
7. **Operative Language**—consists of the terms that answer the what, where, when, and how questions related to the procurement.
8. **Obligations**—concern things that the contractor has promised to do and are signified by the word "must" or "shall." The term used will often be dependent on the preference of the entity's legal counsel.
9. **Representations and Warranties**—includes any representations about the contractor and the contractor's product that the entity has relied on in entering into the contract. Warranties may either be representations of current facts or may relate to a promise of something in the future.
10. **Declarations**—addresses the legal principles that govern the parties' agreement. Declarations are typically standard terms and conditions and any special clauses or conditions developed for the contract.
11. **Closing**—shows that all parties consent to the agreement and indicates where signatures are placed (King, Unesh, and Webb 2021).

Drafting Contract Terms and Conditions

The solicitation forms the foundation of the contract document, so the organization of the solicitation is just as important as it is for the basic contract. To avoid potential interpretation conflicts between parties, contracts must be written to fully disclose and define every detail of the agreement between the parties. Procurement should strive to establish terms and conditions that ensure that both parties to the contract are protected during contract execution.

Since the purpose of a contract is to define an agreement, it is important that the terms and conditions accurately and thoroughly define the rights and responsibilities of the parties involved in the contract. One key to developing a good contract document is the identification, development, and use of some general solicitation provisions that can be used consistently for every solicitation. Terms and conditions that are basic to every solicitation should be established as a standard boilerplate and are referred to as Standard Terms and Conditions. Boilerplate is a common term used to refer to standard clauses used in a solicitation or contract document, often prepared as a preprinted insert. Procurement, in consultation with the entity's legal counsel, identifies the legal issues that they want to be consistent in all contracts. An entity's laws will often require that certain terms appear in every contract. The general terms and conditions, and instructions to offerors, may be sections of a solicitation document's boilerplate. Other topics and information that can be included, but not limited to, as standard terms, include:

- **Definition of terms**
- **The law applicable to the contract**—generally laws governing the entity.
- **Authority of the procurement professional**
- **Public records laws**—state the contract is a public record.
- **Relationship of the parties**—provides that the contractor and its employees are independent contractors and not employees of the entity.
- **General indemnification**—states that the contractor may be required to defend the entity and be liable for any damages or other costs that the entity incurs resulting from the negligence of the contractor under the contract.
- **Subcontracts**—often require the authorized procurement professional's approval.
- **Compliance with applicable laws**—states that the contractor must comply with all laws applicable to the performance of the contract.
- **Force Majeure**—identifies situations in which the contractor will not be held liable for noncompliance of the contract such as Acts of God, pandemics, and labor strikes.
- **Nondiscrimination**—prohibits the contractor from discriminating based on race, color, religion, sex—including pregnancy, sexual orientation, or gender identity, national origin, disability, age—40 or older—or genetic information including family medical history.
- **Ethics**—includes policies on conflicts of interest, gratuities, bribes, and kickbacks.
- **Termination for default**—authorizes the entity to terminate a contract for nonperformance or defective performance.
- **Termination for convenience**—authorizes the entity to terminate a contract if it is deemed to be in the best interest of the entity, provided there is proper notice and provision for certain contractor costs and profits. Termination for convenience is usually exercised when a good or service is no longer needed, or funds are no longer available (King, Unesh, and Webb 2021).

Incorporation by Reference

Standard terms and conditions may be lengthy. One good way to reduce the size of the solicitation is to incorporate terms and conditions by reference. A term can be included in the solicitation stating: *This solicitation incorporates by reference the Standard Terms and Conditions, Form ________, and those terms and conditions are part of the solicitation as if it specifically set them forth.* Procurement may make them available at its office, by fax, or more commonly online (Christensen and Dawson 2021).

Special Terms and Conditions

Terms and conditions can vary according to the specific procurement. A group of terms and conditions that are unique to a particular procurement are referred to as Special Terms and Conditions. Examples of terms and conditions that can be addressed in this section of the solicitation include:

- Shipping terms
- Delivery and installation requirements
- Warranty requirements
- Entity preference programs applicable to the solicitation
- Performance and payment bonds
- Liquidated damages
- Minimum qualifications requirements
- Contract terms and renewal options.

Good Contract Writing Rules

Contracts must be written in plain language and in the present tense. A contract is a concise summary statement of all the terms, conditions, specifications, requirements, and other contents of the solicitation document. These, along with any drawings, plans, addenda, bonds, insurance certificates, and sometimes correspondence between the entity and successful supplier or contractor, will form and serve as the basis of the contract. The following guides should be used when writing a contract:

- Use clear, coherent, and consistent language.
- Divide and caption by section.
- Use present tense.

- Use everyday language.
- Provide remedies should the contractor not perform satisfactorily.
- Use readable typeface and size.
- Use active voice and direct statements.
- Focus on using specific words and avoid using general words. This will ensure that both parties have a clear understanding of expectations (King, Unesh, and Webb 2021).

If a contract dispute arises, a court will view the language for its objective meaning, which is the meaning that a reasonable person would give it and not necessarily the meaning that the drafter intended. When drafting contracts, procurement professionals should ask themselves the following questions:

- What am I trying to say?
- Could the language be interpreted in more than one way?
- How could I say it better? The procurement professional must ensure that contract language is specific and is clearly written. If the language is vague or unclear, the courts will rule against the drafter of the contract.

Planning for Contract Performance

During the contract formation phase, two critical plans should be developed that will be used in the contract management process.

1. **Contract Administration Plan (CAP)**—The CAP is part of the procurement planning process. The CAP defines how the contract will be administered and provides the framework for effective contract administration. The ultimate goal of the CAP is the clear communication of obligations and expectations of the contract. The plan should focus on who, what, when, where, and how the contract will be administered for successful completion. Each CAP will vary according to the scope, complexity, and risks associated with the project, and some routine contracts may only require a two- or three-page document discussing specific issues that should be addressed during contract administration. The CAP is a baseline document for the contract administration phase and should be developed in collaboration with Procurement and key project stakeholders. Some common topics that can be included in a Contract Administration Plan include:

    - description—describes the product or service
    - contract term or performance period

- delivery dates, if applicable
- contract pricing
- payment terms
- special terms and conditions or required documentation
- schedules and meetings
- work authorizations, if any
- warranty provisions
- personnel requirements
- roles and responsibilities
- critical milestones
- dispute provisions
- contract close-out requirements (Christensen and Dawson 2012).

2. **Performance Assessment Plan (PAP)**—During contract formation, procurement and the project team will need to define how work under the contract will be evaluated. The performance assessment plan provides specific information on how performance will be evaluated according to the standards required by the contract. At a minimum, the PAP should provide suppliers with:
   - what tasks will be evaluated
   - when will tasks be inspected
   - what standards will be used
   - how the assessment of performance will be made (King, Unesh, and Webb 2021).

Contract Templates

A contract template is a standard form of an agreement in which information can be filled in and used as a contract. Contract templates provide a structured framework that ensures the procurement process is transparent, fair, and in compliance with regulations. Templates are often used in forming contracts when the same agreement can be used to develop multiple contracts with very few changes. Templates can save time and resources that would normally be spent drafting contracts for each new purchase. Templates also provide uniformity and consistency in contract language. Key considerations in developing templates include:

1. **Identify the Procurement Method**—Is the procurement being solicited as an Invitation for Bids (IFB), Request for Proposals (RFP), Invitation to Tender (ITT)—in Canada, a Request for Quotes (RFQ),

Request for Qualifications (RFQu), or another method? The template that is chosen should align with the specific procurement method.

2. **Understand the Procurement Complexity**—Consider the complexity of the procurement. For a straightforward purchase, a simple template may be acceptable. More complex procurements may require a comprehensive template with detailed sections.
3. **Compliance with Regulations**—Ensure that the template conforms to relevant laws, regulations, and policies governing procurement in the entity. Compliance is crucial in maintaining the integrity of the procurement process.
4. **Incorporate Standard Sections**—Good templates will typically include standard sections such as introduction and background, scope of work or specifications, evaluation criteria, terms and conditions, and submission instructions.
5. **Flexibility for Customization**—Choose a template that allows flexibility for customization. Every procurement is unique, and the template should be adaptable to meet the specific requirements of the entity and Procurement.

Contract Signature Authority

Signature authority is the power given to an individual to act on behalf of the entity in legal, contractual, or financial transactions. It provides the authority for individuals such as a Purchasing Manager the legal right to enter into agreements, sign documents, and make binding decisions that directly impact the entity. Without this assigned type of authority, essential business transactions and the execution of contracts would be jeopardized, leading to possible confusion, disagreements, and potential financial losses.

Signature authority serves to ensure that the right people have the right level of authority to make decisions and make decisions on behalf of the entity. It serves to protect the entity by preventing unauthorized individuals from entering into contracts that could result in potential disputes, litigation, and damaged business relationships. This type of authority should be clearly defined and understood by all stakeholders and will enable entities to establish a strong foundation for operations and minimize the risk of fraudulent or unauthorized agreements.

Types of Signature Authority

Signature authority can take various forms with the most common types including general signature authority, limited authority, and specific signature authority. General signature authority grants an individual the power to act on an entity's behalf in any and all contractual matters. Limited signature authority restricts the authority to specific transactions or decisions. Specific signature authority applies to a particular type of agreement or document. Signature authority can also be limited by the dollar value of the contract.

Procurement professionals need to have a clear understanding of who has been granted signature authority in the entity and what type of authority they possess. Signature authority can vary greatly from entity to entity, and the authority may reside with the Chief Procurement Officer, Chief Financial Officer, or Chief Executive Officer. With some governmental entities, an elected official such as a mayor will have contract signature authority for contracts approved by the governing body (Asheychik 2023).

References

Asheychik, Olga. 2023. "Understanding Signature Authority." PandaDoc. https://www.pandadoc.com/blog/signatory-authority/#:~:text=Signatory%20authority%20grants%20specific%20individuals,on%20behalf%20of%20an%20entity

Christensen, Zac, and Nathan Dawson. 2021. "Contract Management and Performance." NIGP.

Ironclad Journal. 2024. "What is a Procurement Contract?" https://ironcladapp.com/journal/contracts/what-is-a-procurement-contract/

King, Ronald, Kalina N. Unesh, and Christine Webb. 2021. "CPPO Certification Preparation." NIGP.

NIGP. "Dictionary of Procurement Terms." https://www.nigp.org/dictionary-of-terms

NIGP. "Public Procurement Practice, Risk Management." https://www.nigp.org/resource/global-best-practices/Risk%20Management%20Best%20Practice.pdf

Pitzer, Jack, and Khi V. Thai. 2009. *Introduction to Public Procurement.* 3rd ed. Herndon, VA: National Institute of Governmental Purchasing.

Robinson, John. 2019. "Internal Customers: Advice and Experience." NIGP.

Part IV

Post-Award

Chapter 11

Contract Administration

The responsibilities and involvement of the procurement professional do not end with the award of a contract. After the contract award, procurement will be responsible for several functions and activities to ensure successful contract completion. Contract administration requires as much attention from the procurement professional as the other phases of the procurement cycle. However, its importance is often overlooked since it pertains to post-award activities.

This chapter will cover the key functional responsibilities of contract administration and detail strategies and processes that can be used to address quality assurance and contract compliance.

What is Contract Administration?

Contract administration is defined as the key functions that are performed after the parties have signed the contract (NIGP, "Dictionary of Terms"). Contract administration activities are goal oriented and are directed to

DOI: 10.4324/9781003566564-15

ensuring compliance with contract terms and conditions while focusing on the achievement of the stated outputs and outcomes of the contract. The primary functions of contract administration include ensuring that the required documents are received and maintained in the contract file, monitoring supplier performance, and resolving any issues related to the contract. Effective contract management is essential in ensuring that goods and services are received in the right quantity, are of the right quality, conform to contract requirements, and are received on time.

Contract administration activities include a wide range of responsibilities and can also involve managing contract changes, identifying and reporting violations, assisting in resolving contract disputes, and ensuring that all parties abide by contract terms and contractors are correctly compensated.

Public contracts are governed by local, state, and sometimes federal laws and regulations, and the procurement professional should make sure that they are familiar with and have a thorough understanding of the various contracting legal requirements. Policies should be established that define the roles and responsibilities of the procurement professional regarding contract administration and provide clear guidance on their authority (Button 2024).

Key Elements of Contract Administration

The key elements of contract administration include the following:

- **Ensuring maintenance of proper contract documentation**—Documentation will include information related to contractor performance, milestones, payments, and documents required to mitigate risks such as certificates of insurance, performance and payment bonds, contract awards, and approval of any change orders or contract amendments.
- **Managing performance of the contract, including contract compliance**—Managing contract performance can include ensuring milestones are achieved, ensuring compliance with risk mitigation strategies, tracking end user service and satisfaction levels, tracking disadvantaged business participation, reviewing payments for processing, and reconciling invoices against the contract price.
- **Resolving any contract issues or disputes**—Procurement should have the authority to monitor performance and contract compliance by both parties and take appropriate action. Compliance issues that procurement may need to address and resolve include missed or delayed deliveries, goods or services that do not meet specifications,

incomplete or unsatisfactory performance, change orders, unforeseen conditions, and disputes (NIGP, "Global Best Practice, Contract Administration").

Key Functional Responsibilities of Contract Administration

Although end user departments play a key role in contract administration, procurement professionals with specialized procurement knowledge are typically involved in this phase. Procurement's involvement will usually depend on the entity's organizational structure, the size of the entity, and the type and complexity of the procurement. The direct and indirect responsibilities of the procurement professional may include any of the following key functional activities.

Delivery, Follow-Up, and Expediting

Delivery requirements must be clearly stated in the contract and fully understood by all parties. The importance of the delivery schedule and completion of milestones must be emphasized to the contractor. Procurement must ensure that the delivery date and time, the free on board delivery point (FOB), any special delivery or installation requirements, and penalties for non-delivery or late delivery are detailed and clearly expressed in the contract. Delivery terms and conditions cannot be vague or ambiguous. Any such vagueness or ambiguity must be eliminated before issuing a solicitation and proceeding with the contract. Procurement must collaborate with the end user to ensure that delivery terms are not unreasonable and meet the entity's needs. Unreasonable delivery requirements can increase the likelihood of risks and can add costs to the entity.

"Follow-up" and "expediting" are often used interchangeably and have the same basic objective of ensuring on-time delivery. However, they have different meanings. Follow-up involves regular communication with the supplier to review and monitor the status of an order to assure compliance by the supplier. Expediting involves an attempt to improve or reduce the agreed-upon delivery time or schedule.

When follow-up efforts are unsuccessful and deliveries have become delinquent, procurement must consider the following options:

- Authorize additional time for delivery.
- Explore alternative transportation and delivery arrangements.

- Cancel the order and seek another source.
- Accept a substitution offered by the supplier (Pitzer and Thai 2009).

Procurement should consider several factors before deciding on an option that will be in the best interest of the entity. These factors include:

- The needs and requirements of the end user.
- The critical nature of the goods or services required.
- The degree of control over delivery that is available to the supplier. Are conditions such as extreme and unusual weather events or labor strikes that are beyond the control of the supplier causing the delay in deliveries?
- The availability and costs of the item(s) if purchased from another supplier.
- The time required to receive the item(s) if ordered from another supplier (Pitzer and Thai 2009).

With all delinquent deliveries, it is important to document the reasons for delivery issues because the information may be needed to evaluate future offers submitted by the supplier(s) involved (University of Minnesota University Policy Library 2025).

Receiving and Inspection

The purpose of receiving and inspection activities is to determine that the contract is fully performed by ensuring that the product or service received conforms to the specifications and is received in the correct quantity, correct quality, and on time. Proper receiving and inspection methods are critical components of contract administration that provide for early detection of defects and allow for corrective action to be taken. Procurement should have authority over receiving and inspection, with actual tasks delegated to the end user. Procurement must have standard procedures and forms to use for receiving and inspection activities.

Generally, the central procurement office delegates most inspection and receiving tasks to the end user but is available to help when needed. However, in some large governmental entities, the central procurement office has trained inspection staff. Trained staff can assist the entity with inspection and testing, make periodic spot checks, and are typically responsible for inspections of high-dollar procurements or specific items.

The inspection function has three types of categories:

- **In-process inspection**—This type of inspection occurs at the contractor's location while the work is in progress to ensure that the work to date conforms to specifications and contractual agreements.
- **Receiving inspection**—Receiving inspection occurs at the end user's receiving site after supplies are delivered to ensure compliance with specifications and contractual agreements.
- **Final inspection**—This type of inspection involves examining an item to ensure that the item conforms to specifications and contractual requirements before making final payments. Final inspections typically occur in construction, heavy equipment, complex systems, and service contracts.

When it is necessary to conduct a technical inspection, a decision must be made as to whether the inspection is based on attributes or variables. With attribute inspection, an item is either acceptable or unacceptable because it does or does not meet certain specified or required characteristics such as color or size. Variable inspection allows for acceptance within certain tolerances and the item is acceptable or unacceptable based on predetermined factors, such as the time it takes for a computer to boot up or the accuracy of a thermometer within two degrees. A decision on the type of inspection should be based on how critical the quality characteristics are to the entity and the cost and time required for the inspection. Most inspections are conducted on an attribute basis since these inspections are usually faster and less expensive than variable inspections. (Pitzer and Thai, 2009)

Testing

With the purchase of more complex materials or equipment, it may be necessary to include testing as part of a technical inspection. The procurement professional should be aware that even when using detailed, technical specifications for the procurement of some materials such as chemical products or lubricants, it may be difficult to determine if the supplier is furnishing materials that conform to the specifications. With these types of products, it may be necessary to test the materials for a specified time period or conduct laboratory testing. Testing can be time-consuming and requires technical equipment and skilled personnel but may be justified for some materials.

Quality Assurance

During contract administration, quality must be managed carefully to prevent an adverse effect on other operating areas. Different types of materials and equipment will require different types of inspections and skill sets to determine adequate quality. For example, a single individual may be able to determine adequate quality for small purchases or equipment items by a simple examination of an item. For more complex procurements such as software acquisitions, highly technical equipment, or construction projects, specialized teams may be required to determine if the desired level of quality has been achieved.

Defect-prevention strategies are usually more effective and more efficient than defect-detection methods. Prevention methods are proactive strategies that analyze data to predict and control process behavior. The most common approach is statistical process control, a technique to identify the impending production of an unacceptable product before it occurs. Prevention methods make it possible to identify causes of possible defects so that they can be corrected and the process stabilized. A statistical process control system is one of the key building blocks used in implementing a strategy of continuous product or service improvement, which is the focus of quality management. (Pitzer and Thai, 2009)

Methods for Proper Acceptance, Remedies, or Rejection

Proper inspection and testing typically lead to a conclusion that can result in acceptance, rejection, or remedies to address defects. Sufficient time must be allotted for the inspection of goods promptly on arrival, including time to conduct any tests outlined in the specifications.

- **Acceptance**—The acceptance process is a critical function of contract administration. Acceptance entitles the supplier to payment and limits the rights of the entity to seek remedies for defects that are found at a later date. An acceptance clause should be included in the solicitation document during the solicitation process, and at a minimum, within the contract document executed between the entity and the contractor.
- **Rejection**—Rejection is the formal process used by a public entity to officially notify the contractor that a product or service is defective and will not be accepted. Remedies may or may not be pursued before

issuing the official notice, although the options are similar. It is very important to determine the conditions for proper rejection and acceptance. Once a good or service is accepted, an entity's rights to rejection are very limited.

Post-Acceptance Rights

Acceptance substantially limits an entity's ability to reject goods or services if a defect is found at a later date. One of the following conditions must exist for an entity to seek a remedy after a good or service has been accepted.

- **Latent defects**—These defects exist at the time an item is accepted but could not have been discovered through normal inspection procedures.
- **Fraud**—All of the following factors must be present for a public entity to revoke acceptance based on fraud.
  - Misrepresentation of fact, actual or implied, or the concealment of a material fact.
  - Knowledge of reckless or wanton disregard of the facts.
  - Intent to mislead the entity into relying on misrepresentations.
  - Injury suffered by the public entity.
- **Gross mistakes amounting to fraud**—A major mistake by a contractor that is so serious and uncalled for as to not be expected or justified. The requirements to prove a gross mistake are the same as fraud except for proving there was deliberate intent to mislead.
- **Warranties**—Warranty clauses provide the entity a remedy for latent or patent defects discovered after acceptance.

Remedies for Defects in Non-Conforming Products or Services

When defects are discovered in products or services, the public entity can consider three options for seeking remedies before acceptance.

- **Require the contractor to correct the deficiencies**—The contract should include a clause that addresses the correction of defective work by the contractor. The clause should include a statement requiring the contractor to replace or correct defective work found not to conform to the contract requirements at no charge to the entity unless, in the public interest, the entity consents to accept work with an appropriate adjustment in price.

- **Price reduction, acceptance of minor nonconformities**—The doctrine of substantial completion permits an entity to accept a product or service with minor deficiencies or nonconformities when the correction would cause economic waste or financial loss to the contractor. However, the entity is entitled to monetary compensation from the contractor based on the decreased value of the work or the amount of the savings realized by the contractor resulting from the minor deficiencies. Accepting a minor nonconformity does not provide relief for correcting similar defects on existing or future contracts.
- **Correction of defects by the public entity or owner**—Inspection and acceptance clauses typically allow the public entity to repair, replace, correct defective work, or perform the services and charge or offset the costs to the contractor. This remedy can occur after the contractor is allowed to correct the deficiencies and fails to make corrections within a reasonable time period (King, Unesh, and Webb 2021).

Cure Notice

If a contractor fails to perform some provisions of the contract other than those dealing with timely delivery, or fails to make progress that impacts performance altogether, the public entity is required to give the contractor written notice of the deficiency and allow a specified time for the contractor to cure or correct the failure before issuing a termination notice. The procurement professional should emphasize to end users the importance of clearly documenting problems or deficiencies in a contractor's performance. The public entity should reserve the right, unilaterally, to extend the time for cure if it is in the best interest of the entity without waiving the right to default.

Delays in Contract Performance

One of the most common problems in contract administration is unanticipated delays. Delays can result in increased costs, decreased efficiency, and disruptions in critical public services, such as a public school not being completed in time for the opening of the new school year, and can result in failure of the entire project. Failure by a contractor to meet a delivery schedule usually originates from problems that occur earlier in the course of work. Therefore, progressive action should be taken as soon as a potential delay is identified. Actions include determining if the delay will impact delivery or timely completion, the duration of the delay, determining fault, and selecting an appropriate course of action to resolve the problem.

Types of Delays

The following are types of common contract delays.

Excusable Delays

Excusable delays occur as the result of events or circumstances that are beyond the control of the contractor and can affect the contract price, terms, and conditions. These events are not caused by contractor negligence and may excuse delays in performance during the events and under certain conditions caused by them. *Force Majeure* is a term that includes occurrences that are often described as Acts of God or disruptive conditions for which a contractor will not be held responsible. Excusable delays can include extraordinary weather events, epidemics, labor strikes, and sudden legal changes that can prevent one or both parties from fulfilling their obligations under the contract.

Non-Excusable Delays

Non-excusable delays are foreseeable within the contractor's control, and usually result from some deficiency on the part of the contractor. These delays can result from financial difficulties, lack of materials, lack of equipment, lack of personnel, and lack of knowledge.

Compensable Delays

Compensable delays are typically beyond the contractor's control and for which they are entitled to a time extension and additional compensation. Compensable delays are commonly caused by constructive changes which are actions or inactions on the part of the public entity that have not been made through a formal change order but have caused the contractor to perform additional work outside the scope of the existing contract. Common causes of compensable delays include interference, failure to cooperate, nondisclosure of important information, orders to accelerate work, defective or ambiguous specifications, or problems with contract interpretation (King, Unesh, and Webb 2021).

Payment Processes

When the work performed under a contract is successfully completed and has been accepted by the entity, the contractor will need to be paid. Payment of invoices is a key function of contract administration, and prompt payment is important in maintaining good relationships with suppliers. It is also a requirement for receiving some types of United States federal funding.

The contracting officer is typically responsible for enforcing payment rights and responsibilities during contract administration. Entities that pay promptly normally receive good service each time that they conduct business. Prompt payment is also important when there is a discount offered for timely payment or when there might be a penalty for late payment. Procurement should maintain good relationships with the entity's accounts payable and finance departments and emphasize the importance of paying suppliers and contractors promptly.

Several methods exist for paying invoices. These methods apply whether payment is being made the traditional way or electronically. The types of payment methods are as follows:

- **Full payment**—When the goods ordered have been received or services rendered have been determined to meet contractual requirements, payment of the total amount of the invoice is made within the timeframe stipulated in the contract.
- **Advance payment**—Typically, unless they are approved, most entities prohibit the payment of contracted goods and services before receipt. However, with some complex procurements for customized equipment and projects with high startup costs, it may be necessary to make one or more advanced payments to facilitate final agreements or enhance contractual operations. Hazardous waste clean-up is an example of a project where advance payments may be necessary. Advanced payments have also been authorized by some entities to assist small and disadvantaged business firms by providing the necessary capital to start work and perform some contracts. As a word of caution, such payments should be used judiciously since they introduce the possibility of a financial risk, and the entity loses an important leveraging tool if the goods or services are not delivered. To counter the potential risk, some entities require a performance bond before payment is provided.
- **Partial payments**—These payments are directly related to the accomplishment of completed portions of a contract or partial delivery of materials. As a result, there may be several partial payments for several deliveries under one contract.

- **Progress payments**—Progress payments are made to assure acceptable performance and progress on a contract. Payments are made commensurate with the progress made on the contract and serve as a method for financing the contractor throughout the life of the contract. Usually, the aggregate amount of the progress payments is restricted to a percentage of the total contract price.
- **Milestone payments**—These payments are very similar to progress payments and are tied to predetermined milestones. Milestones represent specific events that must be completed at various stages of the contract. Milestone payments are commonly used in construction contracts and software system installations.
- **Assignment of payment**—This is an arrangement where payment is made to an entity other than the contracted supplier of goods and services. The assignment of payments may be made as a result of a contractor's poor credit history or one of the contractor's creditors bringing legal action against the supplier.
- **Incentive contracts**—Incentive contracts include payment terms that allow an entity to pay for the performance of predetermined goals such as reducing costs, improving delivery, and performance above the level specified in the contract. An example of an incentive contract would be providing an incentive payment to a design engineer for early completion of the design for a new bridge or the early completion of an interstate construction project. (King, Unesh, and Webb 2021)

Contract Modifications

With rare exceptions, most contracts will undergo modifications. Modifications may be necessary for many reasons and can include change orders, amendments, and escalation and de-escalation of price. Modifications can alter routine administrative matters within the contract, correct minor errors, or make substantive changes to the terms of the contract by the parties. All modifications can be classified as either bilateral or unilateral.

- **Bilateral modifications** are changes to a contract that require the agreement and signature of both parties. They are typically made when circumstances change the delivery of the contract and are often related to some alteration of one or more substantive terms of the contract. Substantive changes can cause significant changes to the rights and obligations of both parties, and the bilateral execution serves as a protective mechanism so both parties are aware of the nature of the changes.

- **Unilateral modifications** only require execution by the entity's Contracting Officer, and the contractor is not required to sign the modification for it to have full force and effect. Unilateral modifications can occur for two reasons: (1) the right to unilaterally modify the contract has been given to the public entity in the contract itself, or (2) the modification is for a minor purpose (Christensen and Dawson 2021; King, Unesh, and Webb 2021).

Change Order Authority

In most public entities, the authority to issue change orders resides with the Contracting Officer or Chief Procurement Officer. However, procurement professionals need to have a clear understanding of the legal and policy requirements of their entity regarding change order authority and their right to delegate this authority to other procurement professionals. Some public entities have encountered major problems by the actions of unauthorized individuals who have directed a contractor to perform additional work or make a change to contract terms.

Breach of Contract

Breach of contract occurs when one or more parties to the contract fail to perform under the terms of the contract. As previously mentioned under the section *Remedies for Defects in Non-Conforming Products and Services*, a minor failure or deficiency on the part of the contractor or supplier does not permit the entity to avoid the obligation of payment and could provide for a price reduction caused by the defective performance of the contractor. Generally, if a breach is major, all legal remedies including cancellation of the contract can be applied. If the breach is minor or trivial, more limited remedies are available and the contract may not be canceled. Examples of minor breaches can include late deliveries, minor damage, or a shortage in quantity.

Contract Termination

Sometimes circumstances are such that a contract must be prematurely terminated. Termination is a drastic adjustment of the contractual relationship and may be grounds for future litigation. Procurement should proactively include clauses in the solicitation and contract documents that protect the entity from poor contractor performance. These clauses can include warranties, performance bonds, liquidated damages, and grounds for termination for default. Termination is a very complex process and should only begin after thoughtful consideration of the consequences with input from a variety of sources, including legal counsel and the impacted end user. It is important to note that the contractor has the right to appeal any decision made by the procuring entity.

Termination for Default

At the onset, successful contract administration requires that disputes be handled tactfully, effectively, and promptly. The goal of contract administration is to settle claims by mutual agreement. A termination for default clause allows either contracting party the right to cancel the contract, either in whole or in part, resulting from the failure of the other party to perform satisfactorily. The right to terminate for default hinges upon two prerequisites: (1) reasonable grounds for termination, and (2) noncompliance with several procedural notification requirements. This type of termination requires the entity to prove that there is a reasonable likelihood that the contractor will not complete performance before the delivery deadline date. Termination for default should be exercised as a last resort, and discretion should be exercised to ensure that it is the best course of action, that no excusable conditions exist, and that the right to terminate has not been waived through some unintentional action.

Before terminating a contract for default, the procurement professional should consider whether it would be more effective to withhold payment until satisfactory performance is demonstrated, whether there is a reliable alternative source of supply, the added cost of re-procurement, and whether continued performance under a revised delivery schedule would better serve the entity's interests.

Termination for Convenience

Termination for convenience allows a public entity to terminate a contract when the entity's requirements have changed, such as when the contracted goods or services are no longer needed or funding is no longer available. The contractor's performance has no bearing on the decision to terminate for convenience. The contractor is limited to recovering costs and profit only for work completed up to the date of termination. The contractor is not allowed to recover any anticipated profits that will not be realized as a result of termination.

Careful consideration should be given before including a termination for convenience clause in the solicitation document. Depending on the type of product or service purchased, a contractor may be hesitant to respond to a solicitation containing a termination for convenience clause or may include higher pricing. Alternatively, they may counter with their own termination for convenience clause. For example, a contractor submitting an offer for a multi-year grounds maintenance contract may increase pricing out of concern that they may need to purchase additional equipment and have no assurances that the entity will continue payments for the term of the contract. It is recommended that procurement professionals inform prospective offerors of the conditions under which a termination for convenience clause would be exercised (Christensen and Dawson 2021; Formella et al. 2021).

The Contract Transition Plan

Once a contract is awarded, a process should commence to implement the plan with minimal issues or disruption to the entity. A transition plan identifies what is to be done, by whom, and by when. Consideration must be given to the requirements for both the new contractor to transition in and the current contractor to transition out. Not all contracts require a transition plan, but larger, more complex projects or services need a plan to ensure that the incoming and outgoing contractors understand the transition requirements and that there is no lapse in services or coverage to the entity.

Examples of contracts in which a plan will increase the effectiveness of the transition process include janitorial services, ambulance services, security monitoring services, and hazardous waste management services.

Senior contract administrators are more likely to be administering these types of contracts, but it is recommended that procurement professionals be aware of the processes involved (Christensen and Dawson 2021).

Contract Close-Out

Contract close-out is part of the performance monitoring phase of contract management. Close-out occurs when the goods or services required in the contract are accepted, performance is complete, and final payment is made. Contract close-out is an important process for complex procurements, particularly those involving capital projects and extensive service provisions. Or it may be a simple process, such as when a price quote or completed purchase order for simple goods or services is included in the contract file.

By performing a formal close-out process, the procurement professional ensures that both the contractor and entity have completed their contractual obligations and that the contract file contains all records and documents to support the actions taken by the entity during the performance of the contract. In addition, the close-out process ensures the entity has fulfilled its fiduciary responsibility to the public in the expenditure of the public's resources (NIGP, "Global Best Practice, Contract Closeout").

References

Button, Ken. 2024. "Contract Administration vs, Contract Management: How to Go from Administration to Management." June 21. ContractSafe.

Christensen, Zac, and Nathan Dawson. 2021. "Contract Management and Performance." NIGP.

Formella, Richard J., John Adler, T. Suzette Moore, Theresa Bauccio-Teschlog, and Willam J. Tommie. 2021. "Construction Procurement Specialization." NIGP.

King, Ronald, Kalina N. Unesh, and Christine Webb. 2021. "CPPO Certification Preparation." NIGP.

NIGP. "Dictionary of Terms." https://www.nigp.org/dictionary-of-terms

NIGP. "Global Best Practice, Contract Administration." https://www.nigp.org/resource/global-best-practices/global-best-practice-contract-administration.pdf

NIGP. "Global Best Practice, Contract Closeout." https://www.nigp.org/resource/global-best-practices/global-best-practice-contract-closeout.pdf?dl=true

Pitzer, Jack, and Khi V. Thai. 2009. *Introduction to Public Procurement.* 3rd ed. Herndon, VA: National Institute of Governmental Purchasing.

University of Minnesota University Policy Library. 2025. "Administering Contracts for the Purchase of Goods and Services." https://policy.umn.edu/finance/professionalservice-proc03

Chapter 12

Documentation and Reporting

A critical function of public procurement is ensuring that all documents related to a particular procurement are properly maintained and accurate reports are developed that will measure and track the progress of procurement activities. Procurement must ensure that the entire procurement process is managed and supported within the legal framework of the entity's legal requirements. This chapter will cover the importance of proper documentation and reporting, the various manuals and documents essential for effective procurement management, and examine how an effective reporting system can enable Procurement to assess progress in accomplishing the goals and objectives of the entity.

Transparency

Transparency is a core principle of the public procurement process. Transparency can be defined as access to clear, precise, and accurate information that is understandable to all. The goal of transparency is to provide sufficient information related to a particular procurement to suppliers, contractors,

 DOI: 10.4324/9781003566564-16

service providers, and private citizens unless there is a valid legal reason to keep certain information confidential. The way the procurement organization conducts its business transactions affects public opinion and the public's trust. An open and transparent procurement process is essential for any public entity and can result in increased competition and value to the entity.

Transparency can be exhibited in many practices, including published policies and procedures manuals, public advertisement of solicitation, and detailed contract files (NIGP, "Public Procurement Practice, Transparency in Public Procurement"; The Coalition of Government Procurement 2023).

Documentation

To be effective in a procurement operation, all types of documentation must be current, accurate, detailed, indexed, and easily accessible. Proper documentation can be especially challenging because of high workloads and many smaller entities having limited staff. The use of technology and automated procurement systems has made documentation more efficient and streamlined, but Procurement must commit to having the discipline and structure necessary for efficient document management and organization. There are three key elements to procurement documentation: procurement and policy manuals, bid and proposal file checklist, and management reports.

Procurement and Policy Manuals

Policy and procedure manuals must be directly related to an entity's enabling laws and regulations that establish the structure and govern the entity. Manuals must be well organized and should include a clear definition of the purpose of each manual. To provide operational impact and support the procurement operation, the entity's Chief Executive Officer, e.g. School District Superintendent, City Manager, Mayor, etc., should endorse the manual. Since changes are common because of legislative changes or operational changes, manuals should be flexible and produced in a manner that will easily facilitate revision. To enhance transparency and accessibility to the public, many entities maintain their manuals in electronic format and post them on their websites.

When considering the structure of procurement manuals, the procurement official should consider the following terms:

- **Regulation**—A statement by a governing body to implement, interpret, or prescribe a law or policy. Regulations are published by governing bodies to clarify their interpretation of the law and how the law will be implemented.

- **Policy**—A governing set of principles or plan that establishes the general parameters for an entity to follow in carrying out its responsibilities; guiding principles or a high-level overall plan establishing the general goals and acceptable procedures of an entity.
- **Procedure**—The detailed series of related activities that must be completed and the sequence in which they must be done to accomplish a given task. Procedures provide step-by-step instructions for specific tasks and can include a checklist or process steps to follow (Pitzer and Thai 2009).

Policy Manuals

All public entities should develop a comprehensive procurement policy manual that clearly defines authority and responsibility and establishes clear guidelines for procurement professionals to follow when carrying out their duties. Policy manuals contain the key provisions of the enabling legislation and are used to develop a direct relationship between the legal foundation of an entity's procurement program and the procurement rules and policies that guide the entity. Well-developed procurement policy manuals should establish the legal authority of the procurement function, enable uniform procurement policies through the entity, ensure fair and equitable treatment of all parties involved in the procurement process, and build public confidence in public procurement.

Since laws, regulations, and organizational structures can change over time, Procurement should conduct a periodic review of the continued relevance and applicability of procurement policies.

Procedure Manuals

Procedure manuals are written with a greater level of detail and are intended not to just provide guidance but to provide detailed, step-by-step instructions required for completing a procurement action. They outline action-oriented procedures that help improve efficiency, effectiveness, and communication with end user departments. Procedure manuals are distributed to a larger audience and are used by procurement staff and operational staff in departments.

Procedure manuals should be tailored to meet an entity's requirements and should include:

- The procurement goals, objectives, and responsibilities.

- A step-by-step outline of the procurement process including the processing of requisitions, solicitations and price quotes, bid evaluation and awards, issuance of purchase orders and contracts, and contract administration.
- A step-by-step guide on property and supply management programs including inventory control and disposition or transfer of surplus property.
- Other special procedures, including the use of cooperative purchasing programs, state or federal contracts, term contracts, and processing of invoices.
- A list of important forms used in the procurement process, instructions to bidders and general conditions governing contracting, and a glossary of key terms used in the manual.

Supplier or Vendor Manuals

Supplier manuals, sometimes called "How to do Business with the Government" manuals, contain important information to help suppliers better understand the entity's procurement processes and enhance their business opportunities. An effective supplier manual should provide the following information:

- General information about the entity.
- Key contacts with telephone numbers or email addresses.
- How to identify bidding opportunities.
- Describe how the solicitation process is conducted.
- Detail how bids and proposals are to be submitted.
- Provide the standards of conduct expected of procurement staff and vendors including ethical requirements.
- Provide the rules governing communication between suppliers and end user departments (NIGP, "CPPB Prep Guide").

Bid and Proposal File Checklist

A checklist is a useful tool that lists various steps and documents that need to be included in the procurement file. The type of goods and services being procured can determine the required checklist items and must reflect the entity's legal and policy requirements for a particular type of procurement. For example, the procurement file for a solicitation for a large construction project will likely require more documentation than the file for the purchase of new office furniture. Checklists ensure that the proper documentation is maintained and help support award decisions and prepare procurement for compliance audits.

Listed below is an example of a typical construction solicitation checklist for construction services solicitations for a Georgia local government. Reminder, procurement professionals must be careful when developing their bid and proposal checklists to ensure that the checklist items include all documentation that aligns with the entity's legal and policy requirements.

Construction Bid File Checklist

1. ________ Copy—Public Advertisement
2. ________ Advertisement—Georgia Procurement Registry (> $100,000.00)
3. ________ Solicitation Posted to Website
4. ________ Copy of Solicitation
5. ________ Pre-Bid or Pre-Proposal Sign-Sheet
6. ________ Copies of Addenda
7. ________ Bid or Proposal Tabulation
8. ________ Bids or Proposals Received
9. ________ Evaluation Scoring Summary for RFPs and RFQs
10. ________ Certificate of Insurance
11. ________ Bid Bond and Copy of unsuccessful bidders bid bonds
12. ________ Performance and Payment Bonds
13. ________ Notice of Intent to Award
14. ________ Executed Contract and Purchase Order
15. ________ Copy—Approved Change Orders or Supplemental Agreements

Management Reports

Well-developed management reports are essential for an effective public procurement operation. Reporting is a technique for measuring progress or controlled procurement activities from collected data. Management reports enable procurement professionals to analyze data to access progress and readjust activities, if needed, to achieve the entity's goals and objectives. A reporting system should allow an entity to interpret data quickly and meaningfully. Well-developed reports consist of measurements against defined targets.

One of the main benefits of procurement reports is their ability to contribute to cost savings. Through an analysis of procurement spend and processes, procurement can identify ways for cost reduction and increased cost-effectiveness. This can result in more volume purchasing, identifying more cost-effective alternatives, or utilizing cooperative contracts that can lead to cost savings. In addition, procurement management reports can result in enhanced decision-making, risk mitigation related to supplier stability and market conditions, and greater transparency by providing a clear summary of procurement activities.

Since reporting requirements continually change and evolve, reporting systems and mechanisms should be flexible and continually refined. All reports should be practical and useful. Reports that do not furnish useful data and are seldom accessed offer no value in monitoring and improving procurement processes and procedures. With the availability of automated procurement systems, most reports are now generated electronically and are tailored to a specific procurement official or management need (Pitzer and Thai 2009).

Planning Performance Measures

For procurement professionals to know "what" they are measuring, accurate planning must be completed before developing the performance metrics. Ways to accomplish this include:

- Obtaining input from key stakeholders, those to whom performance will be reported.
- Ensuring that measures are simple and relevant to the intended audience.
- Ensuring that measures are specific, consistently applied, and within the control of the procurement function.
- Identifying any dependencies among other functions or departments that will be related to the measures.
- Defining a specific time period for reporting measures that are directly related to the attainment of goals and objectives in the strategic plan.
- Ensuring that the measure represents a balance of the types of measures critical to achieving the specific goals and objectives.

Levels to be Assessed Using Performance Measurement

The performance measurement process can be used at various levels throughout procurement to assess progress toward the completion of the strategic plan. Measures should address:

- Individual performance
- Group performance
- Organizational performance
- Supplier performance. (NIGP, "Global Best Practice—Performance Measurement")

Efficiency versus Effectiveness

These concepts were addressed briefly in Chapter Seven, but let's take a more detailed look at their differences and how both are crucial for the success of the procurement operation. Efficiency represents the ratio of inputs to outputs and refers to maximizing the time, effort, and resources one puts into a specific activity or function. Efficient procurement practices utilize fewer resources to deliver similar or better results and are often defined as the ability to accomplish a desired result with the least amount of time, monetary cost, and effort.

Effectiveness is defined as the degree to which an activity is successful in producing a desired, positive result. Effectiveness focuses on measuring the degree to which procurement meets its goals and objectives and is often associated with improved service quality and customer satisfaction. Although efficiency and effectiveness are different concepts, they can complement each other and drive success. Increasing efficiency can often result in increased effectiveness. For example, implementing a purchasing card program can increase efficiency by reducing the number of purchase orders issued and improving delivery times. Since end users will be empowered to make small purchases quickly with faster deliveries, the program will result in increased effectiveness. To balance the two, procurement should be strategic and consider both concepts when developing goals and objectives, assigning tasks, and establishing deadlines (Pitzer and Thai 2009).

Audits

An audit is a detailed review and examination of documents and business processes by either internal staff or independent experts. Audits conclude with a detailed report and may include a management letter or findings. Practically all public procurement departments will be required to undergo periodic procurement audits, and procurement professionals must maintain detailed, up-to-date files that provide readily available documents and data. Participating in an audit can help procurement staff maintain a professional approach that promotes effective stewardship of public funds and results in the best value for constituents served by the entity. Procurement may be the direct focus of an audit or may be brought into the audit of other departments by providing supporting documentation and data (NIGP, "Public Procurement Practice, Audits").

The three primary audit types are as follows, and each type will generate relevant questions.

Compliance Audit

Compliance audits are conducted to determine the degree of adherence to established laws, regulations, policies, and procedures, and represent the most common type of audit used to review the procurement function. During a compliance audit, auditors will evaluate the procurement function by addressing the following questions:

- Are policies, regulations, and laws being adhered to in procurement processes?
- Were funds spent in accordance with grant or contract requirements?
- Were purchases conducted in a manner that met the policy requirements for competitive quotes or solicitations?
- Has procurement prepared and maintained records of relevant documents including purchase orders, requisitions, and contracts?
- Is delegated authority clearly outlined in the published documents?
- Did procurement document non-compliance when it was identified internally, and were necessary measures taken to ensure future compliance?

Financial Audit

Financial audits are conducted to determine whether all funds are properly accounted for to verify the accuracy of financial statements, and to ensure that financial transactions are recorded and shown accurately in all accounts. Financial audits will typically address the following questions:

- Were public funds spent on goods or services specified in the grant or contract?
- What documents does the entity have that support contracts and grant expenditures?
- Did all financial transactions, including cash, follow the proper procedures, and were those transactions documented?
- Are early payment discounts taken if offered by suppliers?
- Are suppliers being paid promptly?
- Does the entity have appropriate internal checks and balances, and separation of duties for procurement, contracting, and payment?

Performance Audit

Performance audits review all operations of an entity and provide a systematic and independent review of the management and activities of the organization related to the economic, efficient, and effective achievement of objective criteria. A performance audit reviews all operations of a public unit or department and is an increasingly common means of ensuring that officials entrusted with the management of public services and programs are held accountable. Performance audits address the following questions:

- Was departmental performance measured, and did those measurements show efficiency, economy, and effectiveness?
- Was supplier performance measured, and did those measurements show adherence to contract terms, requirements, and conditions?
- What is the level of maverick or rogue spending throughout the entity, and did it lead to supplier allegations of breach of contract? Maverick or rogue spending is when an end user department makes a purchase that does not follow its procurement rules.
- Are solicitations for replacement contracts being started in time to execute a new contract before the expiration of the existing contracts?
- Do procurement professionals and officials receive regular professional development training, and are the entity's employees trained on the procurement process? (NIGP, "Public Procurement Practice, Audits"; Pitzer and Thai 2009).

Preparing for and Participating in an Audit

As stated earlier, procurement professionals must maintain detailed, up-to-date, contract files that are readily accessible. One of the best ways to be prepared for an audit is by conducting regular self-assessments and contract file reviews to ensure that the proper documentation is being maintained. The foundation for audit preparedness and effective self-assessment programs lies in the procurement professional's knowledge of and adherence to laws, regulations, policies, procedures, and processes. In addition, procurement professionals must be knowledgeable of the entity's retention laws and regulations.

Self-assessments should be scheduled regularly to ensure that procurement is operating with efficiency, economy, and effectiveness, and in compliance with applicable laws, regulations, and policies. When determining areas of self-assessment, senior management should include the entire staff. Assigning areas of assessment to staff members builds trust and demonstrates transparency. Assignments may include, but not be limited to, small purchases, sole source and emergency purchases, competitive solicitations, term contracts, procurement cards, and written policies and procedures.

Participating in an audit will differ depending on the type of audit and whether the audit is conducted by internal audit staff, an external auditing firm, a federal auditor, or an independent expert. When an audit is requested, the audit letter usually includes the objective or reason for the audit and a request for specific information and documentation. Procurement managers may also be requested to complete a questionnaire before the start of the audit. When audit personnel arrive, they should be introduced to the procurement staff. Audits can take a significant amount of time, sometimes several weeks or months, and procurement should be prepared to familiarize auditors with documents, describe processes, answer questions, and discuss findings (NIGP, "Public Procurement Practice, Audits").

Contract Close-Out and Closing Out the File

Contract close-out occurs when the performance of the contract is complete. The contract file serves as the official file within the archives, and the procurement professional must ensure that all necessary information is included in the file. Documentation will be relevant to the type and complexity of the procurement, and the close-out file should contain:

- Official copy of the contract and all modifications and changes to the contract, related solicitation documents, and Notice of Award
- Documentation that all reports, deliverables, and items have been received and accepted
- Performance and progress reports
- Validated payment documents
- Documents related to intellectual property
- Required bonds, certificates of insurance, and any correspondence with surety companies
- Reconciliation of overpayments and underpayments
- Conflict of interest forms are completed by each member of the contract administration and evaluation teams
- Documentation regarding any changes in delivery date contract price
- Notice to Proceed
- Transfer of services such as utilities and transfer of warranties from the contractor to the entity
- Documentation of inspection and acceptance
- Documentation of contract close-out (NIGP, "Global Best Practice, Contract Closeout").

It is advised that on all but the simplest closures the procurement professional utilize a checklist for the close-out. It is the responsibility of public entities to ensure that the work under a contract has been completed and the contract is ready for close-out before final payment. By performing a formal close-out, the procurement professional ensures that both the contractor and the entity have completed their contractual obligations and that the contract file includes all records and supporting documentation.

References

NIGP. 2022. "CPPB Prep Guide." NIGP.

NIGP. "Global Best Practice, Contract Closeout." https://www.nigp.org/resource/global-best-practices/global-best-practice-contract-closeout.pdf?dl=true

NIGP. "Global Best Practice—Performance Measurement." https://www.nigp.org/resource/global-best-practices/Performance%20Measurement%20Best%20Practice.pdf

NIGP. "Public Procurement Practice, Audits." https://www.nigp.org/resource/global-best-practices/audits-best-practice.pdf?dl=true

NIGP. "Public Procurement Practice, Transparency in Public Procurement." https://www.nigp.org/resource/global-best-practices/Transparency%20in%20Public%20Procurement%20Best%20Practice.pdf?dl=true

Pitzer, Jack, and Khi V. Thai. 2009. *Introduction to Public Procurement*. 3rd ed. Herndon, VA: National Institute of Governmental Purchasing.

The Coalition of Government Procurement. 2023. "What is Fair and Reasonable Transparency?" September 8. https://thecgp.org/2023/09/08/what-is-fair-and-reasonable-transparency/

Chapter 13

Disposal Methods

The effective and efficient disposal of surplus or outdated materials is essential to the fiduciary responsibility of an entity. As such, it is often Procurement's responsibility to adopt processes and procedures which ensure the efficient, safe, and ethically aligned disposal of excess, surplus, and obsolete goods. While the surplus process will require procurement staff resources, it is an essential step of an asset's life cycle.

Managing a Surplus Program

Reviewing surplus disposal policies and preparing a lessons-learned document are all required actions to manage surplus. A lessons-learned document captures the process used to make decisions regarding surplus management. It is used to track all the issues, both positive and negative, related to the project's processes, people, financials, and technology, and should be maintained until the file is destroyed in accordance with the entity records retention schedule. A periodic review of surplus disposal policies to make any necessary changes or updates is a best practice.

DOI: 10.4324/9781003566564-17

Entity departments may be reluctant to dispose of items because of a variety of reasons such as costs, a hoarding mentality, or a reluctance to deal with the process. Inventory, however, involves costs. Holding costs may include:

- Damage
- Deterioration
- Obsolescence
- Space
- Stocking
- Retrieval
- Labor from receiving
- Quality checks
- Shipping
- Packing
- Theft.

This chapter addresses the methods used to dispose of goods at the end of their useful life or when they are no longer needed. While the disposal is the final step, tracking and reporting is a vital step of asset accountability.

Sources of Surplus

Each day, procurement professionals across the world purchase goods for use by government entities. The goods are often considered assets which are anything the entity owns that could be liquidated into cash. Those goods or assets will at some point no longer be needed by the public entity and will be considered surplus. In its online dictionary, NIGP defines surplus as:

> 1. An overstock situation that occurs when the quantity of goods on hand exceeds the quantity of goods needed. The overstocked goods may be returned to the supplier, sold at auction, or disposed of in a method acceptable to the entity.
> 2. The goods or materials that are obsolete or no longer needed by the agency and are designated for disposal. Surplus becomes available for disposal outside of the entity due to an unforeseen situation that affects the use of the item, for example, chairs or desks that have been replaced with new items. (NIGP, "Dictionary of Procurement Terms")

The NIGP Dictionary of Procurement Terms further defines obsolete supplies or equipment as,

> items that are out of date, no longer in use, or are effectively unusable, e.g., 8-track audio tapes and floppy computer disks. Obsolete supplies and equipment become outdated due to new technology, new regulations, or new procedures instituted by the entity.

As technology evolves, newer technologies such as servers and computer hardware replace existing assets. Equipment such as tasers and defibrillators are replaced when the manufacturer no longer supports the existing models. Ergonomic, electronic sit-and-stand stand desks often replace traditional stationary desks. Body armor becomes obsolete when it reaches its expiration date. Additionally, vehicles and equipment are often replaced when the cost to maintain the assets exceeds their value or when an unforeseen repair is needed that will cost more than the asset is worth.

Excess and Surplus

The terms "excess" and "surplus" are sometimes used interchangeably when referring to property that is no longer needed by the public entity. While both mean more of something than necessary, the term "excess" often has a negative connotation, while surplus is often perceived as abundance. Excess is perceived as being more than necessary, permitted, or desirable. In comparison, surplus is the additional items that are left over when requirements have been met. Often in public entities, the excess is surplussed or disposed of. For example,

- Lake City has a budget <u>surplus</u> vs…
- Umatilla County has <u>excess</u> inventory in its warehouse. OR The <u>excess</u> of imports over exports rose by $1.2 billion.

NIGP defines excess property as,

> 1. Any supplies or equipment, other than expendable supplies having a remaining useful life, that are no longer required by the entity in possession of the material. 2. Material and supplies that are acquired by a government entity but are not required or can no longer be used by the entity and that may or may not have a residual value. (NIGP, "Dictionary of Procurement Terms")

Many of the items purchased are assets that are replacing items such as vehicles and equipment that are past their useful life and are replaced with a newer vehicle. The assets that are no longer needed are considered excess and are surplussed by the entity. For example, when a new asset is added, the entity does not need two assets for the same purpose so they surplus the older asset. Entities consider items that they no longer need and that cannot be used elsewhere in the entity as excess.

Types of Surplus

Every item purchased by a government entity is a potential source of surplus and can be categorized into one of three categories: scrap, waste, or rubbish. NIGP has developed clear differentiation between the terms.

Scrap, Waste, and Rubbish

Scrap, waste, and rubbish are often used interchangeably, but each is slightly different from the other.

- **Scrap** consists of ferrous and non-ferrous metals as well as non-metallic scrap, such as wood, wood chips, paper, plastic, and other materials. Scrap items may have a purpose such as used tires being repurposed into mulch. If the scrap does not have a new purpose then it becomes waste. NIGP defines scrap as, "Salvageable materials with a market value that are damaged, defective, or deteriorated. 2. Remaining residue from operations after a project is completed. The value of such materials exceeds the expenses required to sell them" (NIGP, "Dictionary of Procurement Terms").
- **Waste** may consist of small broken items such as broken staplers, lamps, desks, appliances, etc. NIGP defines waste as, "salvageable materials that are damaged, defective, deteriorated, or residue from operations with little or no market value. The selling expenses exceed the value, and the materials are discarded" (NIGP, "Dictionary of Procurement Terms").
- **Rubbish** is defined by NIGP as "refuse that must be disposed of that does not have any market value." Examples of rubbish are trash, non-recyclable plastics, as well as medical and hazardous waste. Essentially everything that is immediately thrown into a trash can (NIGP, "Dictionary of Procurement Terms").

Tracking and Reporting

Depending on the funding source, surplus items may have different tracking and reporting requirements. Assets that were purchased with grant funds may have additional tracking and reporting requirements included in their grant funding documents that extend beyond the entities' standard policy. In these instances, the stricter of the requirements applies. Therefore, public entities must establish policies and procedures to track inventory and assets. It is also essential that every entity has implemented systems to track assets from receipts to disposal completion.

In general, when evaluating assets for surplus and disposal, various inventory reports can be used to evaluate items for surplus, such as:

- Inventory Status Reports
- Stock-out Reports
- Inventory Aging Reports.

When reviewing inventory reports, some factors to reflect on include:

- Quantity on hand
- Usage over a designated time period, such as month, quarter, and year
- Obsolete and no longer needed items.

Surplus and Disposal Considerations

Surplussing decisions must be made with the entities' best interests in mind. When deciding to surplus an item, several factors must be considered before a decision is made. In deciding whether to surplus an item or not, at a minimum an entity should consider the following factors:

1. Possible future requirements or use
2. Present value of the property
3. Likelihood of locating a buyer
4. Intergovernmental cooperation
5. The general welfare of the citizens.

There are often other considerations that may also affect the handling, tracking, and reporting of the asset, such as the funding and any additional legal requirements.

Funding

When beginning the solicitation process, one of the first questions that must be asked before surplussing an item is, what was the original funding source? Determining the asset funding source may be difficult if the asset has been owned by the entity for a long time. For example, one entity no longer needed its boat motors from a police boat because the motors were being replaced. The police lieutenant thought that the motors may have been bought with grant funds. Unfortunately, that entity could not surplus the boat motors until a final determination had been made on the original source of the funding.

The initial funding source may limit the options available to the entity to dispose of an asset or require the entity to give the sale proceeds back to the original grantor or internal entity fund. For example, an entity may surplus an asset owned by its utility fund. In this instance, the recovered funds for the enterprise fund must be tracked separately from those funds recovered for the general fund. Similarly, assets sold that were initially purchased with grant funds must also be tracked separately and may have additional reporting requirements.

Assets purchased with grant dollars may have additional requirements as well. For example, if an asset was purchased using grant funds, the entity must read the original grant for any requirements for surplussing the item. Some grants may require that the entity request permission before selling an item, while other grants may be silent on the disposal process. In the example of the police boat motors, after much research it was found that the original boat was purchased using United States Department of Homeland Security grant funds; therefore, the surplus requirements provided in the grant award for the boat flowed down to the components of the original asset. While the entity was keeping the original boat, the entity had to follow the grant instructions for surplussing the motors. For United States federal grants, entities are encouraged to review 2. C.F.R 200.312–314 and related federal regulations for current requirements. The entity must maintain a file for its assets with documentation of the original source of funding. It is also strongly recommended to review any grant documents for disposal, tracking, and reporting requirements before deciding to surplus an item ("Code of Federal Regulations").

Legal Requirements

Legal requirements for surplus items will vary from public entity to entity. The most common legal requirements are advertising, notice, and approval. Legal requirements can be found in state and federal statutes, regulations, or local codes. For example, many entities may require that the entity advertise in its newspaper of record before surplussing an asset. The advertising requirement provides public notice that the entity is going to dispose of an asset. Additionally, there may be a required approval process by a governing board or council. Some entities require a resolution to be passed before the surplussing of an item. Often, the legal requirements are based on the value of the asset. For example, an entity may be able to dispose of a broken stapler with the approval documented in an email or surplus form, whereas an asset over $5,000 may require the approval of a resolution by the governing body. It is strongly recommended that public entities have clear policies or municipal codes that outline their specific legal requirements for surplus.

Methods of Surplus

There are many different methods to surplus items. Numerous public entities have adopted acceptable methods in their codes or regulations, while other public entities may allow any of the methods below. Procurement professionals are encouraged to collaborate with their legal and other internal departments when deciding which method to use.

Donations

Donating surplus may also be a method of disposal if it is allowed by the entity's jurisdiction. If it is allowed, there are usually many restrictions and approval requirements to avoid abuse, fraud, and any improprieties or the appearance of any improprieties. Some central, federal, and state or local entities donate surplus property through inter-governmental programs. In the United States, federal surpluses are allocated to several agencies in each state through the General Services Administration (GSA). Since 1987, the GSA of the United States government alone has conveyed over $3 billion worth of property across the United States. Of this, about one-third has been given to state or local governments and non-profit organizations at a substantial discount in price (US General Services Administration n.d.). Similarly, Canada has a GCDonate platform through its GCSurplus program, which is used to facilitate the donation process for Canadian government departments and entities, making it easier to donate surplus moveable assets to designated eligible groups and organizations (Government of Canada 2025).

The donation method has been used successfully by Community Transit in Washington state through its "Van GO" program. Since 2000, Community Transit has granted 158 vehicles to nonprofit organizations in Snohomish County to provide transportation services to residents. Vehicles that are designated for surplus auction are instead granted to nonprofit organizations. Nonprofit organizations then apply for a vehicle grant. Competitive grant applications are scored based on demonstrated community benefit, number of trips provided, service coordination, and clarity and quality of the application (Community Transit n.d.).

Sales to Other Public Entities

Some public entities are required to receive fair market value for their surplus items regardless of whether the items could be used by another public entity. While other entities may allow an item to be transferred to another public entity at or below reasonable market value. For example, instead of donating the items, the public entity establishes the fair market value of the item through research of current market prices and negotiates with another public entity. In some instances, money may be exchanged. In other instances, the selling entity may negotiate that the value of the item offsets its monetary contribution to a project or program. This is often called gifts in kind. For example, one city fire department provided a surplussed air compressor filling station to the regional fire authority instead of a required monetary contribution to a fire training program. In this instance, both public entities benefitted from the exchange. The regional fire authority used the air compressor filling station to train firefighters that the city fire department sent its staff to.

Trade-Ins

Trade-in is another option for disposal. Disposal of surplus equipment through trade-in is an option that can be used when a new asset is required. This may be the best method when an asset is being upgraded such as tasers, firearms, large equipment, or vehicles. The procurement professional may be able to utilize trade-in credits to reduce the purchase price of new goods. When using this method, the procurement professional must take measures to ensure the entity is getting a fair value of the goods being traded in and a good value for the overall procurement.

With this method, the public entity solicits bids for the required new items and includes a line on the price sheet for credit of the trade-in toward the purchase of the new asset. The credit would be deducted from the price paid for the new item(s), thus reducing the total purchase price. While this method may not bring the highest return, it can contribute to a lower administrative cost for storage, transportation, and handling expenses. It also allows a department to reduce its outward expense versus selling an asset and having the funds returned to the entity's general account fund.

Sales to Entity Employees

While rare, some entities choose to sell certain surplus assets, such as computers, to employees for a set price. For example, one entity wanted to improve computer literacy and access for its mostly blue-collar staff. The entity determined it was in its best interest to sell surplus computer towers to its employees for a set price through a lottery-type system that was adopted by resolution. In this instance, the overall business benefit to the entity was considered greater than the revenue that would have been received from selling the computers through a surplus program. However, to eliminate the numerous challenges associated with the ethical considerations and perception of selling items to employees, it is highly recommended to adopt a policy regarding selling to employees. The policy should establish the appropriate organizational boundaries with the intent to avoid any appearances of impropriety in the surplus program. At a minimum, the oversight employees such as the procurement manager, any entity employee involved in the decision to surplus an item, and any elected or governing members should be prohibited from purchasing surplus items from the entity.

Auctions

Of the options available to sell surplus assets, the auction method is the most common. The auction method is popular with citizens who appreciate the opportunity to bid on valuable items. There are two types of auction types. The most prevalent is the English auction. With English auctions, the auctioneer opens the bidding at a reserve price, which may be zero, the lowest price the entity is willing to accept for the item, and auction bidders make higher offers. In contrast, the Dutch auction is descending in price accepted. With a Dutch auction, the auctioneer begins at a high price, higher than they believe the item will get, then decreases the price until a bidder finally calls out, "Mine!" The bidder then receives the item at the price at which they made the call. If multiple items are offered, the process continues until all items are sold (Fine n.d.).

Additionally, there are a variety of different auction formats. The two most used in the public sector are online and on-site auctioneer.

Online Auctions

One of the most popular methods of auctioning items is to contract with an online auction site. Depending on the site and service, this method may or may not require advertising. This approach can provide a creative solution to uncommon surplus dilemmas. For example, because of budget constraints during COVID, a city in Washington state had to cut its downtown beautification program and had to sell its entire inventory of greenhouse-grown plants, which amounted to nearly 10,000 plants. The procurement manager used an online auction site to sell all the plants by staggering the auction closing times during a two-day weekend period, with the designated plant pick-up scheduled for the following Saturday. While the plant auction required significant planning, about 97% of the plants were sold and picked up successfully in a short time frame, allowing the greenhouse operations to shut down before staff layoffs.

On-Site Auctioneer

Some public entities will hire an auctioneer's services and conduct periodic on-site auctions. The advantage of this method is that the items can remain at the entity's location without being transferred to an auctioneer company's site. However, this method requires additional entity staff resources as well as space to store all the items until the sale. Requiring buyers to attend the auction may also limit the pool of interested parties. Any on-site auctions should be publicly advertised in newspapers, trade magazines, or other publications, and electronically through email and web postings. The goal is to notify as many potential buyers as possible to maximize the number of bidders.

Commercial Markets

Certain types of surplus commodities may be best sold through established commercial markets. For example, the produce or livestock grown in connection with agricultural research programs are often sold through this surplus method. Arrangements for sales through commercial markets should be made through a seller who may also be an auctioneer. Like auction services, a percentage of the sales is normally paid for the services.

Sealed Bids

When the quantity of objects is not sufficient to justify an auction, the sealed bid method may be the most appropriate solution. A sealed bid is a formal sale in which sealed bids are required for the items to be purchased. Many public entities require at least one notice of the call for bids in the entity's official newspaper at a minimum of 13 days before the bid opening. A guaranteed deposit is sometimes required, and all the bids must be received before the advertised time of bid opening. The sealed bids are opened publicly, and the public entity reserves the right to reject all the bids or sell only to the highest bidder. This method has been used successfully by a city in Washington state to sell timber from its utility properties. The city's municipal code requires the award to be made to the highest bidder demonstrating the most experience and the best record in water quality protection, including erosion control, site cleanup, rehabilitation, and sanitation. Additionally, any funds received from its timber sales must be deposited and used for water quality improvements per its municipal code.

Spot Bids

The spot bid method of disposal is a sale in which bidders place written offers in a bid box at the location of the sale. Bids for each item are compared and the high bid is announced for each successive item or lot before the next item is called. This method is appropriate when there are only a few items to be sold, particularly if the items are offered on an irregular basis. This method can be organized quickly, therefore eliminating the need to store surplus materials for a longer period. However, it requires interested buyers to travel to the site location, therefore possibly minimizing the potential bidding pool.

Negotiated Sales

This method is often only used when an item cannot be sold through other methods or when no satisfactory bid is received through the sealed bid or spot bid methods. Some entities will allow the officials to negotiate with one or more designated buyers. Some entities require notice to be provided in the entity's official newspaper if this method is used.

Retail Sales Outlet

A retail sales outlet may be considered if the variety, quantity, and value of the items are sufficient to attract numerous buyers and financially support the resources required to manage the inventory, research pricing data, and staff, and to assist customers. Additionally, adequate space in a good location must be available and the scheduled hours of operation should be reasonable and justifiable. A best practice is to conduct a cost-benefit analysis to see whether the endeavor is viable before committing the entity.

Disposal

Disposal is the action or process of throwing away or getting rid of an item. The United States sends about 140 million tons, or about 52% of its 268 million tons of total waste, into landfills each year (McDonald 2022). In comparison, Canada sends about 36 million tons of waste, about 72.5% of its total, to landfills each year (Environment and Climate Change Canada 2024). That amounts to a staggering amount of waste from just two countries. In contrast, Sweden only sends about 1% of its total waste to landfills (Kim and Mauborgne 2021).

There are numerous ways to dispose of surplus that extend far beyond sending items to the landfill. The Institute for Public Procurement's class on Surplus, Disposal, and Close-out identifies seven ways to dispose of surplus. They are listed below.

1. **Reuse**—Also called redeploying, reuse is the most rewarding option for an entity. Redeploying equipment to another department or business unit avoids buying a new asset and saves on procurement costs. It is also the best stewardship of the public's funds from an environmental and social point of view.
2. **Recondition**—Also referred to as refurbishing, it is the method of putting used equipment and parts back in service. It is less expensive than buying new and allows the entity to have products in a like-new state.
3. **Return**—Equipment and parts can sometimes be returned to the Original Equipment Manufacturer (OEM) or the supplier for cash or credit value. An increasing number of OEMs offer buy-back solutions, as they do not want their products to end up in landfills either.
4. **Resell**—Idle assets can be sold again on the open market to resellers. Auction platforms are the most common tools used to sell used machinery and spares, but trades and bartering are other possibilities. Donating is also considered a reselling option, as it increases the entity's involvement and community benefit.
5. **Reclaim**—Chemicals, hazardous substances, and metals can be recovered in a responsible and environmentally friendly way and used again.
6. **Recycle**—Non-ferrous and ferrous metals, plastic, paper, and glass can easily be scrapped, recycled, and sent back to the raw material streams. Procurement professionals sometimes forget the value of raw materials. For example, thieves breaking into construction sites to steal copper. Even waste is not wasted, as it can be burnt for energy "biomass."
7. **Remove**—Surplus assets are sent to the landfills at the expense of the entity. Regrettably, this is often the default decision made by several entities. It is easier to throw something away at the solid ease facility or

laydown yard than looking for a better-adapted solution. Additionally, it is also the most negative solution from an environmental and entity reputation perspective. Fortunately, this can be a last resort choice. It is rare when nothing from a surplus asset can be recycled and properly disposed of. For example, electric car batteries can be dismantled and most of the parts used in a new battery, which reduces the amount of material sent to landfill. Additionally, many items can be scrapped or recycled and sent back to the raw material streams, such as metals, plastic, paper, and glass (Ball, Matthews, and Shaw n.d.).

References

Ball, Roger, Darin Matthews, and Cynthia Shaw. n.d. "Surplus, Disposal, Closeout." NIGP, The Institute for Public Procurement.

"Code of Federal Regulations." The Federal Register. https://www.ecfr.gov/current/title-2/subtitle-A/chapter-II/part-200/subpart-D/subject-group-ECFR8feb98c2e3e5ad2/section-200.312

Community Transit. n.d. "Van GO." https://www.communitytransit.org/van-go

Environment and Climate Change Canada. 2024. "Solid Waste Diversion and Disposal." Government of Canada. https://www.canada.ca/en/environment-climate-change/services/environmental-indicators/solid-waste-diversion-disposal.html

Fine, Leslie. n.d. "Review of Auctions." EconLib. https://www.econlib.org/library/Enc/Auctions.html#:~:text=The%20most%20common%20type%20of,to%20accept%20for%20the%20item

Government of Canada, Public Services and Procurement Canada. 2025. "GCDonate." https://www.gcsurplus.ca/mn-eng.cfm?snc=wfdad

Kim, Chan, and Renée Mauborgne. 2021. "Turning Waste to Energy: Sweden's Recycling Revolution." Blue Ocean Strategy. August 27, 2021. https://www.blueoceanstrategy.com/blog/turning-waste-energy-sweden-recycling-revolution/#:~:text=Only%201%25%20of%20Sweden

McDonald, Juliana. 2022. "How Much Trash Does the U.S. Really Produce?" Dumpsters. July 13, 2022. Updated February 17, 2023. https://www.dumpsters.com/blog/us-trash-production#:~:text=The%20U.S.%20produces%20268%20million

NIGP. "Dictionary of Procurement Terms." https://www.nigp.org/dictionary-of-terms

U.S. General Services Administration. n.d. "The Disposal Process." https://www.gsa.gov/real-estate/real-estate-services/overview/the-disposal-process#:~:text=If%20state%20and%20local%20governments

Appendix A

NIGP Code of Ethics

- The Institute believes, and it is a condition of membership, that the following ethical principles should govern the conduct of every person employed by a public sector procurement or materials management organization:
- Seeks or accepts a position as head (or employee) only when fully in accord with the professional principles applicable thereto and when confident of possessing the qualifications to serve under those principles to the advantage of the employing organization.
- Believes in the dignity and worth of the service rendered by the organization, and the societal responsibilities assumed as a trusted public servant.
- Is governed by the highest ideals of honor and integrity in all public and personal relationships in order to merit the respect and inspire the confidence of the organization and the public being served.
- Believes that personal aggrandizement or personal profit obtained through misuse of public or personal relationships is dishonest and not tolerable.
- Identifies and eliminates participation of any individual in operational situations where a conflict of interest may be involved.
- Believes that members of the Institute and its staff should at no time, or under any circumstances, accept directly or indirectly, gifts, gratuities, or other things of value from suppliers, which might influence or appear to influence purchasing decisions.
- Keeps the governmental organization informed, through appropriate channels, on problems and progress of applicable operations by emphasizing the importance of the facts.
- Resists encroachment on control of personnel in order to preserve integrity as a professional manager.
- Handles all personnel matters on a merit basis, and in compliance with applicable laws prohibiting discrimination in employment on the basis of politics, religion, color, national origin, disability, gender, age, pregnancy and other protected characteristics.
- Seeks or dispenses no personal favors. Handles each administrative problem objectively and empathetically, without discrimination.
- Subscribes to and supports the professional aims and objectives of NIGP - The Institute for Public Procurement.

Appendix B

Resolution 1002

CENTRALIZED PURCHASING

Whereas, a strong, well managed purchasing program is essential to good government, and

Whereas, poorly managed purchasing programs result in inefficient and wasteful government, and

Whereas, improper purchasing results in the loss of public confidence in the integrity of the government, and

Whereas, governmental purchasing functions best in a free and open environment, and

Whereas, openness, centralization, and professionalism serve a government well, and

Whereas, where there is a public record of the acquisition of goods and services there is public confidence, and

Whereas, the centralization of the purchasing authority is the basis for responsibility and accountability of governmental purchasing, and

Whereas, the central purchasing office objectively exercises the purchasing authority of a government, independent of internal special programs and special interests, and

Whereas, professionalism—adherence to high ethical standards—reduces the cost of government, by awarding contracts impartially, and instills public confidence in the integrity of the government,

Now Therefore, BE IT RESOLVED, that the National Institute of Governmental Purchasing, Inc., urgently recommends the adoption of centralized purchasing as the standard government organization

The above resolution was adopted by the Board of Directors of the National Institute of Governmental Purchasing at its official meeting on the 1st day of January, 1989.

I certify that the above resolution was reviewed and ratified by the Board of Directors of the National Institute of Governmental Purchasing at its official meeting on the 11th day of November, 1995.

J. E. Brinkman, CPPO
Executive Vice President and Secretary

Index

Note: Page locators in **bold** refer to tables.

Made in the USA
Las Vegas, NV
19 September 2026

c8b924fd-5759-4a05-97fb-239ae1de39aaR01